AFTER THE PROCLAMATION PARADE.

LIFE IN AN INDIAN OUTPOST

LIFE IN AN INDIAN OUTPOST

By

MAJOR GORDON CASSERLY

ILLUSTRATED

GYAN

Published by

GYAN

Gyan Publishing House
5, Ansari Road
Daryaganj, New Delhi-110002
Phone: 011-47034999, 9811692060
E-mail: books@gyanbooks.com

Distribution Network
gyanbooks.com
India, USA, Canada, UK, Australia, France

ISBN : 978-81-212-6486-0 (PB)
First Published, 1914

2nd Impression 2022

Printed at: Gyan Press, Delhi.

LIFE IN AN INDIAN OUTPOST
Author: MAJOR GORDON CASSERLY

LIFE IN AN INDIAN OUTPOST

BY

MAJOR GORDON CASSERLY

ILLUSTRATED

1914

CONTENTS

CHAPTER I

A FRONTIER POST

CHAPTER II

LIFE ON OUTPOST

CHAPTER V

IN THE JUNGLE

CHAPTER VI

ROGUES OF THE FOREST

CHAPTER IX

A FOREST MARCH

CHAPTER X

THROUGH FIRE AND WATER

CHAPTER XI

IN THE PALACE OF THE MAHARAJAH

CHAPTER XII

A MILITARY TRAGEDY

CHAPTER XIII

IN AN INDIAN HILL STATION

CHAPTER XIV

A JUNGLE FORT

CHAPTER XV

FAREWELL TO THE HILLS

LIST OF ILLUSTRATIONS

LIFE IN AN INDIAN OUTPOST

CHAPTER I

A FRONTIER POST

Our first view of the Himalayas—Across India in a troop train—A scattered regiment—An elephant-haunted railway—Kinchinjunga—The great Terai Jungle—Rajabhatkawa—In the days of Warren Hastings—Hillmen—Roving Chinese—We arrive at Buxa Road—Relieved officers—An undesirable outpost—March through the forest—The hills—A mountain road—Lovely scenery—Buxa Duar—A lonely Station—The labours of an Indian Army officer—Varied work—The frontier of Bhutan—A gate of India—A Himalayan paradise—The fort—Intrusive monkeys—The cantonment—The Picquet Towers—The bazaar—The cemetery—Forgotten graves—Tragedies of loneliness—From Bhutan to the sea.

AGAINST the blue sky to the north lay a dark blur that, as our troop train ran on through the level plains of Eastern Bengal, rose ever higher and took shape—the distant line of the Himalayas. Around us the restful though tame scenery of the little Cooch Behar State. The chess-board pattern of mud-banked rice fields, long groves of the graceful feathery bamboo, here and there a tiny hamlet of palm-thatched huts—on their low roofs great sprawling green creepers with white blotches that look like skulls but are only ripe melons. But the dark outlines of the distant mountains drew my gaze and brought the heads of my sepoys out of the carriage windows to stare at them.

For somewhere on the face of those hills was Buxa Duar, the little fort that was to be our home for the next two years.

For four days my detachment of two hundred men of the 120th Rajputana Infantry had been whirled across India from west to east towards it. From Baroda we had come—Baroda with its military cantonment set in an English-like park, its vast native city with the gaily painted houses and narrow streets where the Gaikwar's Cavalry rode with laced jackets and slung pelisses like the Hussars of old, and his sentries mounted guard over gold and silver cannons in a dingy backyard. Where in low rooms, set out in glass cases, as in a cheap draper's shop, were the famous pearl-embroidered carpets and gorgeous jewels of the State, worth a king's ransom.

Four days of travel over the plains of India with their closely cultivated fields, mud-walled villages, stony hills and stretches of scrub jungle, where an occasional jackal slunk away from the train or an antelope paused in its bounding flight to look back at the strange iron monster. Across the sacred Ganges where Allahabad lies at its junction with the River Jumna. The regiment was on its way to garrison widely separated posts in outlying parts of the Indian Empire and neighbouring countries. Two companies had already gone to be divided between

Chumbi in Tibet and Gantok in the dependent State of Sikkim, and to furnish the guard to our Agent at Gyantse.

The month was December; and they had started in August to cross the sixteen-thousand-feet high passes in the Himalayas before the winter snows blocked them. The regimental headquarters, with four companies, was on its way to embark on the steamers which would convey them a fourteen days' journey on the giant rivers Ganges and Brahmaputra to Dibrugarh and Sadiya in Assam.

At Benares my two companies had parted from the rest and entered another troop train which carried us into Eastern Bengal.

Every day for three or four hours our trains had halted at some little wayside station to enable the men to get out, make their cooking-places, and prepare their food for the day. The previous night my detachment had detrained at Gitaldaha, where we had to change again on to a narrow gauge railway, two feet six inches in width, which would take us through Cooch Behar to our destination. The railway officials informed me that we must stay in the station all night, as the trains on this line ran only by daylight. I asked the reason of this.

"They cannot go by night on account of the wild animals," was the reply.

"The wild animals?" I echoed in surprise.

"Yes; the line runs through a forest, the Terai Jungle, full of elephants and bison. Three months ago one of our engines was derailed by a wild elephant and the driver badly injured. And not long before that another rogue elephant held up a station on the line, stopped a train, blockaded the officials in the buildings, and broke a tusk trying to root up the platform."

And when daylight dawned and I could see the toy engine and carriages, I was not surprised at the fear of encountering an elephant on the line.

Now on our fifth day of travel we were nearing the end of the journey. We had passed the capital of Cooch Behar and were approaching Alipur Duar, the last station before the Terai Forest is reached. Suddenly, high in the air above the now distinct line of hills, stood out in the brilliant sunlight the white crest and snowy peaks of Kinchinjunga, twenty-eight thousand feet high, and nearly one hundred and twenty miles away. Past Alipur Duar, and then hills and snow-clad summits were lost to sight as our little train plunged from the sunny plain into the deep shadows of the famous Terai Forest—the wonderful jungle that stretches east and west along the foot of the Himalayas, and clothes their lowest slopes. In whose recesses roam the wild elephant, the rhinoceros and the bison, true lords of the woods; where deadlier foes to man than these, malaria and black-water fever hold sway and lay low the mightiest hunter before the Lord. And standing on the back platform of our tiny carriage my subaltern and I strove to pierce its gloomy depths, half hoping to see the giant bulk of a wild elephant or a rhinoceros. But nothing met our gaze save the great orchid-clad trees, the graceful fronds of monster ferns, and the dense undergrowth that would deny a passage to anything less powerful than bisons or elephants.

In a sudden clearing in the heart of the forest, the train stopped at a small station near which stood a few bamboo huts and a gaunt, two-storied wooden house in which, we afterwards learned, an English forest officer lived his lonely life. The place was called Rajabhatkawa, which in the vernacular means, "The Rajah ate his food." It was so named because, nearly one hundred and thirty years before, in the days of Warren Hastings, a Rajah of Cooch Behar ate his first meal there after his release from captivity among the hill tribesmen of Bhutan who had carried him away into their mountain fastnesses. They had released him at the urgent instance of a British captain and two hundred sepoys who had followed them up and captured three of their forts.

Among the crowd of natives on the platform at this station were several of various hill races, Bhuttias and Gurkhas, with the small eyes and flat nose of the Mongolian. I was surprised to see two Chinamen in blue linen suits and straw hats, fanning themselves and smoking cigarettes, as much at home as if they were on the Bund in Shanghai or in Queen's Road in Hong Kong. But later on I learned that Rajabhatkawa led to several tea gardens, where Chinese carpenters are always welcome. These men are generally from Canton, the inhabitants of which city emigrate freely. I have met them in Calcutta, Penang, Singapore, Manila, and San Francisco.

On again through the jungle our train passed for another eight miles, and then drew up at a small station of one low, stone building with a nameboard nearly as big as itself, which bore the words "Buxa Road." It stood in a little clearing in the forest, where the ground was piled high with felled trees, ready to be dispatched to Calcutta. This was the end of our railway journey.

The sepoys tumbled eagerly out of the train, threw

their rolls of bedding out of the compartments, fell in on the platform and piled arms, and then turned to with a will to unload the heavy baggage from the brake-vans. A number of tall, bearded Mohammedans, men of the detachment of the Punjabi Regiment we were replacing, were at the station. Their major came forward to welcome me, and expressed his extreme pleasure in meeting the man who was to relieve him and enable him to quit a most undesirable place.

This was a blow to me; for I had pictured life in this little outpost as an ideal existence in a sportsman's paradise.

"What? Don't you like Buxa Duar?" I asked in surprise.

"Like it?" he exclaimed vehemently. "Most certainly not. In my time I have been stationed in some poisonous places in Upper Burmah, when I was in the Military Police; but the worst of them was heaven to Buxa."

I gasped with horror. "Is it as bad as all that? How long have you been here?"

"Three weeks," replied the major; "and that was three weeks too long. Before you have been here a fortnight you will be praying to all your gods to take you anywhere else."

This was pleasant. The subaltern of the Punjabis now came up and was introduced to me. He had been six months in Buxa; and *his* opinion of it was too lurid to print. My subaltern, who had been superintending the unloading of the baggage, joined us and in his turn was regaled with these cheering criticisms of our new home. His face fell; for, like me, he had been looking forward eagerly to being quartered in this little outpost, where, we had been told, the sport was excellent. Fortunately men's tastes differ; and after eighteen months' experience of this much-abused Buxa, I liked it better than any other place I have ever served in in all my soldiering.

I learned from our new friends that the fort was six miles from the railway and fifteen hundred feet above it; so I inquired for the transport to convey our baggage there.

Before leaving Baroda the quartermaster of our regiment had written to the nearest civil official of the district, requesting him to provide me with a hundred coolies for the purpose. There were also, I knew, three Government transport elephants in charge of the detachment quartered in Buxa Duar. These I saw at the station engaged in conveying the baggage of the Punjabis, who were to leave on the following day. I asked for my hundred coolies.

The major laughed when I told him of our quartermaster's requisition. "Your regimental headquarters," he said, "evidently did not realise what a desolate, uninhabited place this is. A hundred coolies? Why, with difficulty I have procured eight; four of them women. You will have to leave your baggage here under a guard, and have it brought up piecemeal on the elephants after our departure. And now, if you will fall in your men, I'll lead the way up to Buxa and gladly take my last look at it."

A baggage guard having been left at the station with our food and cooking-pots, etc., my detachment fell in, formed fours and followed us. From the clearing near the railway a broad road, cut through the forest, led towards the hills. For the first three miles it was comparatively level; and we swung along at a good pace between the tall trees rising from the dense undergrowth. Breaking the solemn silence of the forest, I eagerly plied our new friends with questions on the chances of sport that Buxa afforded. But I found that they had done little in that way and could give me scant information. The subaltern had shot a tiger on a tea garden, but had hardly ever gone into the jungle. I learned, however, that out of the three transport elephants now at my disposal, two were trained for shooting purposes and were remarkably steady. This at least was good news.

Towards the end of the third mile the road began to rise; and when it emerged into a small clearing we halted for a few minutes. We were now at the very foot of the hills; and from here we could see them for the first time since our train had entered the forest. High above our heads they towered. At first low, rounded, tree-clad buttresses of the giant ramparts of India, long spurs thrust out from the flanks of the mountains. Then lofty rugged walls of rock, jagged peaks, dark even in the brilliant sunshine, precipitous cliffs over which thin threads of water leapt and seemed to hang wavering down the steep sides.

In the clearing stood two or three wooden huts; and a hundred yards farther on was a long and lofty open structure, with a thatched roof supported on rough wood pillars. The flooring was of pounded earth with three brick "standings," with iron rings inserted in them; for this was the Peelkhana or elephant stables of the detachment. The clearing was dignified with the euphonious name of Santrabari. Past the Peelkhana the road entered the hills.

At first it wound around their flanks, crossing by wooden bridges over clear streams; then, rising ever higher, it climbed the steep slopes in zigzags. Along above a brawling mountain torrent, tumbling over rounded rocks in a deep ravine it went, across wooded spurs and under stony cliffs. Huge bushes flamed with strange red and purple flowers, thick shrubs hung out great white bells to tempt the giant scarlet and black butterflies hovering overhead. Above our path tall trees stretched out their long limbs covered with the glossy green leaves of orchids. From trunk to trunk swung creepers thick as a ship's hawser, trailing in long festoons or interlacing and writhing around each other like great snakes.

But, as we climbed, the forest fell behind us. The trees stood farther apart, grew fewer and smaller. The undergrowth became denser. Tall brakes of the drooping plumes of the bamboo, thick-growing thorny bushes, plantain trees with their broad leaves and hanging bunches of bananas, the straight slender stems of sago palms with trailing clusters of nut-like fruit springing up from tangled vegetation. A troop of little brown monkeys leapt in alarm from tree to tree and vanished over a cliff. With a measured flapping of wings a brilliantly plumaged hornbill passed over our heads. The road crossed and re-crossed the mountain stream and led into a deep cleft among the hills towering precipitously over us. And looking up I saw on the edge of a cliff the corner of a building. It was the fort of Buxa at last. But before we reached it a few hundred feet more of climbing had to be done; and we panted wearily upward. Through a narrow cutting we emerged on a stretch of artificially levelled soil, the parade ground, and halted gladly. We stood in a deep horseshoe among the mountains, nearly two thousand feet above the plains. Before us, peeping out from low trees and flowering bushes, were a few bungalows; and above them towered a conical peak, its summit another four thousand feet higher still From it right and left ran down on either side of us two long wooded spurs; and on knolls on them stood three white square towers. Behind us, on a long mound, were fortified barracks with loopholed walls. These formed the fort; and this was Buxa Duar. We had reached our destination.

The major first showed our men to their new quarters; and I told them off to their different barrack-rooms, and saw them settled down. Then he and his subaltern led us to the Mess where we met a third officer, the doctor, a young lieutenant in the Indian Medical Service named Smith, who was to remain on in Buxa in medical charge of my detachment. Then ensued the wearisome task of taking over charge of all the Government property in the Station, from the rifle-range and the ammunition in the magazine to picks and shovels, buckets and waterproof coats. We had next to do our own bargaining over the buying of the store of tinned provisions, jams, pickles and wines in the Mess, as well as the scanty furniture in it. Among other things we purchased were two Bhutanese mountain sheep—huge creatures with horns. Meat being a rare commodity in Buxa, the major had bought them from a Bhuttia from across the border. Not needing to kill them at once, he had let them roam freely about the Mess garden until, as he said, they had become such pets that he could not harden his heart sufficiently to order them to be killed for food. My subaltern and I mentally resolved not to allow them to become thus endeared to us by long association.

Dinner in the Mess that night was quite a pleasant function, everyone but the doctor being in the best of spirits. As he was not to take his departure on the morrow, he was not as cheerful as the two Punjabi officers, who were delighted to think that they were so soon to leave Buxa. They had, perhaps, reason to rejoice at their return to civilisation and the society of their kind. They had come there from Tibet, where they had been quartered in the wilds from the end of the fighting in the war of 1904 to the evacuation of the country by our troops. They frankly pitied us for the prospect of two years' exile in this isolated post, where a strange white face was rarely seen. They fully expatiated on the loneliness of it. In a Bhuttia village a few miles over the hills there was an elderly American lady missionary. Down in the forest below a few English tea-planters were scattered about, the nearest fifteen or twenty miles from us. During the winter we might expect an occasional visitor, a General or our Colonel on inspection duty, or a Public Works Department Official come to see to the state of the road or the repair of the buildings. During the rainy season, which lasts seven months, from April to the end of October, with a rainfall therein from two hundred to three hundred inches, we would see no stranger and probably be cut off from outside intercourse by the washing away of the roads. As during those months the forest below would be filled with the deadly Terai fever, we could not solace our loneliness by sport which rendered the remainder of the year bearable. And as the jungle around us, which grew to our very doors would, during the Rains, swarm with leeches which fasten in scores on man or beast if given the chance, we would scarcely be able to put foot outside our bungalows, even if tempted to face the awful thunderstorms and torrential Rains.

All this certainly did not sound cheering; so I changed the subject and asked for information regarding my duties in the Station. I learned that, in addition to my work of my detachment, I would hold the proud but unpaid post of Officer Commanding Buxa Duar—an appointment which would entail voluminous routine correspondence on me. I would also, again without extra pay, represent law and order by being Cantonment Magistrate, third class, with power to award imprisonment up to three months' hard labour. Verily, the duties that fall to the lot of the Indian Army Officer are many and various. Besides being a soldier he is also a schoolmaster, having to set and correct examination papers for certificates of education. He must be something of a master tailor to decide on the fit and alteration of his men's new uniforms; a clerk to cope with interminable correspondence; an accountant to wrestle with complicated accounts. He must be an architect and builder to direct and oversee the erection and repair of the barracks, which is done by the sepoys themselves. Bad for him if he is not a good business man, for he must often give out contracts for hundreds or thousands of pounds, and see that they are properly carried out. A lawyer, to sit on or preside at courts martial, or to administer the law to civilians as

Cantonment Magistrate. And sometimes it falls to his lot to replace the chaplain in a military Station, read the lessons in church, or, perhaps, the Burial Service over the grave of a comrade.

Next morning the detachment of Punjabis marched off; and as we watched their files disappear down the winding mountain road, we three Britishers certainly felt a little isolated and cut off from our kind. Before the small column passed the last bend which would hide them from our eyes, the major turned to wave us a cheery farewell. Poor fellow, not long after, when in command of his regiment, he died of cholera in Benares.

However, our depression was momentary; and we turned away to begin making ourselves acquainted with our new surroundings. Buxa Duar stands guard over one of the gates of India, which opens into it from the little-known country of Bhutan. It commands a pass through the Himalayas into the fertile plains of Eastern Bengal, a pass that has run with blood many a time in the past. Through it fierce raiders have poured to the laying waste of the rich plains below. Back through it weeping women and weary children have passed to slavery in a savage land. And were the strong hand of Briton lifted from it, its jungle-clad hills would see again the blood-dyed columns of fighting men and the sad processions of wailing captives. To-day its gloomy depths are peaceful. But to-morrow, when the menace of a regenerated and aggressive China becomes real, its rocky walls may once more echo to the sounds of war.

Three thousand feet above our heads, two miles away in a straight line, but six by the winding mule track, lay the boundary-line between the Indian Empire and Bhutana—a line that runs along the mountain tops and rarely fringes the plains. It curves round the northern slopes of the conical hill that towers above Buxa, Sinchula, the "Hill of the Misty Pass."

Buxa Duar has been the scene of fierce fighting even in the short history of England's rule in India. It was first taken by the British from the Bhutanese in the days of Warren Hastings, when in 1772 Captain Jones and his small column of sepoys swept them back into their mountainous land. It was given back the following year. In 1864 we again went to war with Bhutan and captured Buxa; and, although throughout the winter of that year, our troops were closely besieged in it, it has remained in our possession ever since. Formerly garrisoned by a whole regiment, it is now occupied merely by a double company—two hundred men—of an Indian Infantry battalion. They are the only troops between the Bhutan border and Calcutta—three hundred miles away.

In all my wanderings I have seldom seen a lovelier spot than this lonely outpost. Nestling in the little hollow on the giant Himalayas, its few bungalows stood in gardens flaming with the brilliant colours of bougainvillias and poinsettias, surrounded by hedges of wild roses, and shaded by clusters of tall bamboos and the dense foliage of mango trees. The encircling arms of the mountains held it closely pressed. The jungle clothed the steep slopes around it, and rioted to our very doors. No sound disturbed its peace, save the shrill notes of our bugles or the chattering of monkeys by day, and the sudden harsh cry of barking deer or the monotonous bell-like note of the night-jar after the sun had set.

The building dignified by the name of fort was in reality an irregular square of one-storied stone barracks, their outer faces and iron-shuttered windows loopholed for rifle fire. They were connected by a low stone wall pierced with three gateways, closed at night or on an alarm by iron gates, which slid into place on wheels. The fort was built on a knoll, which on three sides fell perpendicularly for two or three hundred feet in rocky precipices from ten to forty yards from the walls. On the north face it was only about fifty feet above the parade ground, which was a levelled space two hundred yards long and a hundred broad. This served also for hockey and as a rifle-range; the targets being placed in tiers up the steep hill-side on the east end.

Standing at the front gate and looking northwards towards the mountains, one saw the ground rise sharply to the foot of Sinchula. Dotted about among the trees and set round with orchid-studded, low stone walls or flowering hedges, were four or five single-storied bungalows.

The lowest and nearest to the parade ground of these was the Commanding Officer's Quarters, which I occupied. Higher up to the right, and separated from mine by a deep ravine crossed by a little wooden bridge, was an empty house, known as Married Officers' Quarters. Behind it was a long wooden building raised on pillars, the forest officer's bungalow, to shelter that official in his annual visit. Around it were a few bamboo huts for his native clerks. Past my quarters ran the mountain road which climbed the steep sides of Sinchula, and, degenerating into a narrow mule track, wound round it to the Bhutan frontier. Near my house it was shaded by mango trees which, when the fruit was ripe, were very popular with the wild monkeys. To preserve the mangoes for ourselves, I was then obliged to station a sentry on the road at daybreak to keep the marauders off. In my garden stood a very large mango tree, up which I used in the season to send a small Bhuttia boy to gather the fruit. One day he found a large monkey there before him. It attacked him savagely and I was obliged to shoot it to save him from its fury.

A hundred feet above my house and on the left of the road stood in a terraced garden the Officers' Mess, occupied by my subaltern and the doctor. And three hundred feet higher still was the last building in Buxa, the Circuit House, intended as a courthouse and temporary residence for any civil official who should chance to come there on duty. The three white square towers, which stood on the spurs running down from Sinchula were known as the Picquet Towers, and, conspicuous against the dark mountains could be seen for many miles from the plains below. They were intended to contain in war time small parties of the garrison and hold points which commanded the fort at close range. From one above the east face of the fort even arrows could be shot into the interior of our defences; so its possession was a necessity to us. They were strongly built of stone and loopholed, the door eight feet from the ground, and reached by a ladder, windowless, the only light coming from the loopholes. To the west of the fort beyond the mountain road and behind another spur, was the bazaar or native

BUXA DUAR.
My bungalow in the foreground; the Officers' Mess among the trees.

"THE FORT WAS BUILT ON A KNOLL."

town, which consisted of a dozen wooden huts, and three or four brick houses, in which lived the few *bunniahs* or merchants who resided there to trade grain, salt, and cloth, with the Bhutanese across the border. There were hardly thirty natives in the bazaar, comprising our whole civil population. The "shops" in the one tiny street contained little of use, even for our sepoys' frugal needs, and nothing for ours; so that anything we required had to be sent for from Calcutta—a day and a night by train.

Beside the bazaar was the European cemetery, a mournful enclosure which was dotted with ruinous tombstones of British officers who had been killed or died of disease in this solitary outpost. The most recent grave was that of a former forest officer of Rajabhatkawa who, unable to bear the loneliness of his isolated life, had shot himself in his house in the jungle below. But before our detachment left Buxa another grave was dug here to hold the body of a young captain of my regiment. Though he died of disease, with no doctor there at the time to attend him, yet it was in reality loneliness that killed him; for, depressed by the solitude, he had no heart in him to fight against illness. But the far-flung boundaries of England's Empire are marked everywhere by graves like his.

From the south wall of the fort the ground fell in wooded spurs and rocky cliffs to the forest fifteen hundred feet below. East and west the interminable miles of trees ran on beyond the range of sight, clothing the foot-hills and climbing the steep mountain sides. Here and there a light green island in the darker-hued sea of foliage showed where a tea garden lay in a clearing, the iron-roofed factories, and the planters' bungalows visible through a field-glass. But to the south, beyond the clearly defined edge of the forest, the cultivated plains of Eastern Bengal stretched unbroken to Calcutta—three hundred miles away. South-west, in the Rains when the Indian atmosphere is clearest, we could see the Garo Hills fifty miles away in Assam, lying beyond the broad Brahmaputra where it flows to join the Ganges and pour their united waters through a hundred mouths into the Bay of Bengal—close on four hundred miles to the south of us.

CHAPTER II

LIFE ON OUTPOST

The daily routine—Drill in the Indian Army—Hindustani—A lingua franca—The divers tongues of India—The sepoys' lodging—Their ablutions—An Indian's fare—An Indian regiment—Rajput customs—The hospital—The doctor at work—Queer patients—A vicious bear—The Officers' Mess—Plain diet—Water—The simple life—A bachelor's establishment—A faithful Indian—Fighting the trusts—Transport in the hills—My bungalow—Amusements in Buxa—Dull days—Asirgarh—A lonely outpost—Poisoning a General—A storied fortress—Soldier ghosts—A spectral officer—The tragedy of isolation—A daring panther—A day on an elephant—Sport in the jungle—*Gooral* stalking in the hills—Strange pets—A friendly deer—A terrified visitor—A walking menagerie—Elephants tame and wild—Their training—Their caution—Their rate of speed—Fondness for water—Quickly reconciled to captivity—Snakes—A narrow escape—A king-cobra; the hamadryad—Hindu worship of the cobra—General Sir Hamilton Bower—An adventurous career—E. F. Knight—The General's inspection.

> "Why, soldiers, why should we be melancholy, boys,
> Whose business 'tis to die?"

WITH the easy philosophy of the soldier we three officers settled down rapidly in our new surroundings—new at least to my subaltern Creagh and me. Life was a little monotonous; but we did not grumble more than the Briton considers is his right. Our daily existence did not vary much. Before the sun had risen above the Picquet Towers, my white-robed Mohammedan servant woke me to the labours of the day, as the bugles in the fort were sounding the "dress for parade." Moving noiselessly about the room on bare feet he placed on a small table beside my camp bed, the *chota hazri* or "little breakfast," the light refreshment of tea, toast, and fruit with which the good Anglo-Indian begins the morning. The bad one prefers whisky-and-soda. Then my servitor laid out for me the dull khaki uniform which in India, except on occasions of ceremony, replaces the gayer garb of the soldier in England.

Morning and afternoon we drilled our men, watched them at musketry on the rifle-range, or practised them in mountain warfare up the steep slopes.

We found it difficult to manœuvre off the parade ground, as the hills around were mostly covered with such tangled jungle that one had to hack a passage through it with a *kukri* or a *dah*.* The drill of the Indian Army is precisely the same as for British troops. The words of command are invariably given in English, while only the explanations of movements are made in the vernacular. Thus in action an officer ignorant of Hindustani could take command of a native regiment in a crisis when all its white officers had been killed. Hindustani is a lingua franca invented in India by the Mohammedan armies of invasion from the north for intercourse with the peoples of the many conquered States. It is really a camp language made up of Sanscrit, Persian, Hindi and many other tongues. Even some military words, such as "*cartouche*," "*tambour*," have been borrowed from the French, owing to so many French adventurers having taken service in the armies of native princes in past times. Nowadays the English terms for military things or new inventions are adopted as

* Heavy native knives.

they stand. Hindustani or Urdu is by no means universally understood in India, though most Mohammedans throughout the Peninsula have some knowledge of it; for nearly every race has its own separate language or dialect and there are probably a hundred and fifty different tongues spoken in our Indian Empire. Urdu, however, is a *sine qua non* for the British officer of the native army; and he has to pass at least two examinations, the Lower and the Higher Standard, in it. But in addition he must also qualify in the particular language spoken by the majority of men in his regiment. A subaltern in a Gurkha regiment, for instance, must pass in Gurkhali, in a Mahratta regiment in Mahratti; and so on.

After morning parade I held orderly room, disposed of any prisoners—rare things in the Indian Army—and took reports from the native officers commanding the companies. Then I went to my office where, such is the amount of accounts and correspondence in the Service, I found at least two hours' work. Then I visited the hospital and went on to inspect the lines, as the barracks of native troops are called. The Indian sepoy is not luxuriously lodged. The barrack-rooms in Buxa, better and more substantial than in most places, were single-storied stone buildings roughly paved and furnished only with the men's belongings; for Government does not even provide them with beds. So each of my sepoys had fitted himself out with a *charpoy* or native cot, a four-legged wooden bedstead with a string network bottom which makes a comfortable couch. On this lay his *dhurri* or carpet, and his blankets. Overhead on a rough shelf stood his canvas kit-bag containing his clothing, while on pegs hung his belt, bayonet, and *puggri* or turban. Such luxuries as basins and baths are unknown to the sepoy. He strips to his waist-cloth and even in the coldest weather washes himself under a stand-pipe or pours water over his body from his *lotah* or small brass vessel which he always carries to drink from or use for his ablutions. In personal cleanliness most Indian races are surpassed only by the Japanese; and my men were either Mohammedans or Rajputs whose religions enjoin frequent ablutions.

From the barrack-rooms I passed on to the sepoys' cooking-places. In the Indian Army rations in peace-time are not provided for the men; but, instead, they are given a certain allowance of money above their pay known as "compensation for dearness of provisions." This helps them to purchase their food, which consists in general of *chupatties* or cakes of flour and water, supplemented by *ghee* or clarified butter, various grain-stuffs, curry and sometimes a little meat. Many races eat rice instead of flour. Their method of cooking is primitive. A hole scratched in the ground and a couple of stones make the *chula* or fireplace, in which burn a few bits of wood or a handful of dry twigs. The sepoy mixes his *atta*, or flour, into a paste with a little water in a large brass dish, rolls it into balls and flattens them out into thin cakes on a convex iron plate over the fire, the result being something like crisp, thick pancakes. Having made a pile of these he grinds between stones various spices, such as turmeric, chillies, onions and poppy seed, moistened with water to make his curry, adds some cooked vegetables or a raw onion, and his simple meal is ready.

Among Hindus, men of different castes cook and eat apart. A Brahmin must have his separate fire-place, prepare his own food and eat alone. Other castes are not so particular and can employ cooks. In an Indian regiment each company or double company is generally composed of men of one race; and Government allows and pays two cooks and a *bhisti* or water-carrier to each company, these menials, with Hindus, being necessarily of the same caste as the sepoys they serve. Thus in my own battalion we have a double company of Rajputs, one of Gujars, and one of Rawats—all these being Hindus. The fourth is composed of Mohammedans. Each company is officered by men of their own caste, a *Subhedar* or captain, and a *Jemadar* or lieutenant; and every two companies are under a double company commander and a double company officer, who are British, and with the commandant, adjutant and quartermaster make up the European officers of the regiment.

My double company in Buxa was composed of Rajputs; but, having had to detach signallers, bandsmen, clerks, and other employed men to go with the headquarters to Dibrugarh, some Mussulmans were temporarily attached to bring it up to its original strength of two hundred men. The Rajputs' method of eating their meals is rather peculiar. Before each they must bathe and put on a clean *dhotie*, a cotton cloth wrapped round the waist, passing between the legs and falling to the knees. They must eat inside the *chauka*, a space of ground marked out and swept clean. Food which they wish to carry away and consume outside the *chauka*, as, for instance, if they are going on a long march, must be prepared in a particular way with water instead of *ghee*, which is generally used by them in cooking.

In my daily visit to the hospital I would find our medical officer, Smith, hard at work. For, besides the sick of the detachment, he had to tend any natives from outside who chose to seek the white man's medicine. To help him he had a young Indian sub-assistant surgeon, who, despite the scanty medical training he had received, pined to perform major operations. With little knowledge of surgery he wished to resort to the knife on every possible occasion. Once, when left in sole charge of the hospital, he determined to amputate the leg of a Bhuttia suffering from gangrenous sores. The patient, however, was of a different opinion and during the night stole silently from the hospital and fled in terror across the hills to his village. Like most mountaineers the Bhuttias are very subject to goitre. Two out of every three are the proud possessors of these enormous appendages, in some cases nearly as large as the owner's head. They seemed to regard them as ornaments, and absolutely refused to allow our medico to operate on them. One day there was carried to the fort from Chunabatti, the only village for miles round, a Chinaman suffering from beriberi. This man, who knew no word of any language but his own, had made his way on foot from China across Tibet and Bhutan over the Himalayas endeavouring to reach Calcutta in search of work. Stricken down with this fell disease he had lain for months in the village, living on the charity of the Bhuttias, and was brought to our hospital only to die. Another interesting case was a boy about seven years old who was brought in, absolutely scalped by a blow from

RAJPUT SEPOYS COOKING.

BRITISH AND INDIAN OFFICERS.

the paw of a bear which he had disturbed when gathering wood in the forest. From brow to nape of neck his skull had been left bare to the bone, in which were deep indentations from the animal's claws. The shock of the blow would probably have killed a European, but with the marvellous tenacity of life among savage races, the boy soon recovered.

Our morning's work finished, we climbed up the hill for breakfast in the Mess. This was a long, single-storied stone building with an iron roof, erected on pillars which raised it six feet from the ground. From the tangled wilderness of the garden, bright with the vivid colours of huge bushes of poinsettia and bougainvillias, a flight of steps led up to the railed veranda which ran along the front of the building, and on to which opened the four rooms —the end ones used as quarters by Creagh and Smith, the centre apartments being the ante-room and dining-room. I wonder what some writers of military fiction, who prate glibly of the luxury in which army officers live, would say to the bare rooms and whitewashed walls of our Mess, furnished only with a few rickety tables and unsteady chairs. Or my subaltern's abode. One room, an iron cot borrowed from the hospital, a kitchen table, one dilapidated chair, a tin bath, and an iron basin on an old packing-case, comprised the sum-total of his possessions. Other furniture we could not get in Buxa; for the nearest shops were three hundred miles away in Calcutta. Of course, crockery, cooking-pots, glass-ware, linen and cutlery, we had to provide for ourselves. These we had brought with us. Before long, by dint of colour-washing the stone walls, hanging curtains and draperies of native cloth, and decorating the bare walls with the heads of animals we shot, we succeeded in making the Mess quite habitable and cosy.

We were not much better off in the bare necessities of life. Buxa produced little in the way of food. Chickens—more literally, hens of no uncertain antiquity—and eggs of almost equal age were often procurable locally. But no meat. Sometimes a Bhuttia from across the frontier brought a goat for sale; and, although the Asiatic goat is an abomination, yet such an occasion was a red-letter day for us. Bread was sent us by rail from a railway refreshment-room twenty-four hours away, and did not always arrive. Fresh vegetables we never saw until later on we tried our prentice hands at gardening—and a sorry mess we made of it. In the winter we could add to the pot by the help of our rifles and guns; and venison and jungle fowl were a welcome change from the monotony of our menus. But our staple food consisted of tinned provisions—an expensive and wearisome diet. I dare say the British workman would have turned up his nose at our usual fare; and I could not blame him. Even the water supply in Buxa was a difficult question. Our Mess got its water from a spring in the hills hundreds of yards away, led down in bamboos to the kitchen. The fort was supplied from another spring in the base of the hill on which it was built; and all day long the *bhistis* * toiled up and down bringing the water in goatskin bags. But a few months after our arrival the springs nearly gave out; and I was faced with the necessity of abandoning fort and station, and moving the military and civil population to camp on the banks

* Water-carriers.

of a river miles away in the forest below, when we were saved by timely rain.

Yet despite the simple life we were leading in Buxa my monthly expenses were more than twenty pounds for the bare necessities of existence. I had to pay rent to Government for my bungalow, and a share of the rent for the Mess, as well as my share of the expenses of mess-servants, lighting, and food. My personal household consisted of my "boy" or body-servant, a *dhobi* or washerman, a *bhisti* or water-carrier, a *syce* or groom, and my sword-orderly, a sepoy of the regiment. This last individual, a Mussulman named Mohammed Draj Khan, had been in my service for many years and, with the fidelity of the Indian, was faithfully attached to me. He went with me to China in 1900 with the Indian Expeditionary Force and returned with me again there five years later. When I was going from Hong Kong on furlough to the United States, Canada and Europe, I arranged for him to be given six months' leave to his home in India. But when he heard of it Draj Khan was exceedingly wroth.

"What? Am I not to accompany my Sahib?" he demanded indignantly.

"No; I cannot take you with me to Europe," I replied. "But I have got you leave to go home to your wife whom you have not seen for four years."

"Oh, my wife does not matter," was the ungallant answer; "she can wait. But my place is with my Sahib wherever he goes."

And he has never forgiven me for not taking him; although he still continues to serve me faithfully.

Our sepoys fared better than their British officers. We found on arrival that the local *bunniahs* or shopkeepers were in the habit of supplying the men with very inferior and bad flour and other food-stuffs and charging a high price for them, relying on the monopoly they enjoyed. I determined to follow the example of the United States Government and make war on trusts. So I sent my native officers to Cooch Behar and other towns fifty miles away to purchase supplies, and ordered flour in bulk from a mill under English management in Calcutta. I had it sent by rail to Buxa Road Station, and conveyed thence by our elephants and Bhuttia coolies. An elephant can carry a weight of ten or twelve maunds—a maund being equal to eighty pounds. The sturdy Bhuttias, women as well as men, could come up our steep road, each with a load of two maunds on his or her back. Their burdens were fixed in two forked sticks bound to the shoulders in such a way that when the bearers sat down the ends of the sticks rested on the ground and supported the weight. But when heavily laden a coolie cannot then rise to his feet unaided, unless he first lies down, rolls over on his face, then pushes himself on to his knees with his hands and stands up. In Chemulpo and Seoul in Corea I have seen coolies employ a similar method of carrying their loads.

After breakfast I returned to my house to pass the hours until the afternoon parade. After the dilapidated bungalows of most stations in India, with their thatched roofs sheltering rats, squirrels and even snakes, and their floors of pounded earth and decayed matting full of fleas, ants and the myriad plagues of insect life of the East, my small house seemed luxurious. It was built strongly of rough stone blocks to withstand the awful mountain storms. The roof was of iron which rang like a drum to the

MY DOUBLE COMPANY.

MY BACHELOR ESTABLISHMENT.

heavy rain and monster hailstones of the Monsoon. It contained four small rooms with ceilings and floors of wood, each with its fireplace. For during the winter we found it cold enough to have fires going day and night, the jungle around furnishing us with an ample supply of fuel. The meagre furniture which I had bought from the major of the Punjabis was soon supplemented with a few more articles sent from Calcutta. The little garden contained mango trees and a tree bearing the huge and evil-smelling jack-fruit, of which natives are very fond, though its sickening odour and oversweet taste repel most Europeans. The hedges around my compound were of wild roses. At one side stood my stable and the stone outhouses in which my servants lived; for in India the domestics are not lodged in the bungalow.

The afternoon was occupied with drills, signalling practice and military lectures to the non-commissioned officers.

Buxa offered scant amusement within its limits to us Britishers. We had hockey-matches with the men two or three times a week. Creagh, being a keen golfer, tried to make miniature links about the fort; but, after losing six balls in his first game in the jungle around, he gave it up. We turned our attention to tennis. A comparatively level space hewed out of the mountain-side was fixed on as a court. Rocks four or five feet high were dug out of it; and the elephants were employed for days in bringing up earth from the plains below to spread on it. But more rocks seemed to grow in it and shove their heads through the thin covering of mould, grass came in thick, wiry patches; and altogether our tennis court could not be pronounced a success.

Evening brought with it the dullest hours of the day. The Calcutta newspaper, which arrived by post every afternoon, was soon read; and the English journals sent to us from regimental headquarters were a month old. None of us were keen card players. Our library was small; and, as light literature, drill books soon cease to charm. Our daily life was too uneventful to afford many subjects of conversation; and as topics the incompetency of Naik Chandu Singh or the slackness on parade of Sepoy Pem Singh were not engrossing. England seemed too far away for the discussion of its politics to interest us. The pitiable limitations of men as talkers was painfully evident. Not being women we had no ever-ready subjects of conversation in dress, babies and servants' misdemeanours; and we could not talk scandal about ourselves. So, after the meagre dinner that our Gurkha cook contrived out of the athletic hen or tinned sausage, we threw ourselves into long chairs around the fire; Creagh betook himself to the study of military books for his forthcoming examination for promotion, and the doctor and I thumbed tattered novels we had read a dozen times.

But Buxa was not the loneliest spot in which I have been quartered. As a subaltern I was stationed alone for many months in Asirgarh in the Central Provinces, an old Indian fortress on a hill lost in the jungle. That was solitude itself. My nearest European neighbour was forty miles away. I saw no white face and spoke no word of English for months at a time. Once a year a General was supposed to pay it the compliment of an official inspection, although the garrison consisted only of a British subaltern and fifty sepoys. But I think that after one occasion when the General and his staff officers nearly died on my hands of ptomaine poisoning—really contracted on their journey thither, but ascribed by the uncharitable among my friends to my base devices and resentment at having my peace disturbed by this officious intrusion—this duty grew out of favour with generals who valued their lives. This detachment has since been abolished.

The fortress was wonderfully interesting, with a history reaching back to the eighth century. It had passed through the hands of the various masters of India in turn, and every stone of its walls had a story to tell. Taken by the British from the Maharajah of Gwalior twice, it remained in our possession from 1818, and was formerly garrisoned by a company of Artillery, a British regiment and a wing of a native battalion. Fallen from its high estate, a subaltern and half a company were considered enough for it in my time. And the subaltern combined in his own person the important offices of Commandant of Asirgarh Fortress, officer commanding the troops, officer in charge of military treasure chest, Cantonment Magistrate third class, and Church Trustee. For inside the fort were a Protestant Church in disused barracks, a ruined Catholic Chapel on the altar of which wild monkeys perched, and two cemeteries full of graves of English dead. The post was a lonely one for a young officer. I lived in the only habitable European building, formerly the general hospital, for which I paid twenty-four pounds a year to Government. The dead house was just outside my bedroom window. The interior of the fort, the fifty-feet-high walls of which were a mile and a half in circumference, was crowded with the ruins of an ancient palace, a large mosque, an old Moghul prison with wonderful underground passages and cells, and—most depressing of all—the gaunt wrecks of English bungalows with bare rafters and tattered ceiling-cloths. A fit habitation for ghosts. And ghosts there were. No native would venture about the fort alone at night. Weird tales had my sepoys to tell of the *Shaitans* and *bhuts*, as they termed the spectral beings that wandered within the walls in the dark hours and were seen again and again by my men. They invariably took the form of British soldiers. And actually one night when I was miles away out shooting in the jungle the sentry at the gate turned out the guard to an approaching white officer, whom he took to be me. The whole guard, eleven men in all, swore next day to the ghostly visitant.

Few English folk at home, who fondly picture an officer's life in India as one long round of social gaieties, of polo, sport, races and balls, realise the tragedies of loneliness of many who serve the Empire. Of the dreary solitude of a military police post in the jungles of Burma, of a fort on the Indian frontier, where a young subaltern lives for months, for years, alone. A boy brought up in the comfort of an English home, used to the pleasant fellowship of a regimental mess, is there condemned to isolation from his kind, to food that a pauper would reject, and a lodging a cottager would scorn. Should one of the many diseases of India lay its grisly hand on him he is far from medical aid. He must fight his illness alone, lying unattended in his comfortless quarters. Outside, a pitiless sun in a sky of brass pours down its rays on the glaring, shadowless desert. Inside, the droning whine of the punkah mocks him throughout the weary day, as it scarcely stirs the heated air. Night brings only the more terrible hours of darkness when sleep is banished from the tired eyes and the fever-racked brain knows no relief. Small wonder that too often in his agony he seeks death by his own hand. I have gone through the hell of sickness in a lonely post, when day after day the awful pains of jungle fever tortured me and night brought no relief. I have known what it is to gaze in my delirium at my revolver and think it the kindly friend that alone could end my misery, until a sane moment made me realise that its touch meant death and I had it taken away from me. But I have known, too, many a poor fellow to whom that saving interval of sanity was denied, to whom a bullet through the tortured brain brought oblivion.

In comparison with Asirgarh, Buxa was quite a gay place. I was seldom alone in it, and generally had at least one other white man with me. We were kept in touch with the outside world by a telegraph line, which, however, was constantly being broken by trees blown down by storms or uprooted by elephants. Once a day a sturdy little Bhuttia postman toiled up the hill with our letters. "His Majesty's Mail" carried for his protection a short spear with bells on it to scare wild beasts; but this did not save him from being occasionally stopped by wild elephants and once being treed by a tiger. For sport we had to descend to the forest; though sometimes a barking deer wandered into our gardens from the jungle, and from the Mess veranda we shot a couple on the hillside across a deep *nullah* or ravine.

Between my bungalow and the Married Officers'

Quarters ran another *nullah*. Occasionally, when there was no moon, a panther used to wander down it, calling like a cat in the darkness which was too intense to allow me a shot at the animal. When we came to Buxa we had wondered why the windows of our houses were covered with strong wire netting, and were inclined to be sceptical when told that this was to keep predatory beasts out. But the Punjabi subaltern had been awakened one night by the noise of some animal moving about his room in the Mess, he having left his door open. He seized a handful of matches, struck them and saw a panther scared by the sudden blaze dash out through the door. And twice during our sojourn in Buxa did a similar thing happen.

This particular panther, for we assumed that it was always the same animal, haunted the Station and preyed on the dogs in the bazaar. One day on the road just below the fort it met one of my sepoys who promptly climbed the nearest tree and remained in the topmost branches until his shouts brought some other men to the rescue. Once at night I was roused from sleep by wild cries from a Bhuttia's hut on the spur above our Mess and learned on inquiry that the panther had carried off his dog. Another time, in brilliant moonlight, an Indian doctor then in medical charge of the detachment, who lived in the bungalow next to mine, saw the beast sitting in the small garden intently watching the door of an outhouse in which a milch-goat was kept shut up. The doctor ran indoors to fetch his gun and had an unsuccessful shot at it as it jumped the hedge. Needless to say we made many efforts to compass its death. One night it killed a goat tied up as a bait to a tree within fifteen yards of the fort and was wounded by a native officer waiting for it behind the wall. Yet not long afterwards it climbed into the fort at night and carried off a sepoy's dog. Many a time I sat up in a tree over a bleating goat in the moonlight, but always in vain; and I suppose that panther still lives to afford sport to our successors in Buxa.

Life was well worth living on the days when we could descend into the forest for a shoot. At dawn we started down the three miles of steep road to Santrabari where the elephants awaited us. For work in the jungle these animals, instead of the howdahs or cage-like structures with seats which they carry on shoots in fairly open country, have only their pads, thick, straw-stuffed mattresses bound on their backs by stout ropes. For in dense forest howdahs would soon be swept off. When we arrived at the Peelkhana the *mahouts* made the huge beasts kneel down, or we clambered up, either by hauling oneself up by the tail, aided by one foot on the hind leg held up for the purpose at the driver's command, or by catching hold of the ears from the front and standing on the curled-up trunk which then raised us up on to the elephant's head. One either sat sideways on the pad or astride above the shoulders and behind the *mahout* who rode on the neck with his bare feet behind the ears. Then our giant steeds lumbered off into the forest with an awkward, disjointed stride which is sorely trying to the novice. And sitting upright with nothing to rest the back against for eight hours or more, shaken violently all the time by the jerky motion, is decidedly tiring. Prepared for beast or bird, each of us carried a rifle and a shot-gun, and, separating from the others, went his own way through the forest. Sometimes a *sambhur*, the big Indian stag, was the bag; sometimes a wild boar. Perhaps a *khakur*, the small, alert barking deer, of which the flesh is infinitely more tender than a *sambhur's*, or a few jungle fowl, rewarded our efforts. We carried with us food and water for the day and did not return until evening. Then, after leaving the elephants at the Peelkhana, came the fifteen-hundred-feet climb up the steep road to Buxa. And in a long chair in the Mess the fatigues of the day were forgotten in the pleasure of recounting every incident of the sport.

Sometimes we went out among the hills around us to stalk *gooral*, an active little wild goat. Clambering up the almost sheer sides of the mountains or clinging to the faces of rugged precipices while carrying a heavy rifle was a toilsome task; and too often, after a long and perilous climb, did I arrive in sight of the quarry only to see it disappear in bounding flight over the cliffs.

In our excursions into the forest or by purchase from natives we gradually gathered together a varied collection of pets to solace our loneliness. At different times I possessed half a dozen barking deer fawns, one of which became an institution in Buxa. Scorning confinement she insisted on being allowed to wander loose about the Station, and, soon getting to know the sepoys' meal hours, visited the fort regularly. She was punctual in her attendance at tea-time in my bungalow, being exceedingly fond of buttered toast, and always claiming her share of mine. More than once I have only just been in time to save her from the rifle of one of our rare visitors who, seeing her on the hill-side, took her to be wild. A

A KNEELING ELEPHANT.

small green parrot which I had similarly objected to being shut up and flew freely about the Station. From wherever it happened to be its quick eye always marked my servant bringing my afternoon meal to the bungalow from the kitchen; and, having a strange liking for hot tea, it used to fly in through the open door of my sitting-room and perch on my head. It was little use my objecting to this familiarity; for, if I attempted to dislodge it, it would stick its claws into my scalp and hold on to my ear by its sharp beak until I let it drink from my cup. Its propensity for swooping down in the open on any white man was sometimes alarming to strangers. Once a certain civil official visitor to Buxa who was jocularly reputed to be overfond of alcohol and never far from the verge of delirium tremens was approaching my bungalow when the parrot swept down on him and tried to alight on his hat. Uncertain as to the reality of the vision circling around his head, our visitor uttered a cry of terror and tried to brush the phantom aside until I laughingly assured him that it was a real bird. He revenged himself afterwards by encouraging the parrot in a depraved taste for whisky.

In my afternoon walks I used to be accompanied by a small menagerie. Two small barking deer stepped daintily behind me, their long ears twitching incessantly. A monkey loped on all fours ahead, now and then stopping to sit down and scratch himself thoughtfully. A bear cub shambled along, playing with my dogs and being occasionally rolled over by a combined rush of riotous puppies. On our return to the bungalow we would be greeted by no less than five cats; while from its perch on the veranda a young hornbill, scarcely feathered and possessing a beak almost as big as its body, would survey us with a cold and glassy stare from its unwinking eyes. Once in a beat in the forest my orderly caught a *sambhur* fawn which he bore, shrieking piteously, in his arms to me. In a day or two it was perfectly tame, fed from my hand, and insisted on sleeping on my bed. It was killed by a snake shortly afterwards.

I might almost include in our list of pets our three Government elephants, of which we became very fond. They were named Jhansi, Dundora, and Khartoum. I generally used the last in the jungle; though when looking for dangerous game I preferred Dundora. Jhansi was a frivolous and unsteady young lady of forty years of age; and shooting from her back was impossible. I soon learned to drive them, sitting on their necks and guiding them by pressing my feet behind the ears, as the *mahouts* do. I was sometimes called on to doctor them; and had to perform almost a surgical operation on Jhansi, when wounded by a wild elephant out in the jungle. I had fortunately been taught how to treat their ailments when doing veterinary work in a transport course some years before. Elephants are somewhat delicate animals and liable to a multiplicity of diseases. Accustomed in the wild state to shelter from the noonday heat in thick forests, they suffer greatly if worked in a hot sun and get sore feet if obliged to tramp along hard roads. Domesticated elephants are generally very gentle and docile; though males in a state of *musth* often become very dangerous. Contrary to the usually received opinion they are not intelligent; but they are very obedient. At the word of command they will kneel, rise, pick up an article from the ground or lift a man on to their necks. When a *mahout* is gathering fodder for his charge and sees suitable leaves out of reach at the top of a small tree, he orders his elephant to break the tree down. This it does by curling up its trunk and pressing its forehead with all its weight behind it against the stem and thus uprooting it. When crossing a stream they try to sound the depth with their trunks. A bridge they attempt cautiously with one foot, and, if not satisfied with its strength, will resolutely refuse to trust themselves on it. Though good at climbing up steep slopes they are the reverse when descending. On the level they are fast for a short distance only; but they can cover many miles in the day when travelling. They are excellent swimmers and are very fond of water. In the wild state they bathe whenever they can; and tame elephants thoroughly enjoy being taken into the river and lie in the shallows with a look of blissful content while their *mahouts* wash them and scrub them with bricks. It is extraordinary how quickly they become used to captivity. In a few days they let their keepers feed them, mount them and take them to water. I have seen two, caught only four months before, being driven in a beat for a tiger; and when he was wounded and broke back into thick jungle they followed him unhesitatingly at their *mahouts'* command.

Like all hill-places Buxa was full of snakes. One night in the hot weather when dining on the veranda, we found a viper climbing up the rough stone wall of the Mess just behind our chairs. We vacated our seats promptly and killed it with long bamboos. Another evening I discovered one on my veranda.

Once when camped in the forest with my detachment, the officer who was then with me and I were sitting at a small table having tea when one of the native officers came up. I had a chair brought for him and he sat talking to us until dusk came. My servant placed a lighted lamp on the table. Suddenly the native officer who was sitting a few yards from me said quietly:

"Do not move, Sahib. There is a snake under your chair; and if you try to stand up you may tread on it."

It was difficult to obey him and remain motionless; but, as it was the wisest thing to do, I sat quietly until I saw a small and very poisonous viper emerge between my feet and wriggle off. Then I jumped up, seized the lamp from the table and a cane from my native officer and killed it.

In Buxa one afternoon when I happened to be inspecting the bazaar a native ran up in a state of great excitement to inform me that a "*bahut burra samp*," a *very* large snake, was climbing up the precipice on the west side of the hill on which the bazaar stood. I went with him and found two or three Bhuttias looking over the edge at an enormous serpent which was making its way up the steep face, clinging to projecting rocks and bushes. From its size I took it to be a python, which is not poisonous and kills its prey only by compression. We waited until the snake had got its head and a third of its length over the brink and fell upon it with sticks and clubbed it to death. I had it carried to my bungalow where I measured it and found it to be fifteen feet two inches in length. Preparatory to skinning it, I compared it with the coloured plates in a book on Indian reptiles and found to my horror that it was a king-cobra or hamadryad, the most dreaded and dangerous ophidian in Asia. It is very venomous and wantonly attacks human beings; so that it was fortunate for us that we had caught it at a disadvantage. There is a recorded instance of one chasing and overtaking a man on a pony. It is generally to be found only in the forests of Eastern Bengal, Assam, and Burmah.

When one considers the enormous number of snakes in India it is surprising how seldom they are seen. This is due to their rarely venturing out in the daytime. But I have killed one with my sword when returning from a morning parade in Bhuj and another, a black cobra five feet nine inches long, in my bathroom in Asirgarh. Few Europeans ever get over their instinctive horror of these reptiles; but the natives, thousands of whom die every year from snake-bite owing to their going about with bare feet and legs at night, have not the same dread of them. In fact Hindus hold the cobra sacred, and have an annual festival, the Nagpanchmai, in its honour. I have seen in Cutch the Rao (or Rajah) of that State go in solemn procession on that day to worship it in a temple, accompanied by his strangely-uniformed troops, which included soldiers in steel caps and chain mail walking on stilts. They were supposed to be prepared to fight in the salt deserts and sandy wastes which surround Cutch.

Our first visitors from the outside world reached Buxa about a month after our arrival. They were General Bower, commanding the Assam Brigade to which we belonged, and his staff officer, come for the annual inspection of the detachment. Brigadier-

General (now Major-General Sir Hamilton) Bower is a man whose paths have lain in strange places and whose career reads like a book of adventures. A keen sportsman and a daring explorer of untrodden ways, he was as a captain ordered by the Government of India to pursue the Mohammedan murderer of an English traveller, Dalgleish, through the savage wilds of Central Asia. For months he chased the assassin through sterile regions where no European had ever before set foot and at last hounded him into the hands of the Russians at Samarcand where he killed himself in jail. His capture was necessary to show the lawless tribesmen of Central Asia that a price must be paid for a white man's blood and that the arm of our Government could reach an Englishman's slayer in any land. Readers of E. F. Knight's fascinating book, "Where Three Empires Meet" will remember the author's meeting with Captain Bower in Kashmir in 1891, after the latter's successful pursuit of this murderer, Dad Mohammed. Bower was then starting on his celebrated journey from India overland to China, which he has described in his work "Across Tibet." And since those days his life has not been tame. Ordered to raise a regiment of Chinamen to garrison Wei-hai-wei, he landed in Shanghai with one follower and soon brought a corps of Northern Chinese into being, which, in two years after its raising, fought splendidly in the bloody struggles around Tientsin in the Boxer War of 1900. He afterwards commanded the British Legation Guard in Pekin and found ample scope for all his tact and good temper in the intercourse with the officers of the Guards of other nationalities in the Chinese capital.

He spent three days with us; and though his inspection was thorough, and entailed fatiguing manœuvres through jungle I had hitherto regarded as impenetrable and up mountains I had considered unscaleable, we were sorry when his visit terminated. As a rule one does not hail a General's inspection as a pleasant function. But General Bower proved the pleasantest and most interesting visitor we ever had. Tired of our own thrice-told tales we revelled in the interesting conversation of a man who had seen and done so much in his adventurous career, who had journeyed along untrodden ways, had fought strange foes and carried his life in his hand in wild lands where no king's writ runs. We talked much of Knight, whom I have the good fortune to know, a man who, like the General, might be the hero of a boy's book of romance. His life had been equally adventurous. He fought for the French in 1870, and against them later in Madagascar. In a small yacht he crossed the Atlantic and visited most countries in South America. In his wanderings beyond the frontier of India he came in for the difficult little Hunza-Nagar campaign and fought in it. Author, traveller, war-correspondent, amateur soldier, he has been everywhere, seen and done everything. And, simple and courageous, he is a type of the adventurers who made England great. Romance is not dead while such men as he and Bower live.

With a General on official inspection one is inclined to speed the parting guest; but as General Bower waved his farewell to us from the back of the elephant which was carrying him downhill we were sorry to part with him, and all three hoped to meet him the following year again in Buxa. But when he came I alone was left. Smith had gone to Calcutta, and Creagh was commanding another detachment of the regiment in the heart of Tibet, even farther from civilisation than Buxa.

CHAPTER III

THE BORDERLAND OF BHUTAN

The races along our North-East Border—Tibet—The Mahatmas—Nepal—Bhutan—Its geography—Its founder—Its Government—Religious rule—Analogy between Bhutan and old Japan—*Penlops* and *Daimios*—The Tongsa *Penlop*—Re-incarnation of the Shaptung Rimpoche—China's claim to Bhutan—Capture of the Maharajah of Cooch Behar—Bogle's mission—Raids and outrages—The Bhutan War of 1864-5—The Duars—The annual subsidy—Bhutan to-day—Religion—An impoverished land—Bridges—Soldiers in Bhutan—The feudal system—Administration of justice—Tyranny of officials—The Bhuttias—Ugly women—Our neighbours in Buxa—A Bhuttia festival—Archery—A banquet—A dance—A Scotch half-caste—Chunabatti—Nature of the borderland—Disappearing rivers—The Terai—Tea gardens—A planter's life—The club—Wild beasts in the path—The Indian planters—Misplaced sympathy—The tea industry—Profits and losses—Planters' salaries—Their daily life—Bhuttia raids on tea gardens—Fearless planters—An unequal fight.

ALONG the North-East Frontier of India lie numerous States and races of which the average Britisher is very ignorant. Of late years Tibet has bulked largely in the public eye owing to international and diplomatic intrigues and our little war with it in 1904. But, previously, it was probably best known to the Man in the Street as the country from which according to the Theosophists, "the Mahatmas come from." They must all have deserted it long since; for I never met anyone who had been in

Tibet who had ever heard of them there. Travellers like General Bower who had journeyed through the land from end to end, officers of the Anglo-Indian Army that made its way to Lhasa, others of my regiment who had lived in Gyantse, learned to speak the language and mixed much with the people, were all ignorant of the existence of these mysterious and supernaturally gifted beings.

Nepal is best known as the country which supplies us with the popular little Gurkha soldiers. But Bhutan, which lies along our Indian border, is scarcely known even by name to the crowd. Yet, as long ago as in the days of Warren Hastings, we had diplomatic intercourse with it; and half a century has not elapsed since we were at war with the Bhutanese. Yet, to-day, there are not a dozen Englishmen who have crossed its borders.

Bhutan is an exceedingly mountainous country, twenty thousand square miles in extent, lying along the northern boundary of Bengal and Assam, hemmed in on the west by Sikkim, a State under our suzerainty, and on the west and north by Tibet. A Buddhist land, its system of government is very similar to that of Japan before the Meiji, the revolution of 1868. It was founded by a lama who, after establishing himself as supreme ruler, handed over the control of temporal matters to a layman and a council of elders. Until the other day the country was nominally governed by a spiritual head, the Shaptung Rimpoche, an incarnation of the deified founder, known in India as the Durma Raja, and a mundane monarch whom we term the Deb Raja. They were assisted by a council. The analogy between them and the Mikados and Shoguns of

Japan was very close. To complete it the real control of the land was practically in the hands of feudal barons called *Penlops*, who, like the *Daimios* of old Japan, ruled their own territories, and, when strong enough, defied the Central Government. For the greater part of the last century the *Penlops* of Tongsa were the most powerful among these. The present holder of the title was recently elected hereditary Maharajah of Bhutan. He is Sir Ugyen Wang-chuk, K.C.I.E.—a most enlightened man and strongly in favour of the British. During the war of 1904 with Tibet, he placed all his influence on our side; and, his efforts to prevent bloodshed being unavailing, he accompanied our troops to Lhasa. The Government of India, in recognition of his services rewarded him with the K.C.I.E., and a present of rifles and ammunition. When our present King-Emperor visited India as Prince of Wales in 1906, Sir Ugyen Wang-chuk was invited to Calcutta and saw for himself the wonders of civilisation and learned something of the might of England. It was shortly after his return from India that he was elected Maharajah. Though he is now the real ruler of the country the pretence is kept up of the Government still being in the hands of the Durma and Deb Rajas. On the death of the incumbent of the former position, his reincarnation is sought for among young boys throughout the land, as happens in the case of the Dalai Lama in Tibet.

In former times China held a shadowy claim to the suzerainty of Bhutan; and when, after our war with Tibet, we re-established her influence over that country, the Chinese endeavoured to reassert their hold over Bhutan as well. The Tongsa *Penlop* preferred having the British to deal with and in January, 1910 signed a treaty by which he placed the foreign relations of his country under the control of the Government of India. But otherwise Bhutan is completely independent. We do not interfere in any way in its internal affairs; and while the Bhutanese can enter India freely, no Britisher is allowed into their country without special sanction from our own authorities, which is rarely given.

The first occasion on which the Indian Government was brought into contact with Bhutan was in the time of Warren Hastings. In those days the Bhutanese claimed sovereignty over the forest-clad plains in the north of Eastern Bengal. In 1772 they carried off the Maharajah of Cooch Behar as a prisoner. A small British force pursued them into the hills and made them surrender their captive. Hastings seized the opportunity of their suing for peace to send an Envoy, Bogle, to endeavour to establish trading relations with Bhutan. Bogle entered the country by way of Buxa Duar and was at first well received by the Deb Raja. He gave a flattering account of the people and their customs in his journal; and his description of Bhutan might almost have been written yesterday, so little changed is it. His mission bore little fruit; and the jealousy of strangers, inherent in all Buddhist nations, soon put a stop to any intercourse with India. A long series of raids into our territory and outrages on our subjects along the border was borne with exemplary patience for many years by the East India Company. But at length the ill-treatment of another Envoy, Eden, sent to remonstrate with the Bhutanese, led to our declaring war on them in 1864. Taken by surprise at first, they were driven out of their forts in the Himalayan passes; but they soon rallied, chased one of our columns in disorder out of the country, forcing it to abandon its guns, and penned in our garrisons in the captured forts. But, in the following year, despite their fanatical bravery, they were defeated finally and compelled to beg for peace. The Indian Government deprived them of the Duars, the forest strip of country lying along the base of the Himalayas. The word *duar* means "door," or "gateway," and originally referred to the passes leading through the mountains into India. The Bhutanese pleaded that this deprived them of their most profitable raiding ground and source of supply of slaves. Our Government, moved by this ingenuous plea, compensated them by the grant of an annual subsidy of fifty thousand rupees (now equal to £3333) which has recently been raised to a lakh, which is one hundred thousand. This sum, like similar but smaller amounts disbursed by us to savage tribes along our frontiers, may be regarded as either a species of blackmail or a reward of good behaviour. Should the recipients displease us in the conduct of their relations with other countries or should they allow their unruly young men to raid across our borders, the payment is suspended until amends are made. It generally has the desired effect, and saves a punitive little war. I was surprised, however, to find that the Bhuttias inside our frontier, who were mostly refugees from the exactions and oppression of their own officials, attributed our paying this subsidy to fear of the might of Bhutan, and held it up to my sepoys as a proof of the greatness of their nation

Bhutan to-day stands much where it has for centuries past. Its religion is a debased lamaism and idolatry, which replace the high moral teaching of Buddha. Its impoverished peasants and even the lay officials are heavily taxed to support in idleness the innumerable shoals of Buddhist monks and nuns. Praying wheels and prayer flags and the support of lamas are, as in Tibet, all that is necessary to ensure salvation. Arts and handicrafts are decaying. Trade is principally carried on by the primitive method of barter. Owing to the mountainous nature of the country cultivation is much restricted. The only coins I could find struck in Bhutan were a silver piece worth sixpence, and a copper one worth the sixteenth of a penny. British, Tibetan and Chinese coins are used. Most of our annual subsidy finds its way back into India in exchange for cloth and food-stuffs. When paid by us a large portion of it used to go to the ecclesiastical dignitaries in the capital, Punakha, and the rest was distributed among the various *Penlops*. The Deb Zimpun, the official sent into our territory every year to receive it, now hands it over to the Maharajah, who disburses it.

The roads through Bhutan are mere ill-kept mule tracks. The forests, which are in strong contrast to the usually treeless plateaux of Northern Tibet, though not found at the greatest elevation in the country, are well looked after; and the regulations for their preservation are strictly enforced. A long series of internecine wars has ruined the land; but of late years the predominance of the Tongsa *Penlop* has ensured internal peace. The only buildings of note are the temples, the *gumpas* or large monasteries and the *jongs* or castles, huge rambling edifices of stone and wood. The towns mostly consist of wooden huts. But the Bhutanese are very clever in constructing bridges over the rivers and torrents that traverse their mountainous country. These are sometimes marvels of engineering skill, great wooden structures on the cantilever principle or well-constructed iron suspension bridges, remarkable when one considers the rude appliances at the disposal of the builders.

There is no regular army in Bhutan, each *Penlop* and important official maintaining his own armed retinue; but every man in the country is liable for service. Their weapons are chiefly single-edged straight swords and bows and arrows. The swords are practically long knives and are universally carried as cutting tools, for use in the forests. There are very few modern fire-arms in the country. The Deb Zimpun, in his visit to Buxa to receive the subsidy, was accompanied by his guard of sixty men without a gun among them. He told me that he possessed a fowling-piece himself which he had left behind, as he had no cartridges for it.

Although Bhutan now possesses a Maharajah, the government is still carried on on feudal lines. The *Penlops* rule their own territories without much outside interference. Under them are the *jongpens* or commanders of *jongs*, who act as governors of districts. Each *Penlop* has a *tarpon* or general to command his troops. Under the *jongpens* are lesser officials known as *tumbas*. There is no judiciary branch, and justice is rudely administered. A murderer is punished by the loss of a hand and being hamstrung, or sometimes is tied to the corpse of his victim and thrown into a river or over a precipice. The exactions of the officials drive many refugees over our border; and the hills around Buxa were peopled almost entirely by Bhuttias who had fled from slavery and oppression.

The Bhuttia is a cheerful, hard-working and easily contented individual. He is naturally brave, and has the makings of a good soldier in him. He is generally medium-sized, broad and sturdy, with thick muscular legs such as I have only seen equalled in the chair coolies of Hong Kong and the rickshawmen in Japan. The northern Bhutanese are fair and often blue-eyed. Their Tibetan neighbours hold them in dread. The dress of a Bhuttia man is simple and consists of one garment shaped like the Japanese kimono, kilted by a girdle at the waist to leave the legs free. Their heads and feet are generally bare. The costume of the richer folk, except on occasions of ceremony, is very much the same; but they generally wear stockings and shoes or long Chinese boots. But even the Maharajah often goes barelegged. The Bhutanese women are the ugliest specimens of femininity I have ever seen. In the south they cut their hair shorter even than the men do. But when they can they load themselves with ornaments of turquoises or coloured stones.

Around Buxa the Bhuttia inhabitants build, high upon the steepest hills, villages of wooden, palm-thatched huts supported on poles which raise them well off the ground. Their household utensils and drinking vessels are usually made of the useful bamboo. Around their houses they scratch up the ground and plant a little; but their chief employment is as porters or as woodcutters in the Government forests. They never seek for work in the tea gardens near; though on these the coolies are well paid and have to be brought from a long distance away in India. But the Bhuttia is essentially a hillman; and life in the steamy heat of the Bengal plains would be unendurable to him.

A thousand feet above Buxa, on the slopes of Sinchula, stood a hamlet of a dozen huts. Learning that the inhabitants were celebrating a yearly festival, Smith and I, accompanied by a native officer, set off to visit it. As we climbed the steep hill-side we heard fiendish yells and shrieks, and conjectured that we were coming upon a devil-dance at least. But we only found the men of the village engaged in an archery contest. Two targets were placed about a couple of hundred yards apart; and a party at either end shot at them. The small marks were rarely hit, even when we placed rupees on them to stimulate the competitors; but most of the arrows fell very close to them. A good shot was hailed with vociferous applause by the marksman's team, a bad one by the shrieks, groans and derisive laughter we had heard. When the contest was over we were invited to try our skill and luckily did not disgrace ourselves. Then the bows of the contestants were stacked together on the ground and hung with garlands and leafy branches. The men sat down in two lines forming a lane to the bows; and each drew out from the breast of his kimono a small wooden or metal cup. Several women appeared from the village, bearing food and drink in cane baskets or gaily decorated vessels made of bamboo. We learned that the feast lasted six days and that each one of the principal villagers acted as host and provided the provender a day in turn and his womenfolk dispensed his hospitality. To-day's entertainer began the proceedings by filling his own cup, advancing to the pile of bows, bowing profoundly before it several times and pouring the contents of his cup on the ground. As he did so he muttered some words. Then he turned about and walked back. The other men, as they sat cross-legged on the ground, shouted out a long utterance which I took to be a form of grace before meals, and ended with a series of ear-piercing yells which would have done credit to a pack of mad jackals. The effect of the contrast between the fiendish noises they made and their beaming countenances was comical. Then the hostesses passed down the lines of men, handed them platters and heaped rice and other food on them. The cups were filled first with the vile-smelling and worse-tasting native liquor, and afterwards, when emptied several times, with tea. Undisturbed by our presence the guests made a hearty meal, the host walking up and down the lines and encouraging them to enjoy themselves, while his women brought fresh relays of victuals. But at last their appetites were satisfied. Then the ladies of the hamlet who had been watching their lords and masters from a respectful distance came forward. In addition to their ordinary garments they wore capes of black velveteen, only donned on occasions of ceremony; and their necks were hung with chains of imitation turquoises and large, coloured stone beads. To the monotonous accompaniment of two tiny hand-drums, beaten by men, they performed a mournful and exceedingly proper dance. This the

" THE LADIES OF THE HAMLET CAME FORWARD."

BHUTTIA DRUMMERS.

men applauded languidly. Among the women I was struck by the European-like features of the very ugliest of them. She was fair-haired, high-cheek-boned and long-nosed. She contrasted strongly with the Tartar type of features of those around her. I learned that she was the illegitimate daughter of a Scotch military surgeon who had formerly been quartered in Buxa. She was married to a Bhuttia, and, judging from her silver ornaments, was quite a person of importance in the hamlet. But as I saw her afterwards working as a coolie and passing with heavy loads up and down through Buxa, it was evident that her economical father had not left her beyond the necessity of toiling for her daily rice.

The dance finished the festivities for the day. We were led in procession by the revellers through the village with songs and beating of drums; and, having bestowed a few rupees on them, we departed amid a loud chorus of thanks.

Some time afterwards I was present at a similar festival in Chunabatti, the large village containing nearly a thousand Bhuttias, a few miles over the hills from Buxa. Here the American lady missionary had resided for over fifteen years; and I asked her for some explanation of the festival. But she confessed that, even after her long residence among the villagers, she knew nothing of their beliefs, religion or ceremonies. I may mention that she had never made a convert. But as far as I could see these cis-border Bhuttias were even more ignorant of their faith than the dwellers in Bhutan. There were a few prayer flags fluttering on the hill above the village; but *chortens* and praying wheels were conspicuous by their absence, though there was enough water-power in the mountains for the latter to ensure salvation for millions of believers in their efficacy. The village possessed one lama, who was treated with scant respect. I often saw him teaching the small boys to read the Hindi characters, which are the same as used for the written Tibetan language.

This Chunabatti festival was celebrated in the same manner as the one we had seen before, with eating, drinking, dances by the women, and archery contests by the men. Some of the small boys were brought out to practise with the bow; and many of them shot quite well. But there was absolutely no trace of religious celebration.

To-day the boundary-line between Bhutan and India lies generally along the summits of the last mountain-chain above the plains. Dense jungle clothes the sides of the hills and descends to meet the upward waves of the Terai Forest, which stretches along the foot of the Himalayas through Assam, Bengal, and Nepal. The mountains are cloven by deep and gloomy ravines through which swift-flowing rivers like the Menass, Raidak, Torsa, and Tista pour their waters to swell the Brahmaputra and the Ganges. Some of these torrents disappear underground a few hundred yards from the hills and leave a broad river-bed empty for miles, except during the Rains. But farther away they suddenly appear again above the surface and flow to the south. The character of the jungle in the region where they reappear is damper and more tropical than near the mountains, and has earned for the forest the title of Terai, which means "wet." Streams which on the level of Santrabari reached the plains, there vanish, to come again above the ground near Rajabhatkawa.

CHUNABATTI.

The long belt of the Terai Jungle is nowadays patched with clearings for tea gardens; for the Duars' tea is famous. Mixed with tea grown near Darjeeling at an elevation of six thousand or seven thousand feet it forms a favourite blend. But the sportsman, no matter how fond he may be of the "cup that cheers," cannot view without regret the clearing away of thousands of acres of forests that shelter big game. And an artist would not consider the destruction of the giant, orchid-clad trees with the festoons of swinging creepers compensated for by the stretches of more profitable low green tea-bushes in symmetrical and orderly rows.

Nor do the other signs of man's handiwork on a tea garden compensate for the natural beauties they replace. Hideous factories, gaunt drying and engine-houses with stove-pipe like chimneys rising above corrugated iron roofs, villages of dilapidated thatched huts sheltering the hundreds of coolies employed on the estate, and the unbeautiful bungalows of the Europeans in charge. For on each garden there are from one to four Britishers. The larger ones have a manager, two assistants, and an engineer; on the smaller ones the manager perhaps combines the functions of the others in his own person.

A planter's life is a lonely one. The gardens are generally a few miles apart. Men busy, especially in the gathering season, from dawn to dark have little inclination to go visiting after the day's work is done, even if the roads were better and freer from the danger of meeting a wild elephant on them at night. But in each little district a club-house is built in some central spot within comparatively easy reach of all the gardens around. It is generally only a rough wooden shed; but in the small clearing around it a few tennis courts, or perhaps a polo ground, are made. And here once a week all the planters of the neighbourhood, with an occasional lady or two among them, repair on horseback through the jungle. There may be flooded rivers to cross, wild beasts to avoid; but, unless writhing in the grip of the planters' plagues, malarial or blackwater fever, all will be there on club day. Like the Bhuttias in our village feast one of the number takes it in turn to act as host. He sends over from his bungalow, miles away, crockery, glasses, a cold lunch, and, possibly, tea. For planters are not fond of it as a beverage. Then men, who have not seen another white face for a week, foregather, do justice to the lunch, play tennis or polo, and take a farewell drink or two when the setting sun warns them to depart. Then into the saddle again and off by forest road and jungle track to another week of loneliness and labour. What tales they have to tell of the wild beasts they meet on their way home in the deepening gloom! But the planter fears nothing except wild elephants; and not them if he is on horseback and a good road. Two men from the same garden who used to linger longest at the bar came one evening upon a tiger, another time upon a fine specimen of the more dreaded Himalayan bear, right in their path. They were unarmed, but their libations had added to their natural courage. Without hesitation, they dug spurs into their unwilling ponies and with demoniac yells charged straight at the astonished wild beasts. In each case tiger or bear found this too much for his nerves and promptly bolted into the jungle.

There are few finer bodies of men in the world than the planters of India. Educated men, they lead the life of a *gaucho*. Hard riders, good shots, keen sportsmen, they are the best volunteers we have in the Indian Empire; and more than once some of them have worthily upheld the fame of their class in war.

During the last Abor Expedition of 1912 several of the Assam Valley Light Horse, a Planters' corps, gave up their posts and went to the front as troopers.

It is well to be content with your lot. From our cool hills I used to look down on the bright green patches of the gardens in the dark forests below and pity the poor planters in the humid heat of the summer months. But when I visited them I found that their sympathy went out to us in Buxa. On one occasion my host pointed to the dark wall of hills on which three tiny white specks, the Picquet Towers of my fort, shone out in the sunlight. With a sigh of compassion he said:

"Whenever we look up there and think of you poor fellows shut up in that isolated spot we pity you immensely and wonder how you can bear the dreadful loneliness of it. Down here we are so much better off."

As he spoke we looked towards the mountains, and at that moment a dark cloud was drawn like a pall across their face. Its black expanse was rent by vivid lightning; and the hollow roll of distant thunder in the hills told us that one of the frequent storms was raging over my little Station, while we stood in brilliant sunshine. And certainly at the moment Buxa looked a gloomy spot.

Tea growing seems a profitable industry. I heard

of estates which paid a profit of sixty per cent, and noticed with regret fresh inroads being made in the forest for more ground to plant in. Of course with a new garden one must wait five years or so for any return on the capital invested. And the initial expenses of clearing and preparing the soil, buying machinery and erecting factories, are great. The coolies must be brought from a distance, as the country around is too sparsely populated to supply a sufficiency of labour. And before quitting their houses they demand an advance of pay to leave with their relatives, and not infrequently abscond after getting the money. Each company sends a recruiting agent to collect these coolies who are well paid according to the Indian labour-market rates. And the father of a family is better off than a bachelor; for women and children help to gather the leaves, and each worker brings in his or her basket to be weighed, and payment is made by results. One sees the mothers with their babies on their hips moving among the bushes and plucking the tender green shoots. The whole process of manufacturing, from the planting and pruning, the gathering of the leaf, and the withering and drying, down to the packing of the tea ready for the market is interesting. Little goes to waste. The floors of the factories are regularly swept, and the tea-dust thus collected is pressed into blocks to form the brick-tea popular in Central Asia and used as currency in the absence of money.

But tea growing is not all profit. Sometimes a hailstorm ruins the year's crop, frost blights the plants, and losses occur in other ways. The planters rarely own their gardens, but are usually in the service of companies in England. They are not overpaid; a manager in the Duars generally receives six hundred rupees a month, together with a house, allowances for his horse and certain servants which make his salary up to another hundred, in all about forty-seven pounds. But an assistant begins on less than twenty pounds a month. Engineers, who look after the machinery, are better paid; and some economically minded companies promote the engineer to be manager, and so save a salary. The expenses of living are not great, and a frugal planter—if such a being exists—can save money.

To those fond of an outdoor existence the work is pleasant enough. Early in the morning manager and assistants mount their ponies and set out to ride over the hundreds of acres of the estate, inspect the plants, visit the nurseries, and watch the coolies at work among the bushes or clearing the jungle. Then through the factory and, if it be the season, see the baskets of leaves brought in and weighed. And back to a late breakfast, where tea rarely finds its way to the table, and a siesta until the afternoon calls them forth to ride round the garden again. It sounds an easy life and idyllic, but the planters say it is not.

In any land the sight of the rich plains stretching away from the foot of the barren hills is always a tempting sight to the fierce mountain dwellers. And for the Bhutanese it must have been a sore struggle to curb their predatory instincts and cease from their profitable descents on the unwarlike inhabitants of Bengal. Wealth and women were the prizes of the freebooter until the shield of the Briton was thrust between him and his timorous prey. Yet even to-day, although their nation is at peace with us, the temptation sometimes proves too much for lawless borderers. And parties of raiders from across the frontier swoop down on the Duars. A tea garden, when a store of silver coin is brought to pay the wages of the hundreds of coolies, is their favourite mark. The few police scattered far apart over the north of Eastern Bengal are powerless to stop a rush of savage swordsmen who suddenly emerge from the forest, loot the *bunniahs* and the huts on a garden, and disappear long before an appeal for succour can reach the nearest troops. With the fear of the white man before their eyes they do not seek to meddle with the Europeans in their factories and bungalows. But the fearless planters do not imitate their forbearance. In one garden a terrified coolie rushed to the manager's house to inform him that Bhuttias were raiding the village. Without troubling to inquire the number of the dacoits the planter called his one assistant; and taking their rifles the two Englishmen mounted their ponies and galloped to the village. They found it in the hands of about sixty Bhuttias, armed with *dahs*, who were plundering right and left. The planters sprang from their saddles and opened fire on them. The raiders, aghast at this unpleasant interruption to their profitable undertaking, strove to show a bold front. But the pitiless bullets and still more the calm courage of the two white men daunted them; and they fled into the friendly shelter of the forest. That garden was never attacked again.

I was surprised to learn that on such occasions the planters had never sent information to the detachment at Buxa. But they told me that, as they never saw anything of the troops there, they almost forgot their existence. They added that the raiders came and went with such rapidity that it was hopeless for infantry to try to catch them. I determined to alter this state of affairs. So, shortly after our arrival, I took almost all my men out on a ten days' march, lightly equipped, through the jungle district to show that we were not tied to the fort and that we could mobilise and move swiftly if needed. I also devised a scheme by which, on the first intimation of a raid reaching me, mobile parties of my detachment would dash off at once over the hills to secure all the passes near and cut off the retreat of the invaders, while other parties, descending into the forest, would shepherd them into their hands.

CHAPTER IV

A DURBAR IN BUXA

Notice of the Political Officer's approaching visit—A Durbar—The Bhutan Agent and the interpreter—Arrival of the Deb Zimpun—An official call—Exchange of presents—Bhutanese fruit—A return call—Native liquor—A welcome gift—The Bhutanese musicians—Entertaining the Envoy—A thirsty Lama—A rifle match—An awkward official request—My refusal—The Deb Zimpun removes to Chunabatti—Arrival of the treasure—The Political Officer comes—His retinue—The Durbar—The Guard of Honour—The visitors—The Envoy comes in state—Bhutanese courtesies—The spectators—The payment of the subsidy—Lunch in Mess—Entertaining a difficult guest—The official dinner—An archery match—Sikh quoits—Field firing—Bhutanese impressed—Blackmail—British subjects captured—Their release—Tashi's case—Justice in Bhutan—Tyranny of officials—Tashi refuses to quit Buxa—The next payment of the subsidy—The treaty—Misguided humanitarians.

SOON after our arrival in Buxa I received a letter from the Political Officer in Sikkim, Tibet, and Bhutan informing me that he proposed to visit our little Station and hold a Durbar there in order to pay over to a representative of the Bhutanese Government the annual subsidy of fifty thousand rupees. He requested me to furnish a Guard of Honour of a hundred men for the ceremony. The news that Buxa was to rise to the dignity of a Durbar of its own and be honoured with the presence of the Envoy of a friendly State was positively exciting. True, neither the Durbar nor the Envoy were very important; still, with them, we felt that we were about to make history. The officer who has charge of our political relations with these three countries resides at Gantok, the capital of Sikkim, and, until recently, administered the affairs of that State. Of late years the Maharajah has been admitted to a share of the Government.

In Chunabatti lived two natives of Darjeeling, British subjects, who were paid a salary by our Government to help in transacting diplomatic affairs with Bhutan. They were officially styled the Bhutan Agent and the Bhutanese interpreter. Their knowledge of English, acquired in a school of Darjeeling, was not extensive; and their acquaintance with Hindustani was on a par. They were men of a Tibetan type, dressed like our Bhuttias, except that they wore a headgear like a football cap and also gaily striped, undoubted football stockings.

Shortly after the receipt of the Political Officer's letter, one of these men, the Agent, came to my bungalow one afternoon and informed me that the Bhutan Government's representative had arrived in Buxa and was lodged in the Circuit House. The Agent wished to know when I intended paying an official call on this personage. I had sufficient acquaintance with the ways of Orientals to be aware that this was an impertinence, for it was the place of the Envoy to make his visit first to the officer commanding the Station; but, like the Chinese, who have a childish desire to assert their own importance on every occasion, he was endeavouring to steal a march on me. So I assumed a haughty demeanour and informed the Agent that I would be prepared to receive the Envoy at my house in two hours' time, as he must first call on me. The Agent at once agreed that this was the proper course, as, indeed he had known all the time.

I sent an order to the fort for a native officer and twenty men to parade in full dress at my bungalow in a couple of hours, and then prepared to hold my first official reception. Punctually to the time named a ragged procession of sixty bareheaded, barelegged Bhuttias, armed with swords and every second man of them disfigured by an enormous goitre, descended the road from the Circuit House. From my doorstep I watched them coming down the hill. They escorted a stout cheery old gentleman in dirty white kimono and cap and long Chinese boots. He was accompanied by the Agent and the interpreter and followed by two coolies carrying baskets of oranges. This was the Bhutan Envoy, the Deb Zimpun, a member of the Supreme Council of Punakha and Cup Bearer to the Deb Raja, when there is one. The Guard of Honour presented arms as I advanced to meet and shake hands with him. I addressed him in Hindustani; but the old gentleman grinned feebly and looked round for the interpreter. The latter explained that the Deb Zimpun spoke only his own language; but that he would interpret my greeting. I then formally welcomed the Envoy to India, and invited him to inspect the Guard of Honour, such being the procedure with distinguished visitors. He was quite pleased at this and passed down the ranks, looking closely at the men's rifles and accoutrements. He noticed that two or three of the sepoys, who had been called from the rifle-range and had dressed hurriedly, wore their pouches in the wrong

THE DEB ZIMPUN'S PRISONERS.

"FROM MY DOORSTEP I WATCHED THEM COMING DOWN THE HILL."

place and pointed it out to me. When he had minutely inspected the Guard I led the way into my bungalow and begged him to be seated. He took off his cap politely, and, sitting down, produced a metal box from the breast of his robe, took betel-nut out of it and began to chew it. An attendant holding a spittoon immediately took up his position beside him. The Agent and interpreter stood behind us and translated our remarks to each other. The remainder of the motley crew remained in the garden or crowded into the veranda, scuffling and shoving each other aside in their attempts to get near the open door and look in at us.

At first the conversation, consisting of the usual formal compliments full of hyperbole, did not flourish; and the Deb Zimpun's eyes roamed round the apartment as he gazed with interest at my trophies of sport, pictures, photographs, and curios. When the interpreter had finished explaining some extravagant phrase, the Envoy asked eagerly if I had a gramaphone. He was visibly disappointed when I replied in the negative, and said that he had seen one on a previous visit to India and was much interested in it. To console him I took out my cigar-case and offered him a cheroot, which he accepted and smoked with evident pleasure. I asked him if he would like a drink; and the interpreter replied that the Deb Zimpun begged for two whiskies-and-sodas. I wondered if he wanted to consume both at once or thought that my hospitality stopped at one. But when the drinks were brought by my servant, I found that they were wanted by the interpreter himself and his friend the Agent, as the Envoy did not like whisky. I am sure that the old gentleman never asked for them at all; so it was a piece of distinct impertinence on the part of the interpreter, who was only an under-strapper. I was struck all the time by the contrast between his casual manner to me, an officer of his own Government, and his servile deference to the Deb Zimpun who treated him as an individual altogether beneath his notice.

When the conversation again languished I produced some luridly coloured Japanese prints of the capture of Pekin by the Allied Troops, which I had bought in Tokio after the Boxer War. I thought that they might serve as a useful lesson of the weakness of the Chinese, who endeavour to intrigue against us in Bhutan. These gaudy pictures delighted the Deb Zimpun. He asked to have all the details explained to him and seemed so interested that I made a present of the prints to him to start a Fine Art Gallery with in Punakha when he returned to the capital. This gift quite won his heart. He called into the room the coolies carrying baskets of oranges and brown paper bags of walnuts and presented them to me. The fruit, which was grown in Bhutan, was excellent; and only in Malta have I tasted better oranges. This terminated the visit; the Envoy rose, accepted another cigar, shook hands, and took his departure.

Next day Creagh and I dressed ourselves in full uniform and, accompanied by an escort of sepoys, proceeded up the hill to the Circuit House to return the visit. We were met on the veranda by the Deb Zimpun and, chairs being placed for us, we three sat down. The interpreter was again present, being temporarily attached to the Envoy's suite. I learned that the Deb Zimpun was allowed by our Government the sum of two thousand rupees (about £133) for his expenses while he remained in India. He must have saved most of this money; for I found that he lived chiefly on the contributions, voluntary or otherwise, of the Bhuttias residing in our territory.

A servitor came forward and filled two glasses with Bhutanese liquor from a bamboo bottle. They were offered us; and my subaltern and I made a heroic attempt to drink the nauseous-looking stuff. But the smell was enough. The taste! A mixture of castor and codliver oil, senna and asafœtida would have been nectar compared with it. We begged to be excused, on the plea that we had been teetotallers all our lives. I then ordered my present to be brought forward. It was a haunch of a *sambhur* which I had shot two days before. The gift was a great success. The Deb Zimpun's eyes glistened and he showed his teeth, stained red with betel-nut chewing, in a gracious smile. His unkempt followers crowded around us, looked hungrily at the meat, and seemed to calculate whether there was enough to go round. The Maharajah of Bhutan, as a good Buddhist, had recently decreed that for two years no animals were to be slaughtered for food in his country. So this venison was a luxury to them all. Before the excellent impression of our gift could die Creagh and I rose to take our leave and departed hurriedly.

But we were not to escape so easily. Hardly had we reached the Mess on our return when we were informed that the Deb Zimpun had, as a special mark of favour, sent his two best musicians to play for us. So we came out on the veranda and found two swarthy ruffians squatting in the garden, holding silver-banded pipes like flageolets. We seated ourselves and the performance began. I have patiently endured Chinese, Japanese, and Indian music, have even listened unmoved to the strains of a German band in London; but the ear-piercing, soul-harrowing noises that these two ruffians produced were too much for me. We wondered, if these were the Envoy's best musicians, what his worst could be like. I hurriedly presented each of them with a rupee and sent them away, more than compensated by the money for their abrupt dismissal.

On the following day we invited the Deb Zimpun to lunch with us in the Mess and instructed our Gurkha cook to do his best, which was not much. We found that our guest, having visited India before and having accompanied the Tongsa *Penlop* to Calcutta, was quite expert in the use of a knife and fork, and enjoyed European fare. He was very temperate and refused to touch liquor. But he was not imitated in this by his suite. After lunch he told us that his lama, who was sitting with the rest of his followers in the Mess garden, was anxious to taste whisky, of which he had heard. We invited the priest in and poured him out a stiff five-finger peg of neat Scotch whisky. The holy man smelled it, raised the glass to his lips, and elevated it until not a drop was left. He could not apparently make up his mind as to whether he liked the liquor or not. So we offered him another glass. He accepted it and disposed of it as promptly. We looked at him in astonishment; but it had no effect on him. I told the interpreter to ask him what he thought of whisky.

"I don't like it much; it is too sweet," replied the lama.

We officers glanced at each other; and the same

idea occurred to us all. It happened that some time before we had got a small cask of beer from Calcutta, which, owing to the journey or the heat, had gone very sour and tasted abominably. A large glass of this delectable beverage was offered to the holy man. As he drained it a beatific smile spread over his saintly but exceedingly dirty face and he put down the empty glass with a sigh.

"Ah! that is good. That is very good," he said to the interpreter. "I would like more."

So he was given another large tumblerful. Then, absolutely unaffected by his potations, he left the Mess reluctantly. After this experience we kept this beer, while it lasted, for Bhuttia visitors, and found it a popular brand.

After lunch I brought the Deb Zimpun down to shoot on the rifle-range, as he had expressed a wish to that effect through the interpreter. He seemed to understand the mechanism of the Lee-Enfield and made some fair shooting at a moving target at two hundred yards. When my score proved better than his he said laughingly that the rifle was not the weapon with which he was best acquainted, but that he would challenge me one day to a match with bows and arrows. By this time the old man and I had become quite friendly, and we had all taken a liking to him. He had invited me to pay a visit to Bhutan and promised to obtain the permission of the Maharajah for me to enter the country.

Consequently I was not pleased when next day I received a letter from the civil authorities of the district informing me that the Deb Zimpun was occupying the Circuit House without permission, and requesting me to remove him and his retinue to

Chunabatti. The Political Officer had asked that he might be allowed to reside in it; but, as on a previous occasion he and his followers had done so and left it in an absolutely uninhabitable state, this permission was now refused. The letter stated that it had cost two hundred rupees to clean the house and make it fit for European occupation again. I thought that this was but a small sum, after all, compared with the two thousand the Government were already expending on him. And to turn the Envoy of a friendly State out of the house he was occupying in all good faith seemed an insulting course. If he refused to vacate it peaceably, I presume I was expected to use force, which would probably result in bloodshed. As to the issue there could be no doubt, as the swords and bows of his followers would be poor things to oppose to our rifles. But it seemed to me that this would be giving rather too warm a reception to an official visitor and guest of the Government of India. So I refused to comply with the wishes of the civil authorities, much to the relief of the Political Officer when he arrived and was informed of the matter. He told me that had I acted otherwise it would have given dire offence in Bhutan just at a time when our Government were particularly anxious to be on good terms with the Bhutanese. I only understood what he meant when, more than a year afterwards, I heard of the signing of the treaty with the Maharajah, which placed the foreign affairs of the country under our control.

But, unfortunately, the Agent had received the same instructions as I; and, to avoid trouble, he induced the Deb Zimpun to go to Chunabatti and reside in his home. The Envoy was very displeased at having to leave the Circuit House. I offered to place the empty bungalow, known as the Married Officers' Quarters, at his disposal; but the old gentleman, though very grateful and thanking me warmly, declined, as he did not want to make another move.

The day after our luncheon-party to the Deb Zimpun a detachment of native police came from Alipur Duar escorting a train of coolies carrying wooden boxes which contained the fifty thousand rupees of the subsidy. These were handed over to me; and I placed them in our guard-room under a special sentry. Lastly the Political Officer, Mr Bell, arrived by train from Darjeeling, which is three days' ride from Gantok. He was accompanied by a portly Sikkimese head clerk in wadded Chinese silk coat and gown, another clerk and a couple of pig-tailed Sikkimese soldiers in striped petticoats and straw hats like inverted flower-pots ornamented with a long peacock feather.

On the day after his arrival the Durbar was held. On the parade ground a few of our tents were pitched to form an open-air reception hall. A Guard of Honour of two native officers and a hundred sepoys in their full-dress uniform of red tunics, blue trousers and white spats, was drawn up near it; and the boxes of treasure were brought down and deposited on the ground beside the tents. The only outside visitors were the nearest civil official, the Subdivisional Officer of Alipur Duar, and his wife and children; the three British officers and the native officers not required with the Guard joined them in the tents. Mr Bell, wearing his political uniform, descended on to the parade ground from my bungalow and was received with a salute by the Guard of Honour.

Then to the beating of tom-toms and the wild strains of barbaric music a double file of Bhuttias advanced across the parade ground escorting the Envoy, who was riding a mule. We hardly recognised our old friend. He was magnificently garbed for the occasion in a very voluminous robe of red silk embroidered with Chinese symbols in gold, and wore a gold-edged cap in shape something like a papal tiara. At the tail of the procession came a number of coolies carrying baskets of oranges and packages wrapped up in paper.

In front of the tents the Envoy dismounted. The Political Officer came forward to shake hands with him; and the Deb Zimpun threw a white silk scarf around his neck. This scarf is called the *Khatag* and is the invariable Tibetan and Bhutanese accompaniment of a reception. It is also sent with important official letters. Bell now presented each of us formally to the Envoy, who shook hands solemnly and hung us with scarves. The scene in its picturesque setting of mountains and jungle was a striking one. The Political Officer in his trim uniform and the British officers in their scarlet tunics were outshone by the gaudier garbs of the Asiatics. The Deb Zimpun's flowing red robe, the head clerk in his flowered black silk Chinese garb, the Sikkimese soldiers in their bright garments and the Bhutanese in their kimonos, made a blaze of varied hues. Along one side of the ground was the scarlet and blue line of the Guard of Honour, the yellow and gold *puggris* or turbans of the native officers and the gold-threaded cummerbunds, or waist-sashes, of the sepoys shining in the brilliant sun. Above the Guard the slope and wall of the fort were crowded with the other men of

THE DURBAR IN BUXA.

the detachment in white undress, mingled with native followers in brighter colours. Down the other side of the parade ground was a long line of Bhuttia men, women, and children.

When we were seated the Deb Zimpun produced a document accrediting him as the duly appointed envoy and representative of the Bhutan Government to receive the subsidy. This having been perused by the Political Officer and his head clerk and the official seals inspected, the boxes of money were formally handed over. The usual procedure was to have one of them opened and the contents counted, but on this occasion the Deb Zimpun accepted them as correct and ordered his escort to take charge of them. They were hoisted on the backs of porters who took them off to Chunabatti. Then coolies came forward with the Envoy's basket of oranges and the packages, which we found to contain cheap native blankets worth a couple of shillings each. Oranges and blankets were given to each of us. But as the Government of India has made a strict rule that no civil or military officer in its service is to accept a present from natives, the blankets were taken charge of by Bell's clerks to be sold afterwards and the proceeds credited to Government. We were allowed to keep the oranges. This proceeding terminated the Durbar.

As the officers of the detachment had invited the visitors to lunch, we now adjourned to the Mess. Although our guests consisted only of the Envoy, Bell, the Subdivisional Officer, Mr Ainslie, and his wife and two children, our resources were sorely strained to provide enough furniture for them. The doctor had to sit on a box. The head clerk acted as interpreter and stood behind the Political Officer's chair. A special shooting-party having descended to the jungle the previous day to replenish the larder, the menu was almost luxurious.

After luncheon the Ainslies departed to Santrabari, where they were encamped, having declined our hospitality in Buxa. As Bell was desirous of entertaining the Deb Zimpun himself, he had arranged a dinner to him and us in the forest officer's empty bungalow that evening. So it devolved on me to keep our old gentleman amused until dinner-time, while the Political Officer wrote his despatches. I took our guest down to the rifle-range and kept him busy there till sunset. Then we had to go to my house, where I tried to entertain him by showing him old copies of English illustrated journals. But these require a deal of explanation to the untutored Oriental, who cannot understand the portraits of the favourites of the stage in the scanty costumes in which they are frequently photographed. And I was distinctly embarrassed by some of the Deb Zimpun's questions.

At dinner-time Bell preceded us from my bungalow, where he was staying, and was ready to receive us on the veranda of the forest officer's house when, escorted by servants carrying lanterns, we toiled up the steep path to it. Dinner was laid in the long, draughty centre room in the rambling wooden edifice; and as the night was cold the apartment was warmed by an iron stove. The furniture was scantier and worse than in the Mess. When we sat down to table the Deb Zimpun's rickety chair collapsed under his weight and sent him sprawling on the floor. It was an undignified opening to our official banquet.

The old man presented a ludicrous spectacle as he lay entangled in his red silk robe with the gold-trimmed papal cap tilted over his eye; but we rushed to help him up and controlled our countenances until we found him laughing heartily at his own mishap. Then one glance at our host's horrified expression set us off. A fresh chair was with difficulty procured and we sat down again.

After dinner we gathered round the stove in informal fashion and smoked, the Deb Zimpun helping himself steadily to my cigars. With the aid of the head clerk, who was present to interpret, the conversation grew almost animated. Our old gentleman expressed himself deeply gratified by the kindness he had received from the officers of the detachment, particularly the offer of a military bungalow, and said that if he returned to Buxa the following year he hoped to find us all there again. Me he personally regarded as a brother. We drank his health, a compliment he quite understood, and with difficulty refrained from singing "For He's a Jolly Good Fellow." When he departed we escorted him as far as the Mess and bade him a vociferous "Good night," to the amazement of the squad of ragged swordsmen and lantern-bearers who were accompanying him back to Chunabatti.

Next day Bell left us to return to Sikkim; and we expected the Deb Zimpun would also take his departure for Bhutan with the subsidy. But day after day passed without any sign of his going, and we began to wonder at his remaining after the purpose of his visit was completed. I invited him to lunch with me again. One afternoon he appeared at the head of his wild gathering, all of them carrying bows. He had come to challenge me to an archery contest. We set up targets on the range at a distance of two hundred yards. He defeated me easily, and chaffed me gaily over his victory. To retrieve my honour I sent to the fort for some Sikh throwing quoits, formerly used as weapons in war. They are of thin steel with edges ground sharp, and when thrown by an expert will skim through the air for nearly two hundred yards and would almost cut clean through a man if they struck him fair. They ricochet off the ground for a good distance after the first graze. We set up plantain tree stems as targets, for the soft wood does not injure the edge. I showed the Envoy how to hold and throw the weapon; but his first shot went very wide indeed and nearly ended the mortal career of one of his swordsmen. However, he improved with a little practice, and insisted that all his followers should try the sport.

A day or two after this my detachment did its annual field firing. This is a most practical form of musketry, consisting of an attack on a position with ball cartridge, the enemy being represented by small targets, the size of a man's head, nearly hidden behind entrenchments or suddenly appearing from holes dug in the ground. I invited the Envoy and his suite to witness it. The Deb Zimpun was deeply interested. He followed us everywhere as we scrambled up and down steep hills firing on the small marks dotted about between the trees, in the jungle and at the bottom of precipices. The attack was arranged to finish up on the parade ground where we could make use of the running and vanishing targets in the rifle butts. The Bhuttias were immensely delighted with the crouching figures of men drawn swiftly across the range and saluted with bursts of rapid fire from the sepoys' rifles. But they broke into an excited roar when our men fixed bayonets and charged the position with loud cheers; and I looked back to find the Bhuttias following us at a run, waving their swords and yelling wildly. When I went round to inspect the targets and count the hits, the Deb Zimpun and his followers accompanied me and were much impressed by the accuracy of the shooting. They talked eagerly, pointed out the bullet-holes to each other, and shook their heads solemnly over them. The interpreter told me that they were saying that they would be sorry to face our soldiers in battle after seeing the range, accuracy, and rapidity of fire of our rifles. The Deb Zimpun returned with me to my bungalow and enjoyed a meal of tea, cake, and chocolate creams as heartily as a schoolboy. On departing he shook my hand and bade the interpreter express the interest with which he had watched the field firing.

But alas for the inconstancy of human friendships! Our pleasant intercourse was destined to an abrupt termination. The very next day I was informed that the genial old gentleman had been levying blackmail on Bhuttias residing in our territory and had seized and imprisoned in the house in which he resided a man, three women, and three children, intending to carry them off to Bhutan. The unexpected appearance of a score of my men with rifles and fixed bayonets changed the programme; and the prisoners were removed to our fort until Government should decide their fate. As we marched them through Chunabatti the villagers flocked round us and called down blessings on our heads for saving their friends.

One old lady, the wife of the male prisoner, fell on the ground before Smith, who had accompanied me, embraced his legs and kissed his feet, much to our medical officer's embarrassment.

Much correspondence and a Government inquiry resulted in the freedom of the wretched captives. But before their release the Envoy, in response to impatient letters from the Maharajah who was none too well pleased with the delay in his return with the subsidy, marched off over the hills to Bhutan without a farewell to us.

The case of the man who had been seized is a typical example of the justice meted out in uncivilised countries. He was named Tashi and had been born in Buxa before its capture by the British in 1864 and its subsequent incorporation in our territory. After the war his family retired across the newly made boundary. His father possessed land in a village close to the frontier, which was in the jurisdiction of a certain *jongpen*. He acquired more several miles away in a district governed by another *jongpen*. On his death he left everything to Tashi, who continued to reside in the first village. The second official objected to this and eventually confiscated the land in his district and applied it to his own use. When Tashi threatened to appeal to the Supreme Council at Punakha he sent a party of his retainers to slay him as the easiest method of avoiding litigation. When the other *jongpen* remonstrated against this invasion of his district and proceeded to repel it by force, his brother official pointed out to him that he could not do better than follow the good example set him and seize Tashi's remaining property. The advice seemed good; and the first *jongpen* determined to kill Tashi himself. He sent several soldiers to put him to death; but as they learned on arrival that the unfortunate owner of this Bhutanese Naboth's vineyard had several stalwart sons and possessed a gun, the gallant warriors contented themselves with establishing a cordon round the village and sending for reinforcements. The luckless Tashi realised that discretion was the better part of valour. He bribed some of the soldiers to let him pass through the cordon at night and with his family and five cows, all that he could save from the wreck, he escaped into British territory. But the two Ahabs were not satisfied. It was always believed that Tashi had managed to take some hoarded wealth with him, although he lived in a poor way and worked hard for his living in India. And this belief accounted for his capture on this occasion. On previous visits of the Envoy he and his family had taken the precaution to leave Chunabatti before his arrival.

After his release Tashi resolutely refused to quit Buxa.

"The Commanding Sahib is my father and my mother," he declared. "He has saved my worthless life," for he had been informed that he would be put to death as soon as he was out of British territory; "and I will not leave his shadow, in which I and my family will dwell the rest of our lives." However, he thought that this might not prove sufficient shelter from the weather; so he built a bamboo house in the cantonment limits and announced that he felt safe at last under our protection. Like all Asiatics he considered that my interference on his behalf had constituted a claim on me. However, as he was a useful man, I found employment for him and allowed him to continue to reside in Buxa.

In the following year the Political Officer, accompanied by Captain Kennedy, I.M.S., passed through Buxa on their way to Bhutan, where the subsidy, now doubled, was paid in Punakha, the capital, and the treaty by which the country was placed under British protection signed by the Maharajah. So the Deb Zimpun and I never met again.

There is a certain type of individuals with malformed minds who moan over the subjugation of the countries of barbarous nations by civilised Powers. Do they honestly believe that the cause of humanity is better served by allowing the noble savage to plunder and slay the weak at his own sweet will rather than by subjecting him to the domination of Europeans, be they French, Germans, Russians, Italians or British, who guarantee freedom of life and property in the lands under their rule? Liberty, with these barbarous races, means the liberty of the strong to oppress the weak. Here, in the borderland of Bhutan to-day, the peasant can till the soil, the trader enjoy his hard-earned wealth, where, before the *pax Britannica* settled on it, rapine, blood, and lust went unchecked, where no man's life nor woman's honour was safe from the fierce raiders of the hills. We hold the gates of India. Inside them all is peace. Beyond them, oppression, injustice, murder!

CHAPTER V

IN THE JUNGLE

An Indian jungle—The trees—Creepers—Orchids—The undergrowth—On an elephant in the jungle—Forcing a passage—Wild bees—Red ants—A lost river—A *sambhur* hind—Spiders—Jungle fowl—A stag—*Hallal*—Wounded beasts—A halt—Skinning the stag—Ticks—Butcher apprentices—Natural rope—Water in the air—*Pani bel*—Trail of wild elephants—Their habits—An impudent monkey—An adventure with a rogue elephant—Fire lines—Wild dogs—A giant squirrel—The barking deer—A good bag—Spotted deer—Protective colouring—Dangerous beasts—Natives' dread of bears—A bison calf—The fascination of the forest—The generous jungle—Wild vegetables—Natural products—A home in the trees—Forest Lodge the First—Destroyed by a wild elephant—Its successor—A luncheon-party in the air—The salt lick—Discovery of a coal mine—A monkey's parliament—The jungle by night.

FROM the dense tangled undergrowth the great trees lift their bare stems, each striving to push its leafy crown through the thick canopy of foliage and get its share of the sun. The huge trunks are devoid of branches for many feet above the ground; but around them twist giant creepers which strangle them in close embrace and sink their coils deep into the bark. Here and there a tree, killed by the cruel pressure, stands withered and lifeless but still held up by the murderous parasite. From bole to bole these creepers, thick as a ship's hawser, swing in festoons, coiling and writhing around each other in tangled confusion. Tree-trunk and bough are matted with the glossy green leaves and trails of mauve and white blossoms of innumerable orchids. The trees are not the slender palms that fill the pictures of tropical jungles by untravelled artists, but the giants of the forest—huge *sal* and teak trees and straight-stemmed *simal* with its buttressed trunk star-shaped in section with its curious projecting flanges.

Through the leafy canopy high overhead the sunlight can scarcely filter, and fills the forest with a pleasant green gloom. The undergrowth is dense and rank—tangled and thorny bushes, high grass, shrubs covered with great bell-shaped white flowers—so thick that a man on foot must hack his way through it. But here and there are open glades where the ground is covered with tall bracken. Near the hills and in the damper jungle to the south the bamboo grows extensively. Beside the river-beds are patches of elephant grass, eight to ten feet high, with feathered plumes six feet higher still. This is so strong and dense as to be almost impenetrable to men, but everywhere through it wild elephants have made paths. Wherever the big trees have been felled and the sun can reach the ground the vegetation grows more luxuriantly. And, in the southern belt of the forest, where the water from the hills rises to the surface again, the jungle is wilder and more tropical. Here are huge tree-ferns, the under sides of the fronds studded with long and sharp thorns. Cane brakes, through which none but the heaviest and strongest animals can make their way, abound.

Through the tangled confusion of undergrowth and twisted creepers my elephant forces a passage with swaying stride, as a steamer ploughs her way through a heavy sea and shoulders the waves aside. I am sitting on Khartoum's pad near the *mahout* perched astride her neck, guiding her by the pressure of his feet behind her huge flapping ears. A network of leafy branches of low trees bound together by lianas bars her progress. At a word she lifts her trunk and tears it down, while the *mahout* hacks at bough and creeper with his *kukri* or heavy, curved knife. As she moves on she plucks a small branch and strikes her sides and stomach with it to drive off the flies which are annoying her. For thick as her skin is, yet the insects which prey on her can pierce it and drive her frantic. And once, feeling a sudden pain in my instep, I looked at my foot and discovered an elephant fly biting through a lace hole in my boot. Khartoum, having driven off the pests temporarily, lifts the branch to her mouth and chews it, wood and all. Bechan, her *mahout*, espies a small creeper which is highly esteemed by the natives as a febrifuge and is considered a good tonic for elephants. So he directs her attention to it. Out shoots the snake-like trunk and tears it from the tree around which it is growing; and, crunching it with enjoyment, she strides on through the undergrowth. Suddenly Bechan, in evident alarm, kicks her violently behind the left ear and beats her thick skull with the heavy iron goad he carries, the *ankus*, a short crook with a sharp spike at the end. Khartoum stops short, then moves off to the right. Thinking that he has seen some dangerous wild animal I whisper in Hindustani, "What is it, Bechan?" "Bees," he says shortly and points apparently to a lump of mud hanging from a low branch right in our former path. Then I understand that he would be far less alarmed at the sight of a tiger. For a swarm of wild bees is regarded with terrified respect in India. The lump of mud is a nest; and, had we continued on our original course and brushed against it, we would have been promptly attacked by a cloud of these irritable little insects whose stings have killed many a man. So we prudently give the nest a wide berth. The wild beasts of the forest are not its only dangers. As again Khartoum tears her way through some low-hanging branches, I feel a sudden sting and burning pain in the back of my bare neck. I put my hand to the spot and my fingers close on a big red ant which, knocked from a bough, has fallen on me and is avenging its being disturbed by burying its venomous little fangs in my flesh. Though I crush it, the pain of its bite lingers for hours. Sometimes one dislodges a number of these insects when forcing a passage through dense jungle; and they at once attack the man or animal they alight on. So it is necessary to keep a sharp look-out for them as well as for bees. Nor are these the only perils that lurk in the trees. Though in the jungle serpents do not hang by their tails from every branch, as we read in the books of wonderful adventures that delighted our boyhood, still there is supposed to be one poisonous snake in the Terai which lies along the branches, and if dislodged strikes the disturber with deadly fang. I fortunately never saw one; though in another place I have shot a viper in a tree.

We plod steadily on through the jungle. A gleam of daylight between the stems of the trees shows that we are approaching a *nullah*. Khartoum comes to a stop on the edge of the steep bank of a broad and empty river-bed. After the gloom of the forest the bright transition into the glaring sunlight is dazzling. To the right I can now see the mountains towering above us; and, two thousand feet up, on the dark face of the hills, the three Picquet Towers of Buxa shine out in the sun. At our feet on the white sand lie huge rounded rocks which have been rolled down from the mountains by the furious torrents of the last rainy season. The river-bed is dry now; but were we to follow it a few miles to the south, we would find at first an occasional pool and then further on the water appearing above the surface and flowing on in a gradually increasing stream. For these smaller rivers are lost underground in the boulder formation near the foot of the hills and rise again ten miles further south.

Our elephant slips and stumbles over the polished, rounded rocks until she reaches the opposite bank. Up it she climbs at so steep an angle that to avoid sliding off I have to lie at full length along the pad and hold on to the front edge of it until she regains level ground. We pass from the glare of the sunlight into the cool shade of the forest, and the trees close around us and shut off the mountains from our view. As we push our way through the undergrowth the *mahout* stops the elephant suddenly. "*Sambhur!*" he whispers. Following the direction of his outstretched arm my eyes see nothing at first but the tangled vegetation, the straight tree-trunks and the curving festoons of creepers. But gradually they rest on a warm patch of colour and I make out the form of a deer scarcely visible in the deep shadows. "*Maddi*" (a female) grunts Bechan disgustedly and urges on his elephant. For he knows the Sahibs', to him, ridiculous forest law, which ordains that females are not to be slain, although their flesh is more toothsome than that of a tough old stag.

It is a *sambhur* hind. Apparently aware of her immunity she stands watching us unconcernedly. Accustomed to the wild species, other animals allow tame elephants to approach close to them until they discover the presence of human beings on their backs. So this hind looks calmly at Khartoum. Her long ears twitch restlessly, but otherwise she is motionless; and I can admire her graceful form and the rich brown colour of her hide at my ease. But at last it dawns on her that there is something wrong about our elephant. She swings round and crashes off through the undergrowth and is lost to sight in a moment. And we resume our course.

Across our path from bush to bush great spiders have spun their webs; and Khartoum, pushing through them, has accumulated so many layers of them across her face as to blind her. So the *mahout* leans down and tears them off. These spiders are huge black insects measuring several inches from tip to tip; and their webs are stout and strong almost as linen.

Something scuttling over the fallen leaves in the undergrowth draws my attention and I raise my rifle, only to lower it when, with a frightened squawk, a jungle hen flutters up out of the bushes and flies away among the trees. These birds are the progenitors of our ordinary barnyard fowl, and so like them that once close to Santrabari, when out with a shot-gun, I let several hens pass me unscathed, under the impression that they were fowls belonging to our *mahouts*. And when in the heart of the forest I first heard the cocks crowing I thought that we were near a village. In Northern India these jungle cocks are beautifully plumaged with red, yellow, and dark green feathers and long tails. In Southern India they are speckled black and white with a little yellow. When in the forest villages the tame roosters crow, their challenge is taken up and repeated by the wild ones in the jungle around. And the natives often peg out a cock and surround him with snares to catch the wild birds which come to attack him.

But now Bechan suddenly stops Khartoum and whispers excitedly, "*Sambhur nur!*" "A stag." For a moment I can see nothing in the tangled bit of jungle he points to. Then suddenly the deepened blackness of a patch of shadow reveals itself as the dark hide of a *sambhur* stag. We have almost passed him. He is to my right rear; and I cannot swing round far enough to fire from the right shoulder. But I bring up the rifle rapidly to my left and press the trigger. As the recoil of the heavy .470 high-velocity weapon almost knocks me back flat on the pad I hear a crash in the brushwood. "*Shabash! Luga!* (Well done! Hit!") cries Bechan and slips from the neck of the elephant to the ground. Drawing his knife he dashes into the jungle. For, being a Mussulman, he is anxious to reach the stricken stag and *hallal* it; that is, let blood by cutting its throat while there is life in it. For the Mohammedan religion enjoins that an animal is only lawful food if the blood has run before its death. This is borrowed from the Mosaic Law and is really a hygienic precaution against long-dead carrion being eaten.

From the elephant's back I cannot see the quarry now, but I slip down to the ground and leave Khartoum standing stolidly, contentedly plucking and chewing leaves from the trees around. Following Bechan's track I find him holding the horn of a still feebly struggling *sambhur* and drawing his knife across its throat. The animal is a fine old stag about fourteen hands high. The bullet has broken its shoulder and pierced its heart. But such a wound does not necessarily imply instantaneous death. I have seen a tiger, shot through the heart, dash across a *nullah* and climb half-way up the steep bank until laid low by a second bullet. And *sambhur* and other deer stricken in the same manner will run a hundred yards before dropping. But this stag will never move again of its own volition. As the blood gushes from the gaping wound in the throat the limbs twitch violently and are still. Then Bechan raises its head for me to photograph. This done I look at my watch. It is almost noon and I have been on the elephant's back since six o'clock, so I am glad of a rest; and, sitting on the ground with my back against a tree, I pull out sandwiches and my water-bottle and have my lunch. But, having on a previous occasion been disturbed by a rogue wild elephant, I lay my loaded rifle beside me.

Bechan is busily employed. He cuts off the head, *grallochs* the stag and begins to flay it. After my lunch I get up to help him; for a sportsman in India soon learns to turn his hand to this gruesome task. It is a long job; and the *sambhur* is a heavy weight when we come to turn him over. The skin, parti-

A SAMBHUR STAG AND MY ELEPHANT.

BRINGING HOME THE BAG.

cularly on the belly, is covered with ticks, some big, bloated and immovably fixed, others small and agile. We have to watch carefully lest any of them lodge on us, which they are apt to do; for, with its jaws once clenched in the skin, this insect can only be got rid of by cutting the body off and then pulling the head away, which generally takes a bit of one's skin with it. And the irritation of a bite lasts for months.

At last the animal is completely flayed and the skin rolled up into a bundle; for it makes excellent leather, and is much used in India for soft shooting-boots and gaiters. Then Bechan displays his aptitude for the butcher's trade. With his heavy curved *kukri* he divides the carcass, hacking through the thick bones with powerful blows. Having cut it into portable pieces (for a whole *sambhur* weighs six or seven hundred pounds) he leaves me wondering as to where the rope to tie them up will come from. He looks around him and then goes to a straight-stemmed small tree with grey and black mottled bark. He cuts off a long flap of this bark, disclosing an inner skin. In this he makes incisions with his knife, pulls a long strip of it off and cuts it into narrower strips. He hands one of these to me and tells me to test its strength. Pull as I will I cannot break it. This is the *udal* tree which thus provides a natural cordage of wonderful strength. It is very common in the forest. Making a hole between the bones of a haunch Bechan passes a length of this fibre through and knots it. Then it takes all our combined strength to lift the haunch and bear it to where Khartoum is still patiently waiting. With difficulty we raise and fasten it to the ropes around the pad. And when at last we have secured all this meat, destined for hungry officers and sepoys in the fort and the *mahouts* and their families in Santrabari we look like butchers' apprentices. My khaki shooting-garments are stained, my hands are covered with blood and grime. I gaze around me hopelessly for water, though I know we are miles from a stream. But the resources of this wonderful jungle are not exhausted. Bechan points to one of the myriad lianas criss-crossing between the trees.

"*Pani bel.* The water creeper," he says. I have heard of this extraordinary plant and look carefully at it. It is about two inches in diameter, four-sided rather than round, with rough, corrugated, withered bark, in appearance similar to the corkwood bark used for rustic summer-houses in England. Bechan walks to a hanging festoon of it and cuts it through with a blow of his *kukri.* Nothing happens. I am disappointed; for I had expected to find it tubular and see a stream of water gush out. But the interior is of a white pulpy and moist material. Then Bechan strikes another blow and holds up a length of the creeper cut off. Suddenly from one end of this water begins to trickle and soon flows freely. I wash my hands, using clay as soap. Bechan then tells me to taste the water. Holding the cut creeper above my head I let the water drain into my mouth and find it cold and delicious as spring water. This useful *pani bel*, like the *udal*, is found everywhere in these forests; and, as I am anxious to learn all I can of jungle lore to instruct my sepoys, I carefully note the appearance of both.

We have consumed two hours in the task of flaying and cutting up the *sambhur*. We sit down to rest and smoke before moving on again. I light a cigarette and Bechan pulls out the clay head of a hookah and fills it with coarse native tobacco.

Then at length, with Khartoum hung round with meat and looking like a perambulating butcher's shop, we move on again. After we had been going for ten minutes we come to a spot where a number of trees, some nearly two feet in diameter, have been uprooted, and their upper branches stripped off. This is the work of wild elephants, which push down the trees with their heads to reach the leaves in the tops. We find their trail in the long grass and bushes—not wide, for elephants move in single file, so that it is difficult to tell whether one or twenty have passed. However here and there tracks diverge from the main trail and rejoin it further on, showing where one of the animals has wandered off to one side in search of some succulent morsel; and in the sandy bed of a dry stream we find their footprints, huge, almost circular impression in the dust. Each elephant seems to step exactly in the marks of the leader. Even tame ones advancing over open country will walk in single file if left to themselves. We reach a spot where the herd had evidently passed the night. All around the grass is pressed down and shows where the huge beasts lay down to sleep. Wild elephants usually halt from about 10 p.m. to 4 a.m., then move and feed until 10 or 11 a.m., when they stop and shelter from the heat of the day in thick jungle. About three or four o'clock in the afternoon they get on the move again; and if they come upon water then they bathe. They travel about twenty or thirty miles in the day, though if alarmed will keep on for double that distance.

While we are following this trail a loud crash ahead of us awakens the silent forest. I think at once that it is caused by the herd in whose tracks we are. But Bechan, who is a man of few words, mutters "*bunder*." And I look up and see a troop of monkeys leaping through the upper branches and hurling themselves in alarm at the sight of us from tree to tree. But their insatiable curiosity brings them back to peep at us. Once this curiosity in one developed into impertinence; and the impudent little beast deliberately pelted me. It happened that day that when on foot I had been attacked by a rogue elephant which I had only brought down with a bullet in the head fifteen paces from me. Ruffled by the encounter I was going back to camp, seated on Khartoum's back. Passing under a big tree a jungle fruit fell on me. Then, raising my head, I saw a monkey in the tree grimacing and grinning derisively at me. Coming after the elephant's attack his insolence seemed to add insult to injury, and I felt tempted to reward it with a bullet. But it would have been unnecessary cruelty; and I passed on leaving him still mowing and making faces at me.

We leave the elephants' trail and emerge on a "fire line": for in these Government forests parallel belts, about twenty yards broad, are cleared annually in an attempt to confine the ravages of the jungle fires in the hot weather. They run east and west and are a mile apart, so that they serve not only as roads, but also as guides to one's whereabouts in the forest. As we come suddenly out on the fire line we see two or three fox-like animals playing in it. They are the dreaded wild dogs which do infinite damage to game. Even the tiger regards them with dislike and fear; for, small as they are, they will worry him in a pack, chasing him night and day and giving him no rest. They keep him always on the move, remaining out of his reach until he is exhausted from fatigue and want of sleep. They are pretty little animals, generally reddish, with sharp ears and bushy tails. As soon as these stray dogs in the fire line see us they bolt off into the jungle before I can get a shot at them; for on account of the harm they do to the game every sportsman tries to kill them. I once came upon a *sambhur* and her fawn being attacked by a number of these jungle pests. The hind was circling round, trying to keep between her offspring and the enemy, and striking at the assailants with her sharp hoof. Whilst some of the dogs engaged her in front others tried to dash in at the fawn, retreating at once when the angry mother swung round at them. They had already hamstrung the poor little beast and torn out one of its eyes; so, when they fled as soon as they caught sight of my elephant and the hind ran off, I put the wretched fawn out of its misery with a merciful shot.

Across the fire line we entered the jungle again. Along a branch over our heads a small animal runs swiftly and leaps into a neighbouring tree. It is a giant squirrel, a pretty animal with long and bushy tail and thick black fur, except on the breast, where it is white. It peeps at us from behind the tree-trunk and then is lost to sight in the foliage.

Khartoum pursues her leisurely way through the forest; for, in thick jungle where we must swerve aside to avoid trees and hack a path through creepers and undergrowth, we hardly go a mile an hour. But on a road I have timed her to walk at the rate of four miles an hour. Suddenly my eye is caught by a flash of bright colour; and I see a *khakur* buck and doe bounding through the trees ahead. Laying my hand on Bechan's shoulder I make him stop the elephant. Then as the graceful little deer cross our front in an open glade I fire and drop the male in its tracks. The doe bounds off in affright. As the *mahout* picks up the pretty animal, too dead for him to *hallal* it, binds its legs together and hands it up to me to fasten on the pad, only the thought of its succulent flesh reconciles me to the slaying of it. The *khakur*, or barking deer, as it is called from its cry, which is similar to a dog's bark, is of a bright chestnut colour and has a curious marking on the face like a pair of very black eyebrows raised in surprise and continued down the nose. The male has peculiar little horns with skin-covered pedicles about three inches long, from which project the brow antlers and the upper tines, which curve inward towards each other. These horns are small, six inches being considered a very good length. The buck has, in addition, a pair of sharp, thin, curved tusks in the upper jaw, which it uses as weapons of offence. Satisfied with our bag we turn Khartoum's head towards home, and reach Santrabari before dusk.

Such is a typical day in the jungle. Sometimes, though rarely, I was unsuccessful in procuring something for the pot. But on one day I shot three *sambhur* and a *khakur*. My Rajput sepoys would not eat the flesh of the former; for, like most Hindus, they imagined that its cloven hoof made it kin to the sacred cow. But the Mussulmans of the detachment, and the *mahouts* and their families, and our coolies were grateful for the meat.

Tough as a *sambhur's* flesh is, we officers were glad of it ourselves when nothing better offered. But our Hindus rejoiced exceedingly whenever one of us brought home a wild boar; and the Mohammedans were correspondingly disgusted, as pork is anathema to them. The slaying of a boar with a gun in open country where pigsticking is possible is as great a crime in India as shooting a fox in a hunting county in England; but in the forest it is permissible. There were a few *cheetul* or spotted deer very like the English fallow deer in our jungles; but I only saw one herd and secured one stag all the time I was at Buxa. They usually frequent more open forests; and the spots on their hide assimilating to the dappled light and shade of the sun through the leaves is a good example of Nature's protective colouring. Thus the black hide of the *sambhur* stag blends easily with the dark shadows of the denser forest and makes them very hard to see.

One does not often meet the dangerous beasts of the jungle by day. Tigers and panthers, though frequent enough, generally move only by night. Yet I often saw on the tree-trunks long scratches where these animals had cleaned and sharpened their claws, just as the domestic cat does on the legs of chairs and tables. They keep out of the way of elephants; and so I sometimes must have passed some great feline, whose fresh tracks I had just observed, sheltering in the undergrowth and watching us as we went by. I have seen high up on the stems and branches other scratches which showed where a bear had climbed in search of fruit. These animals, the dreaded large Himalayan variety, usually dwell in the hills and descend into the forest by night, so that they are rarely met with by daylight. The natives regard them with terror; for, if stumbled upon accidently by some woodcutter, they will probably attack him and smash his skull with a crushing blow of a paw. In our stretch of jungle I only came across one rhinoceros and a herd of six bison, which, being protected by the rules of the forest department, we could not shoot. Once my elephant put up a stray bison calf which looked at us with mild curiosity until my orderly climbed down and tried to catch it. It trotted off out of his reach and stopped to look back at him. We drove it for a mile before us, hoping to shepherd it into camp and capture it; but we lost it in thick jungle. Wild elephants I occasionally came across, and had a couple of unpleasant adventures with them.

The fascination of a day's sport in the heart of the great forest is beyond words. Even if nothing falls to one's rifle the pleasure of roaming through the woodland is intense. Of the world nothing seems to exist farther than the eye can see down the short vistas of soft green light between the giant trees. Lulled by the swaying motion of the elephant—not unpleasant when used to it—one's senses are nevertheless keenly on the alert; for every stride may disclose some strange denizen of the jungle either to be sought after or guarded against. And the beauty of it all. The fern-carpeted glades, the drooping trails of bright-coloured orchids, the tangled shadows of the dense undergrowth, the glimpses of never-ending woodland between the great boles. And always the hush, the intense silence of this enchanted forest.

The generous jungle provides everything that savage man needs. The profusely growing bamboo will make his house or bridge the streams for him. Its delicate young shoots can be eaten. Its bark gives excellent lashing. Slit longitudinally it will serve as an aqueduct and convey the water from the mountain torrents to his door. Cut into lengths it makes cups and bottles for him. Should he need a cooking-pot, a length of bamboo cut off below a knot can be filled with water and placed on the fire; and the water will be boiled and food cooked long before the green wood is much charred. For food the forest offers deer, pigs, and fowl. There are several varieties of edible tubers. The unopened flowers of the *simal* tree are eaten as vegetables; while its seed makes a good nourishing food for cattle, and the cotton of its burst-open pods is used for stuffing pillows. The *pua*, a shrub with hairy shoots and dark grey bark gives the fibre which can be woven into cloth or made into fishing-nets, twine and net-bags. There is a creeper, the bark of which, bruised and thrown into a stream, stupefies the fish and brings them floating to the surface, where they can be easily caught. The *pani bel* gives man water to drink. And, if he is ill, another creeper makes an excellent febrifuge, while the gum of the *udal* tree is used as a purgative, and fomentations of the leaves of a shrub called *madar* are excellent for sprains and bruises. Food, drink, clothing, houses, household utensils, medicine; what more does savage and simple man require?

The jungle was called upon to provide me with an

abode; for camping in tents in the forest was a very unsafe proceeding, owing to the wild elephants which might rush over the tents at night or, from sheer curiosity, pull them down and stand on them to the detriment of the occupants. So I got Bhuttia coolies to build a bamboo hut for me up in the trees. Twenty-two feet from the ground they constructed a platform supported by the tree-trunks and branches; and on this they erected a cosy three-roomed dwelling with walls of split bamboo and roof thatched with grass. It was reached by ladders. Although it shook to the tread of anyone walking about in it, it was very strong. Split bamboo partitions divided it off into the three apartments, sitting, bed and bathroom. It was quite a romantic dwelling, such as a boy steeped in the lore of Robinson Crusoe or Jules Verne would have loved. I named it Forest Lodge and regarded it with pride. I thought it safe from the destructive tendencies of wild elephants; for it was supported entirely by the neighbouring trees, with the exception of one long bamboo pole helping to hold up the roof. But once when it was left empty some mischievous elephant discovered it. How it entered into his thick skull to do it I do not know; but he dragged on the bamboo pole until he brought the whole in ruins about his ears. However, I had it built up again, this time with an open lower story surrounded by a bamboo wall to be used as a dining-room. On its apparently frail flooring of split bamboo I once entertained eight planters who had ridden over to see Forest Lodge the Second and who, with my junior officer, myself, and three servants, made a total of thirteen persons standing on the floor at the

FOREST LODGE THE FIRST.

FOREST LODGE THE SECOND.

same time. When shooting or when in camp in the forest with my detachment, for I often brought my sepoys down to teach them jungle lore and practise them in bush warfare, I always occupied it. It was never again dismantled by elephants; though a similar but smaller building close by, occupied by my servants, was several times destroyed by them.

The fact was that its position invited attack. It stood near a path, much frequented by elephants, leading to a salt lick in the hills a few hundred yards away. This was in a curious amphitheatre in the foothills where landslips had left exposed precipitous slopes of a curious white earth impregnated with some chemical salts, probably soda or natron, of which wild animals are extremely fond. Bison, elephants, and deer of all sorts used to come here at night to eat this earth; and tigers prowled around it in search of prey. Native *shikarees* (hunters) erected *machâns* or platforms over it to pot the deer at their ease. This amphitheatre was almost a complete circle, save for one narrow chasm which must have been cut by the force of water. It was a winding gully, in places scarcely broad enough to allow the passage of an elephant with a pad on its back. I wondered what happened when two tuskers met in the narrow path. Its perpendicular sides were formed of the same white clay; but at their bases were seams of coal, black and shining where freshly exposed. When I saw them I thought that I had made a valuable discovery of mineral wealth. But when I broke off lumps of the coal and placed them on my camp fire I found that they would not burn; and I learned that there is coal in these hills which is a thousand years too young and, so, valueless. Thus faded my dream of the boundless wealth the jungle was to give me.

Forest Lodge was a constant source of interest and wonderment to all the monkeys in the neighbourhood. They used to gather in the tree-tops around and hold conferences to discuss it. Perched on the branches mothers with small babies clinging to them, sedate old men and frivolous youngsters scratched themselves meditatively and chattered and argued as to what manner of strange ape I was who had thus invaded their realm. When restless young monkeys wearied of the endless discussion and started to frivol, the elder ones seemed to rebuke their levity, and when this failed to have the desired effect would spring with bared teeth on the irreverent youth to chastise them; and the meeting then broke up in disorder.

When my detachment was encamped around Forest Lodge the scene at night, as I looked down from my windows, was truly Rembrandtesque. Their fires glowed in the trees, lighting up the dark faces of the sepoys and revealing with weird effect the huge forms of our transport elephants restlessly swaying at their pickets, ears flapping and trunks swinging as the big beasts incessantly shifted their weight from foot to foot. Around the bivouac was built a zareba of cut thorny bushes; and the guards mounted with ball cartridge in their pouches, not merely because it is the custom of the Service, but to repel any prowling dangerous beasts that might be tempted to visit the camp by night; for within fifty yards of a sentry I had a shot at a bear; and a tiger killed a *sambhur* not a hundred yards from the zareba. And once I sat at the window of my tree-dwelling listening to a tiger prowling around for a long time, uttering short snorting roars but never approaching near enough to give me a shot at him.

The voices of the men in the camp sounded loud through the silent forest and must have astonished the wild animals making their way to the salt lick close by, for at night all the jungle is awake. The beasts of prey wander from sunset to sunrise in search of a meal; and the deer must be on the alert against them. Only in the hot hours of the day dare they repose in security and lie down to sleep in the shade of the undergrowth. Even then they start at every sound, and the snapping of a twig brings them to their feet; for to the harmless animals life in the jungle is one constant menace. The birds and the monkeys in the trees alone can devote the dark hours to slumber; there is no rest at night for anything that dwells on the ground.

Now gradually the sepoys' voices die away and the flickering fires burn low. The forest is hushed in silence, broken only by the eerie cry of the great owl or the distant crash of a tree knocked down by a wild elephant.

CHAPTER VI

ROGUES OF THE FOREST

The lord of the forest—Wild elephants in India—*Kheddah* operations in the Terai—How rogues are made—Rogues attack villages—Highway robbers—Assault on a railway station—A police convoy—A poacher's death—Chasing an officer—My first encounter with a rogue—Stopping a charge—Difficulty of killing an elephant—The law on rogue-shooting—A Government gazette—A tame elephant shot by the Maharajah of Cooch Behar—Executing an elephant—A chance shot—A planter's escape—Attack on a tame elephant—The *mahout's* peril—Jhansi's wounds—Changes among the officers in Buxa—A Gurkha's terrible death—The beginner's luck—Indian and Malayan *sambhur*—A shot out of season—A fruitless search—Jhansi's flight—A scout attacked by a bear—Advertising for a truant—The agony column—Runaway elephants—A fatal fraud—Jhansi's return.

WHAT animal can dispute with the elephant the proud title of lord of the forest? All give way to him as he stalks unchallenged through the woodland. The vaunted tiger shrinks aside from his path; and only the harmless beasts regard him without dismay, for he is merciful as he is strong. And the shield of the British Government is raised to protect him from man; for the laws of its forest department ordain that he must not be slain.

The stretches of jungle along the foot of the Himalayas harbour herds of wild elephants, which, thus saved from the sportsman's rifle, increase and multiply. These useful and usually harmless animals are far from being exterminated in India. Free to wander unscathed in Government forests, their numbers are not diminishing. The continuity of the Terai saves them from capture; for the ordinary *kheddah* operations, which consist of hemming a herd into a certain patch of jungle and driving it into a stockade of stout timbers is useless in forests where the animals can wander on in shelter indefinitely. This method is costly; for it requires the services of a trained staff of hunters and large numbers of coolies, and may take months. It was once tried near Buxa and, after a great expenditure of money, labour and time, did not result in the capture of one elephant. So the Government has adopted here another system. It lets out the *kheddah* rights to certain rajahs and big *Zemindars* (landholders) who furnish parties of hunters and tame elephants to go into the jungle and pursue the herds. Once on the trail of one they follow it persistently and keep it constantly on the move. When a calf elephant becomes exhausted and falls behind the others, the men fire on the mother and drive her off or kill her, surround the youngster and secure it by slipping ropes on its legs. It is then fastened between tame elephants and led off, a prisoner.

This method is responsible for the existence of a number of dangerous "rogue" elephants in the jungles near Buxa; for the worried herds break up and some of the males take to a solitary life. And of all the perils of the forest the rogue is the worst. The tiger or the panther rarely attacks man; and when it does, it is only for food. The bear, when unmolested, is generally harmless. But the vicious rogue seems to kill for the mere lust of murder. Occasionally a tusker, not belonging to a harried herd, develops a liking to a lonely existence and strays away from the others of his kind. Probably because he is an old bachelor and deprived of the softening influence of the female sex, he becomes surly and dangerous. He may take to wandering into cultivation at night and feeding on the crops, as wild elephants often do. The villagers naturally object to this, light fires around their fields, and turn out with torches, horns and drums to scare the intruders off. The herds are generally easily stampeded; but sometimes the surly old tusker, enraged at having his meal of succulent grain disturbed, charges the peasants and perhaps kills one or two of them. This not only destroys in him the wild animal's natural dread of man, but seems to give him a taste for bloodshed quite at variance with the elephant's accustomed gentleness of disposition.

The tales told me when I first went to Buxa of the ferocity and lust of cruelty of rogues seemed incredible. I heard of them deliberately entering villages on tea gardens, breaking through the frail structures of bamboo and tearing down hut after hut until they reached the houses of the *bunniahs*, or tradesmen who dealt in grain and food-stuffs. Then they feasted royally on the contents of the shops. Roads cut through the forest lead from the railway line to the gardens or from village to village; and along these come trains of bullock carts loaded with grain. Wild elephants used to lie in wait in the jungle until these were passing, then charge out on them, kill the drivers and bullocks and loot the grain.

While I was at Buxa two cases occurred of such

attacks on carts close to Rajabhatkawa Station. In one the drivers got away safely; but a woman with them tripped and fell to the ground. The elephant overtook her, deliberately put his foot on her head and crushed her to death. In the other case the natives all escaped; but the rogue killed several of the bullocks, broke up the carts and hurled one on to the rails, where it lay until removed by the railway company officials who actually prosecuted the owner for obstructing the line. The station at Rajabhatkawa was attacked on one occasion. A tusker elephant suddenly appeared on the metals. The staff rushed into the building and locked themselves in. An engine happened to be standing in the station and the driver blew the whistle loudly to scare the animal off. The sound only infuriated the elephant; but, probably not liking the appearance of the engine, he ignored it, attacked the platform and tried to root it up. In doing so he broke off one of his tusks and, screaming with pain, rushed off into the jungle. I think that this was a brute with which I had a fight afterwards.

The rogues did not always grasp the fact that every bullock cart passing through the forest was not necessarily loaded with grain. On one occasion a convoy of convicts loaded with iron fetters was being taken to Alipur Duar in carts, escorted by armed native police. Suddenly from the jungle through which they were passing rushed out a wild elephant which charged the procession furiously. Drivers, police, prisoners, leapt from the carts and fled in terror. The wretched convicts, hampered by their leg-irons, stumbled, tripped and fell frequently. But fortunately for them the rogue was too busily engaged in chasing the frightened bullocks, killing them and smashing up the carts in a fruitless search for grain, to pay any attention to the men; and they all escaped.

A vicious elephant's method of slaughtering its human prey is particularly horrible. Our nearest planter neighbour, Tyson of Hathipota, was a man who knew the Terai well, having lived in various parts of the Duars, and had had much experience in big-game shooting. He told me of a terrible case which he had seen when on a visit to a forest officer in the Western Duars jungles. Into his host's solitary bungalow one day rushed two terrified forest guards to tell him of an awful spectacle which they had just witnessed. They had been lying hidden watching a well-known native poacher fishing in a preserved river. He was on the opposite bank and the stream at that part was unfordable. While they were discussing a plan to capture him, they saw a wild elephant appear out of the jungle behind the poacher and stealthily approach him. To their horror the brute suddenly rushed on the unsuspecting man, knocked him down, trampled on him and then, placing one foot on his thighs, wound its trunk round his body, seized him in its mouth and literally tore him to pieces. The story seemed too horrible to be true; but the forest officer and Tyson visited the spot and found the corpse of the luckless poacher crushed and mutilated as the eyewitnesses to the tragedy had narrated. The elephant's footprints were clearly visible. I could hardly credit the story until a similar case came to my own notice.

Another instance of unprovoked attack was related to me by Captain Denham White, Indian Medical Service, who had formerly been doctor to the Buxa detachment. An elephant had been reported to be committing havoc in the forest in the vicinity; and the then commanding officer and Denham White endeavoured to find and shoot him. They searched the jungle for a week in vain. Then White vowed that the animal was a phantom elephant and refused to accompany the commandant on the eighth day of the hunt. Taking his orderly with him, he went fishing in a river which flowed through the forest. The water in it was low; and the greater part of the bed was dry and covered with loose, rounded boulders which had been swept down from the hills during the Rains. White was busily engaged with his rod and line when he heard the orderly shout. Turning, he saw to his horror a large tusker elephant descending the steep bank and coming straight towards them. It was the missing rogue. The two men ran for their lives. The elephant pursued them, but, slipping and stumbling over the loose boulders, was unable to move quickly. Denham White, and his orderly gained the opposite bank and reached a road along a fire line and got away. It was fortunate for them that they had a good start and were close to this road; for in the jungle they would inevitably have been overtaken and killed.

A good runner may outpace an elephant on level ground for a short sprint. But in thick jungle a man has a poor chance. Undergrowth and creepers that bar his progress will not hinder an elephant, which can burst through them easily. He cannot escape up a tree; for the large ones in the forest are devoid of branches for many feet from the ground, and any tree slender enough for him to grasp and climb could be easily knocked down by the elephant.

But I am not sure that the animal would have sufficient intelligence to do so in order to reach the man.

I was not long in Buxa before making the acquaintance of a rogue. About three weeks after my arrival I was out in the forest on Khartoum, accompanied by her *mahout*, Bechan, and a *shikaree* or native hunter. Early in the day I shot a *sambhur* stag. The two men slipped off the elephant to *hallal* it; and I followed to photograph the dead beast with a hand-camera. The *mahout* was holding up the head in position for me, when we heard a sudden crashing in the jungle behind us. Bechan dropped the head in evident alarm and said:

"Sahib, that is a wild elephant. I believe it has been following us; for I heard it behind us as we came along."

Hardly had he spoken, when the head of an elephant appeared above the undergrowth. It was a male with a splendid pair of long curved tusks. The moment it caught sight of us it stopped. New to the jungle, I was under the impression that all wild elephants were inoffensive creatures. So I was rejoiced at this opportunity of photographing one, for such pictures are very rare; and, camera in hand, I started towards it. But the moment Khartoum saw the intruder, she stampeded, followed by her *mahout*. The *shikaree* yelled:

"It's a mad elephant. Shoot, Sahib, shoot, and save our lives!" And he bolted.

The newcomer still stood motionless, looking at me; and I smiled at my men's alarm. Still I thought it advisable to put the camera down and take up my rifle. It was unloaded; so I slipped in a couple of solid bullets instead of the "soft-nosed"

"THE MAHOUT WAS HOLDING UP THE HEAD."

ones used for animals less hard to pierce than elephants or bison. But I had no intention of firing; for the forest regulations impose penalties up to six months' imprisonment or a fine of five hundred rupees for killing an elephant. I looked regretfully at the fine tusks; they would have been a splendid trophy. Still smoking my pipe I walked towards the animal which had not moved but was regarding me with a fixed stare. I halted and, taking off my big sun-helmet, waved it in the air and shouted:

"Shoo! you brute. Be off!"

My voice seemed to enrage the elephant. Up went its head, it curled its trunk, uttered a slight squeal and charged at me. I dropped on one knee and aimed at its forehead. With the fear of the forest department before my eyes, I hesitated to press the trigger until the huge bulk seemed almost towering over me. Then I fired. As if struck by a thunderbolt the elephant stopped dead in its furious rush and sank on its knees only fifteen paces from me. But even then I did not realise what an escape I had had. My first thought, as I picked up my pipe and stood erect was: "How can I hide the body, so that the forest officer will never know of my crime?"

So dense was the undergrowth that I could not see the prostrate animal in it. Rifle-butt resting on the ground, I pulled at my pipe perplexedly. I wondered how I could explain my act to the forest authorities. I knew, of course, that I had not to fear imprisonment; but a fine seemed certain. And a worse penalty might be inflicted, the cancellation of my shooting-licence. And I shuddered at the thought of two years in Buxa Duar if I were not allowed to solace my solitude by sport. It never occurred to me that the fact that I would have been killed if I had not fired would be accepted as a sufficient excuse for breaking the Draconic laws of Government.

Suddenly the elephant rose up, turned and dashed away blindly into the forest. My bullet had only stunned it. Bursting through the tangled undergrowth, snapping tough creepers like thread, trampling down small trees and smashing off thick branches, it rushed off mad with pain and terror. Long after I had lost sight of it I could hear its noisy progress through the jungle. I was intensely relieved at its recovery and departure, and did not realise that it was fortunate for me that it did not renew the attack.

I inspected the spot where it had fallen. The ground was ploughed up by its toes where it had been suddenly stopped in its charge; and the undergrowth was crushed flat from the weight of its body. There was a fair amount of blood on the leaves and grass around. I measured the distance to the spot where I had knelt. It was exactly fifteen paces; so I had not fired a moment too soon. While I stood disconsolate the *shikaree* returned. He explained that after the shot he had listened for my dying shrieks and, not hearing them, concluded that I had come off victorious in the encounter. He endeavoured in vain to convince me that I had been right to fire. Shortly afterwards Bechan returned with the still terrified Khartoum; and he agreed with the other man. It occurred to me that the elephant might have fallen again further on; so I thought it advisable to follow him and if I found him dying, put him out of pain. But Bechan and the *shikaree* absolutely refused to go with me; so I started off on foot. But in fifty yards I realised that I would certainly lose myself in the jungle, so I was obliged to return ignominiously to them.

Next day, however, Bechan's courage was restored; and he took me again to the spot. We had no difficulty in picking out the tusker's trail. A broad, almost straight track led away for hundreds of yards. The undergrowth was trampled down, small trees broken off and the ground covered with branches snapped off by the animal's body in its blind haste. At one place the beast had stopped and kicked up some earth to plaster on its wound, as elephants always do. We followed the trail for nearly three miles and then lost it where it mingled with innumerable old tracks of other elephants.

When I knew more about these animals I was not surprised that my shot had not killed the rogue. The front of an elephant's skull is enormously thick and the brain is very small. A bullet in the head not reaching the brain will never kill the brute on the spot, and is not necessarily fatal. Sanderson, the great authority on elephant-shooting narrates many such cases and says:

" It will be evident, on an examination of the skull, that if the brain be missed by a shot no harm will be done to the animal, as there are no other vital organs, such as large blood-vessels etc., situated in the head. It thus happens that, in head shots, if the elephant is not dropped on the spot he is very rarely bagged at all. A shot that goes through his skull into his neck without touching his brain may kill him, but it will take time. I have never recovered any elephant that has left the spot with a head shot. The blood-trail for a few yards is generally very thick; but it often ceases as suddenly as it is at first copious. Elephants are sometimes floored by the concussion of a shot, if the ball passes very close to the brain; large balls frequently effect this. No time should be lost in finishing a floored elephant, or he will certainly make his escape. Many cases have occurred of elephants which have been regarded as dead suddenly recovering themselves and making off."

The position of the head held high in charging protects the one deadly spot in the forehead; and, to quote Sanderson again:

"To reach the brain of a charging elephant from in front the bullet must pass through about three feet of curled trunk, flesh and bone. It is thus occasionally impossible to kill an elephant if the head be held very high."

I could have finished off the tusker at my ease as he lay on the ground, had it not been for my loyal obedience to the regulations. On my return to Buxa I sent a telegram, followed by an official letter of explanation and apology, to the forest officer. His reply filled me with annoyance when I learned that my scruples had been uncalled for and that I could have slain the brute, and probably would have been allowed to keep the tusks. His letter said:

"Rajabhatkawa,
"14-1-09.

"My Dear Casserly,—Yours of 11-1-09 *re* elephant. You were undoubtedly justified in shooting at it; and I must congratulate you on a very narrow escape. In defence of self or property or cultivation you may shoot at any elephant but as far as I read the Act, which is somewhat vague, you must not pursue the elephant further unless it is a 'proclaimed' rogue; that is, proclaimed by Government. There are a number of solitary male rogue elephants about that are always dangerous and should be shot at on sight, especially if you have an elephant with you. If you can tell me the approximate height of this elephant and if a single or double tusker and any distinguishing peculiarities, I will write to the deputy commissioner and get it proclaimed. We had a man killed in one of our forest villages at Mendabari recently; and our *babus* were held up the other day by a rogue. But this animal has one tusk broken off short. A double tusker killed one of our sawyers near here and was proclaimed and a reward of fifty rupees and the tusks offered. Possibly this was your elephant. "Yours etc., etc."

Rogue elephants, like man-eating tigers, are honoured with a notice in Government gazettes. Shortly afterwards I received a copy of such a gazette, which read:

"A reward of fifty rupees is offered for the destruction of each of the rogue elephants described below:

(1). One single-tusker height 9′ 10″. This animal killed a man on 2nd January, 1909, and frequents the Borojhar Forest and western portion of the Buxa reserve and does considerable damage to crops in the adjoining villages.

(2). One double-tusker with large tusks. Height 9′ 10″. This animal charged Captain Casserly and his elephant on the 30th Mile line of the Buxa reserve and was only turned by a shot at close quarters.

Not long afterwards, when on a visit to the Maharajah of Cooch Behar, I was taken by his second son, Prince Jitendra, to inspect the Peelkhana. There I saw an example of how easily elephants recover from terrible wounds. Securely chained to a tree at a distance from the other animals was a large tusker which, while the Maharajah had been having a beat for tiger a few weeks before, had suddenly gone mad and attacked the other elephants. Prince Rajendra, the present Maharajah,* had ridden up close to it and fired two shots at it from his heavy cordite rifle. One bullet struck it in the head, the other in the shoulder. Yet here it was feeding in apparently the best of health. Below the right eye was the scar of an almost healed wound; while in the shoulder a hole was still visible but nearly filled up. And five years before, when suffering from a similar attack of madness, it had been shot by the Maharajah with his ·500 rifle, and had completely recovered in a very short time from the wounds then received.

In the days of a previous commanding officer of Buxa a tame elephant had been condemned to death on account of old age and infirmity and was handed over to the detachment to be shot. A squad of sepoys with ·303 Lee-Enfield rifles was drawn up five paces in front of it and fired a volley at its forehead. But the elephant only winced at the blows and stood its ground. Then the men drew off to one side and aimed at its heart. A volley here killed it. The British officer had the head skinned and found that the first bullets had only penetrated a very short way into the skull, some of them being flattened against the bone.

* He died in 1913, since this was written.

On the other hand cases have occurred of elephants succumbing easily to chance shots from small-bore rifles. On a tea garden not far from Buxa a rogue had been destroying the crops in the cultivation. A young planter sat up in a *machân** in a tree near the fields to watch for it. He was armed with a ·303 carbine. He fell asleep and suddenly woke up to find the elephant passing right underneath him. Without taking aim he fired blindly into the dark mass below his *machân*. The elephant rushed off. The planter remained on his perch until daylight, and, descending, met his manager and told him what he had done. The latter was an experienced sportsman and inveighed forcibly at the useless cruelty of firing at an elephant with such a small bullet, which could only wound and infuriate the animal. While he was speaking a coolie ran up to inform that the elephant was lying dead a few hundred yards in the fields. The bullet, entering the back from above, had been deflected by bones and had taken an erratic course through the body, seeming to have pierced every vital organ in it in turn.

I heard of a case in Assam where a planter, carrying a ·303 rifle, was walking along a road when he was suddenly charged by a wild elephant. He fired at its mouth. The animal turned and ran away. As it did so the planter fired again and hit it under the tail. The elephant staggered on a short distance and then fell dead. One of my sepoys, when on guard at Santrabari, fired at a wild elephant which was attacking our tame ones in the stables. The man used his Lee-Enfield rifle and scarcely waited to take aim.

* A platform erected in a tree at a height above the ground.

Yet the animal, a *muckna* or tuskerless male, dropped dead within a few yards.

Our tame elephants were taken into the forest every day to graze. One morning Jhansi was out in charge of her *mahout* about two miles from Santrabari, when a single-tusker rogue suddenly charged out of the jungle at her. The terrified *mahout* flung himself off her neck and crept away through the undergrowth. The rogue hurled himself against Jhansi and knocked her down by the force of his attack. He drove his one tusk deep into her back and drew off to gather impetus for a fresh charge. Jhansi scrambled to her feet and bolted. The brute pursued her, prodding viciously at her hind quarters; but being a fast mover, she outstripped him and got back to Santrabari. Her vicious assailant followed her for a short distance and then returned to search the undergrowth for the *mahout* but, luckily for the latter, without finding him. Jhansi was brought up to the fort for me to doctor. I found a round punctured wound several inches deep in her back; and on her rump were several smaller holes and cuts made by the rogue elephants she was an excellent patient and stood the cleaning and disinfecting of her wounds admirably.

This unprovoked attack made it imperative that I should try to put an end to the rogue's career; for, if he remained in our neighbourhood, the *mahouts* would be afraid to take their animals out to graze. So I instituted a hunt for him. Creagh had been transferred to Gyantse in Tibet, his place being taken by a junior captain of the regiment named Balderston. A young Irish lieutenant in the Indian

Medical Service was now our doctor, as Smith had gone to another corps. As it was during the rainy season when the Terai Jungle is filled with the deadliest malarial fever, it was impossible to camp in the forest. But I came down from the hills every day and searched far and wide for the outlaw and soon found terrible traces of his presence. The body of a Gurkha, killed by him, was discovered on a path through the jungle. The man had been proceeding along it on foot when he had been met and attacked by the rogue. His head and body had been crushed flat and stamped into the ground, the legs torn off and hurled twenty yards away. The elephant had evidently placed his foot on the body, taken the legs in his mouth and torn the poor wretch to pieces. The sight made me long to meet the brute and put an end to his vicious career. But though we searched the jungle day after day, we never met him.

However, during the hunt, our doctor, who was new to big-game shooting, had the usual beginner's luck and secured the record *sambhur* head for the district. The *sambhur* in these jungles belong to the Malayan species which, probably owing to the dense forest they inhabit, have much shorter though thicker horns than the so-called Indian *sambhur* found in other parts of the Peninsula. The stags are generally darker, the old ones almost black or slate-coloured; and their tails are more bushy. While the record Indian head is fifty and an eighth inches, Lydekker gives the longest Malayan antlers as thirty and an eighth inches; though an officer formerly in Buxa shot one with horns thirty-three inches in length.

As killing deer is prohibited in Government jungles

during the hot weather and Rains, that being the close season, I had warned Balderston and the doctor not to fire at any we met with. And besides this, I did not want to run the risk of alarming the rogue for which we were hunting. But one day we came suddenly upon a large *sambhur* stag. It was the first specimen of big game that the doctor, new to India, had ever seen. He became greatly excited and raised his rifle. Balderston, behind whom he was seated on Dundora, warned him not to fire; but, misunderstanding in his excitement, he pulled the trigger. The bullet struck the *sambhur* in the fore-leg; and the beast went off limping. Shooting a stag in the close season is a dire offence in the sportsman's eye; and Balderston and I abused the unfortunate doctor roundly. However, as it would have been sheer cruelty to allow a wounded animal to get away, I ordered our *mahouts* to pursue. We came up to the stag in about half an hour; and I shot him through the heart. On measuring the horns we discovered them to be thirty-three inches long, which equalled the record Malay *sambhur* I have mentioned.

About three weeks after we gave up the search for the rogue and were satisfied that he had left our jungles, our three elephants were taken out to graze in the forest by the coolies who assist the *mahouts*. It was the duty of these men to remain with their charges; but, as it happened to be pay-day in Buxa, they shackled the elephants' forelegs with chains and left them to feed, while they themselves climbed up to the fort for their salaries. On their return, several hours later, they found Khartoum and Dundora browsing placidly on the trees; but Jhansi had disappeared. She had contrived to slip her shackles, which lay on the ground. The *mahouts*, searching for her, came on the track of a herd of wild elephants, which had passed close to our tame ones. It was conjectured that Jhansi, remembering her recent unpleasant adventure with the rogue, had become alarmed at the sight of them, got rid of her chain and fled away in an opposite direction. But, unlike the previous occasion, she did not return to Santrabari. At the time I happened to be on leave in Darjeeling; so Captain Balderston took our trained company scouts to look for her. Each man carried his rifle and ball cartridge to protect himself if necessary. It was well that they did; for on the second day of their search one of them was wantonly attacked by a large bear. A bullet from the sepoy's rifle taught it that it had not a helpless woodcutter to deal with; and, howling with pain, it ran off.

On my return I borrowed elephants from the forest officer and started out on a systematic hunt for the truant. As in the army an officer generally has to pay for any article of Government property lost while in his charge, I was afraid that I might be called upon to replace Jhansi. The cost of a female elephant runs into hundreds of pounds; so I did not relish the prospect. I telegraphed to the brigade headquarters announcing Jhansi's loss; and when the reply came I opened it in fear and trembling. It only referred me to a certain paragraph in the Army Regulations for India. I consulted it at once, and to my relief found that it merely directed me to advertise the loss of a Government elephant in a newspaper. Not knowing which journal Jhansi was in the habit of perusing, and wondering if I was supposed to word the announcement in the phrasing of the agony column, "Come back to your sorrowing friends and all will be forgiven," I eventually tried the columns of a Calcutta daily. But it did not bring the truant back. As month after month went by, I lost hope of ever seeing her again. Whenever I heard that a *kheddah* party had captured an elephant which evidently had once been tame I sent off Jhansi's *mahout* to inspect the prisoner.

It often happens that animals which have been in captivity for some time escape and take to the jungle again. If caught they are soon discovered to have been domesticated; and *mahouts* of lost elephants are sent to view them, as their former charges will always recognise and obey them. I heard of a case of attempted fraud, with a fatal ending, in this connection. A *mahout* falsely claimed an elephant as his and mounted it. The animal, enraged at being handled by a stranger, dragged him off her neck and stamped him to death before the horrified spectators could intervene.

Eight months after Jhansi's disappearance I was informed by the *mahouts* that she had suddenly come out of the jungle and approached the Peelkhana. She stood at a safe distance watching her former comrades. When the men went towards her to secure her, she fled into the jungle. I ordered the *mahouts* to leave food in her stall and not to attempt to interfere with her unless she came right into the stables. Next day she made her appearance at feeding-time. The men took no notice of her, placed the usual meal of rice and leaves before Dundora and Khartoum and deposited her allowance in her "standing." Jhansi marched boldly in and began to eat it; and the men crept in behind her and slipped the iron shackles on her legs. She showed no resentment and continued feeding unconcernedly, and afterwards she gave no trouble, did her usual work, and seemed to feel no regret at the loss of her freedom.

CHAPTER VII

A FIGHT WITH AN ELEPHANT

We sight a rogue—A sudden onslaught—A wild elephant's attack—Shooting under difficulties—Stopping a rush—Repeated attacks—An invulnerable foe—Darkness stops the pursuit—A council of war—Picking up the trail—A *muckna*—A female elephant—Photographing a lady—A good sitter—A stampede—A gallant Rajput—Attacking on foot—A hazardous feat—A narrow escape—Final charge—A bivouac in the forest—Dangers of the night—A long chase—Planter hospitality—Another stampede—A career of crime—Eternal hope—A king-cobra—Abandoning the pursuit—An unrepentant villain—In the moment of danger.

KHARTOUM stepped along at her usual deliberate pace through the jungle, occasionally raising her trunk to sweep the leaves off a branch and cram them into her mouth, or plucking a tuft of long grass to brush away the troublesome flies. On her neck the *mahout* swayed to the motion, while I sat nursing my heavy ·470 cordite rifle and talking to my orderly, Draj Khan, seated behind me on the pad. He carried a ·303 carbine. We were passing through a patch of thin forest bare of undergrowth, when Bechan pulled up suddenly and whispered:

"*Jungli hathi!* (A wild elephant)."

About sixty yards ahead a large tusker was standing apparently half asleep under the trees, its right side towards us. I wondered if, since it was alone, I could consider it an outlaw which it would be justifiable to shoot. The probabilities were, as there were no signs of a herd in the vicinity, that it was a rogue. While I was mentally debating the question I slipped a couple of solid cartridges into my rifle. As I did so the elephant turned its head slowly and I saw that it had only one tusk.

"*Sahib! Sahib! wuh budmash hai!* (It is the rogue!") whispered Bechan excitedly.

At that moment it caught sight of us. Without hesitation, it turned and charged straight at us. There was no doubt now of its being a rogue; and probably it was Jhansi's assailant and the murderer of the Gurkha. I wished to wait until it was near enough for me to make sure of a fatal head-shot; but Khartoum became alarmed and tried to bolt. The *mahout* did his best to stop her.

"Shoot, Sahib, shoot! My elephant will not stand," he cried, beating her savagely with the iron *ankus*.

So, as I could not get a shot at the head as the animal came through the trees at us, I fired at its shoulder in the hope of laming it and bringing it to a stand, so that I could finish it at close quarters. But it did not seem to feel the bullet and never checked in its stride. I was being favoured with a spectacle which it is not given to many sportsmen in India to witness. Sanderson says of it that

"the wild elephant's attack is one of the noblest sights of the chase. A grander animated object than a wild elephant in full charge can hardly be imagined. The cocked ears and broad forehead present an immense frontage; the head is held high with the trunk curled between the tusks to be uncurled in the moment of attack; the massive forelegs come down with the force and regularity of ponderous machinery; and the whole figure is foreshortened, and appears to double in size with each advancing stride. The wild elephant's onslaught is as dignified as it seems overwhelming."

I confess that at the moment I was little disposed to admire the spectacle. Khartoum plunged and swayed until I was nearly shot off her back. If she stampeded our position would be extremely dangerous, for we would probably be swept off her back by the branches and creepers; and to be thrown to the ground in front of the pursuing rogue meant a certain and awful death. Bechan, hammering furiously at Khartoum's thick skull, yelled at me to fire; and my excited orderly kept urging me to "kill the *budmash*." I fired again, and the tusker, checked in his rush, swung off to one side. As he passed us among the trees, I gave him a third bullet in the ribs at forty yards. The report of my rifle had an almost instantaneously calming effect on Khartoum. She desisted from her efforts to bolt; and when I ordered the *mahout* to follow the fleeing rogue, she obeyed him and moved off quietly. We came on him about a quarter of a mile away in much denser jungle. He was standing sideways to us; and I took a steady shot at his ear, which should have been fatal. But instead of dropping to it, he swung round and charged us again. I told my orderly to aim at his knee, while I fired at his forehead. The two shots rang out together; but the apparently invulnerable brute only turned and fled. He was, however, limping badly; and I quickened his flight with another bullet. This time Khartoum had stood like a rock. We urged her on after him and overtook him partially concealed behind a stout tree-trunk. He seemed on the point of collapsing on the ground. But the moment he caught sight of us he charged again. My orderly and I aimed at the same spots as before and fired together. But the brute bore a charmed life. He swung off and dashed into thick jungle, but not before I could get another shot at him. The undergrowth closed around him and hid him from our sight. We followed at once on his track and found the bushes and grass splashed with blood. Every moment I expected to come upon him lying dead or dying. None of our shots had missed him; so he carried eight bullets from my heavy rifle and two from Draj Khan's carbine. It seemed impossible that he could live long. The trail was an easy one to follow and we found no difficulty in distinguishing it from old tracks; for he was evidently limping badly. One of his forelegs seemed to be useless; and where he had passed across a dry river-bed we found the impressions of three sound feet and the marks of the fourth trailing helplessly. But for all that we did not overtake him until we had covered three miles. We came upon him standing head towards us under a tree in thorny undergrowth. We stopped Khartoum about thirty yards from him; and he never moved as we took deliberate aim. We fired; and the shock of my heavy bullet in the skull drove him back on his haunches in the undergrowth. But again he recovered his footing and dashed away before we could get in a second shot. I was absolutely amazed at his tenacity of life and began to think that it was useless wasting lead on him; but we forced our way through the thorns and followed until the sun sank low in the sky. Then, marking a spot where the trail led across a broad and empty river-bed, I gave the order to turn Khartoum's head towards camp, resolved to take up the pursuit next day. I thought it highly probable that we should find the animal dead; for he now had twelve bullets in him.

At the time the detachment was inhabiting a stockaded post we had built in the jungle; and the men were out practising bush warfare in the forest every day. The spot where I first encountered the rogue was hardly a mile from this post. It was imperative that I should find and finally dispose of him, for I could not expose my sepoys to the danger of an unexpected meeting with him while engaged in their work; and the jungle would be absolutely unsafe while he was in the neighbourhood. He was almost undoubtedly the elephant which had wounded Jhansi and killed the Gurkha; and there were probably many more crimes to his account. His first unprovoked attack on us, and the daring of his repeated charges after being wounded, showed that he was a vicious and formidable brute; and the forest would be uninhabitable until he had been slain or driven far away.

When we reached camp that night I held a council of war with Captain Balderston and our native officers. It was resolved that I should take out with me next day one of our *subhedars*, a fine old Rajput named Sohanpal Singh, and his orderly on a second elephant. We determined to bring blankets and food with us, so that we could follow the trail for days if necessary, bivouacking wherever night found us. I hoped that, badly wounded as the animal was, the

SUBHEDAR SOHANPAL SINGH.

pursuit would not be a long one; but I was prepared to carry it on for days, if necessary.

At daybreak we started out, Sohanpal Singh and his orderly on Dundora, while Draj Khan and I led the way on Khartoum. The three were armed with Government ·303 rifles, while I had my cordite rifle. Our blankets were strapped on the pads, and our haversacks were filled with food. I carried a loaf of bread and a tin of corned beef in mine; while my Thermos flask was filled with limejuice and boiled water. Thus equipped, we started out amidst the cheers of the sepoys, who had been deeply interested in the account of the fights we had had on the previous day. Our route lay by a jungle village called Rungamutti, two miles from our stockade; and a couple of hours after we had passed it we picked up the elephant's trail.

The jungle across the river-bed where we had stopped the pursuit was at first fairly open; and I hoped that we should find our quarry in it. We came on the spot where he had passed the night. The grass was pressed down all around and was covered with blood. This was encouraging; and we went on full of hope. Suddenly through the trees we caught sight of an elephant standing sideways to us. The *mahouts* halted their animals and we brought our rifles to the ready.

But Bechan whispered, "That is not the *budmash*, Sahib. See, it has no tusks."

It was a *muckna* or tuskerless male. These are generally timid beasts, being constantly bullied in the herds by the males provided by Nature with weapons of offence. As soon as this one caught sight of us it bolted away through the jungle. We watched its headlong flight and then continued on the trail. A mile or two further on the jungle had the appearance of an English wood and the ground was carpeted with ferns. In an open glade we saw another elephant. It was a female; and, although it turned its head and looked at us, it did not evince any alarm. So I determined to try to secure a photograph of it. I handed my rifle to Draj Khan and took up my Kodak. The wild elephant stood still while I opened and adjusted the camera and pressed the bulb. As soon as the click of the shutter announced that the operation was over, she turned and moved slowly off into the jungle, while I waved my hat to her and expressed my thanks for her courtesy in waiting until I had taken her portrait. Unfortunately I had been too far off to secure a really good photograph, which was to be regretted, for such pictures are, naturally, extremely rare.

After her departure we moved on again. The forest grew denser; and the thick and entangled undergrowth delayed our progress; for, of course, a tame elephant with a pad and men on her back cannot slip through it as easily as an unencumbered wild one can do. So we were continually obliged to make detours and could not follow the trail closely.

About eleven o'clock in the morning a sudden crash in the jungle a hundred yards ahead of us startled our elephants. Before the *mahouts* could stop them they swung round and stampeded. It was my first experience of being bolted with; and it was decidedly unpleasant. Dundora, which had been behind, was now leading, and dashed through the trees, followed closely by Khartoum. As the noise had apparently been caused by the rogue, I tried to turn round on the pad, ready to fire. And doing so, while at the same time endeavouring to hold on and dodge the boughs and creepers overhead, was no easy task. Over and over again I was nearly swept off. Luckily the *mahouts* soon got their elephants in hand and stopped them. Then we cautiously advanced again, expecting every moment that the rogue would charge out on us. But when we reached the spot whence the noise had proceeded we found by the trail that he had been lying down and, startled by our appearance, had risen and fled. We urged our elephants forward. The chase was becoming exciting. We followed as fast as we could go, hoping every minute to catch sight of the quarry. The jungle was growing more difficult and we made slow progress.

At last, after three hours, we heard him. He was concealed in a dense thicket of thorny undergrowth. We skirted cautiously round it, hoping to see him and get a shot. But, although we could hear him, he was completely hidden. At length my native officer said:

"Sahib, why should we men be afraid of an animal? Let us attack him on foot."

The plucky old man had, in his own country and armed only with a sword, ridden at a tiger; but he did not realise that we were now facing a far more dangerous foe. His proposal was madness. The jungle was almost impenetrable, and we could not see five yards ahead in it. But before I could dissuade him the gallant old Rajput slid from Dundora's back, followed by his orderly, and walked towards the thicket. It was useless to try and stop him; so, cursing his foolhardiness, I dropped to the ground with Draj Khan. As I had the best rifle I pushed the others aside and got in front. But I had to reckon with the devotion of the native soldier for his British officer. They tried to prevent me from taking the post of danger and pulled me back. We had a ridiculous struggle for precedence, which was liable to be turned into a tragedy by the rogue's appearance at any moment. With difficulty I had my own way; though I certainly felt no desire to go first into what I knew was a mad undertaking. But it was only when I tried to force my way into the thicket that I fully realised our folly. The tangled vegetation was composed of thickly interlaced thorny bushes; I can only compare it to strong fishing-nets studded freely with hooks. Torn and bleeding from a dozen scratches I tried to worm my way in. Then to my horror I heard the rogue bursting through it at us. I was pinned down by the thorny branches, bound around by pliant creepers, unable to stand upright or even raise my rifle. I certainly thought that my last hour had come; for, securely pinioned by the cruel vegetation, I was helpless. The men behind me were in the same plight. But at that moment the *mahouts* saved us. Realising our extreme danger, they bravely urged their elephants into the thicket after us. The rogue at the sight of them stopped dead. Though he was not five yards from me, I could not distinguish him clearly, so dense was the undergrowth, but could only make out portions of his body through the tangle. He retreated a few paces, and we tried to scramble out. I could not turn; but shoving my legs out backwards, I tore myself free from the vicious thorns and retired face to the foe. My rifle was at full cock and I was afraid that the triggers might be caught by the twigs, but I dared not lower the hammers. Foot by foot I forced my way back slowly and painfully. When I reached the edge of the thicket, my men, who had extricated themselves, seized me and dragged me out. We looked at each other. I don't know what colour I was; but my men were as nearly pale as it is possible for a native to be. Even my brave old *subhedar's* courage was shaken. He had lost all desire to enter the thicket again, for the danger had been really great. Had the rogue not stopped of his own accord nothing could have saved me, and probably the others, from a most unpleasant death. Of course I ought never to have attempted to enter the undergrowth, as I had fully realised the foolhardiness of it; but I could not allow my sepoys to believe that I was afraid. However, everybody now had quite enough of the attack on foot and gladly mounted the elephants. We did so one by one, the others standing with rifles ready to repel an assault. We circled round the thicket cautiously, hoping to find an easier line of approach. Suddenly our vicious antagonist came charging through the dense undergrowth straight at Khartoum. I halted her ten yards from the edge of the covert. I could vaguely make out the rogue's vast bulk bursting through the tangle, and raised my rifle. Half his body was clear of the jungle, the head thrown up, the trunk curled and the single tusk pointed menacingly at me, when I fired straight at his forehead. The force of the blow drove him back on his haunches into the undergrowth; while the native officer and the two orderlies poured a volley into his side, one of the men getting in a second shot. I could not see him clearly enough to give him the other barrel, and I expected to hear him collapse at last. But, inconceivable as it seems, he recovered himself, swung about and bolted out of the other side of the thicket. I could hardly believe it; but we heard him plainly enough as he dashed off through the jungle. I began to think that it really was useless to waste lead on him; but we followed. He was lost to sight; but the trail was plain. I looked at my watch; it was two o'clock in the afternoon. From that hour until night fell we kept up the pursuit. Obliged to desist owing to the darkness, I determined to bivouac in the forest. We were now too far from the camp to return to it. So we made our way along a river-bed until, near the foot of the hills, we found water in it. Then dismounting we let our elephants drink and prepared for the night. As the tracks of wild animals abounded in the sand near the edge of the water, for the stream disappeared into the ground here and it was the last drinking-place for miles, I ordered fires to be lit around us; for, in the dark, wild elephants attracted by Dundora and Khartoum might rush over us, or a hungry tiger might be unable to resist the temptation of an easy meal provided by sleeping men. My companions ate the *chupatties* or flour cakes they carried with them; while I dined on my bread and preserved meat. Then, telling off one of our number to keep watch in turn, we rolled ourselves in our blankets and lay down to sleep. A chill wind blew down from the mountains and the damp sand made a cold bed; but in a few minutes everyone but the sentry and I was asleep. I heard our elephants chained on the bank tearing the branches from the trees near them. A sudden spurt of flame from the fires lit up their huge bodies, which were vague and shadowy in the flickering light. I looked at the stars overhead and the faint outline of the mountains towering over us, until at last fatigue overpowered me and I slept.

At daybreak next morning we turned out. On going to wash in the stream we found the "pugs"* of a panther in the sand about fifty yards from our bivouac, while a couple of hundred yards farther away the huge footprints of elephants were plainly visible; so our fires had probably saved us from some unwelcome visitors. I had to make a frugal breakfast on the heel of the loaf and the last fragments of tinned meat, washed down by a drink from the stream. The blankets were rolled up and strapped on the elephants' backs; and we started to pick up the trail. We found it without difficulty and followed it all day. It led us towards the south away from the hills. But we could not come up with the rogue. Night found us in the vicinity of a tea garden, the manager of which I had met once; so I determined to claim his hospitality. When we reached his bungalow I learned that he had ridden over to a neighbouring estate, but was expected back to dinner. His native overseers took charge of my party and found them food and shelter. After a long wait in the bungalow I yielded to the persuasions of the owner's servant and ate the excellent dinner he provided for me; then I lay down in the guest-room and fell asleep. At midnight I was awakened by the return of my unwitting host, who, however, made me thoroughly welcome when he discovered me. And next morning before I started off on the pursuit again he loaded me with supplies.

* Footprints.

To record the incidents of what proved a long, weary and fruitless chase would fill a volume. For nine days more we followed the trail, never far behind the rogue but never catching sight of him. He led us first into the dense and tropical vegetation of the jungles around Rajabhatkawa, where we forced our way through luxuriant tree-ferns, their undersides studded thick with long curved thorns. On the second day we were passing through tall elephant grass with waving plumes that nodded high over our heads. We followed a path made by the passage of wild animals. The two orderlies were on foot in front, picking up the trail, when we heard, fifty yards ahead, the rogue crashing suddenly through the jungle. The startled men turned and ran towards our elephants which, alarmed at the sight of their terror, turned sharp and stampeded. Having been leading, I now found myself looking down the muzzle of Sohanpal Singh's rifle as he swung round ready to fire over Dundora's tail if the rogue chased us. Luckily in the tall grass there was no danger of our being swept off the pads; and the *mahouts* soon stopped their animals and brought them back. But when we got clear of the cover we found that it lined the bank of a broad, empty river-bed across which our prey had escaped while our elephants had been retreating. In the sand we found his unmistakable track with the useless foreleg dragging helplessly over the ground. Had our animals not bolted at the critical moment we would have reached the river-bank in time to have a clear shot at him as he crossed in the open. For the remainder of the chase we never got so close to him again.

Wherever night found us we bivouacked; unless

a lucky chance brought us near a tea garden, where I sought the planters' unfailing hospitality. Men whose names I did not know welcomed me with the cordiality of old friends and made me and my train comfortable for the night. I found that I was known to most by reputation as the lunatic who had walked up to a notorious rogue elephant with only a camera in his hand. All gladly aided me in my venture; for I learned that the brute I was pursuing was infamous throughout the district. Everyone had a tale to tell of him, and never to his credit. On one garden he had entered the coolies' village and, finding a native baby in his path, had picked it up in his trunk and hurled it on to the roof of a hut. Alarmed by its cries the parents had rushed out only to be met and trampled to death by the murderous brute. On another garden the manager and a friend were strolling in the dusk along a road within two hundred yards of the bungalow. Smoking and chatting, they were all unconscious of the fact that this rogue was stalking silently towards them intent on murder. Suddenly the planter's terrier saw it and rushed barking at it. Frightened as all elephants are of dogs, the animal turned off the road and plunged in among the tea bushes; and it was only then that his intended victims perceived him. My bullets were by no means the first that he had received. He had been shot at and wounded over and over again. One planter advised me, if I eventually succeeded in killing him, to exploit his body as a lead mine.

Hope springs eternal in the sportsman's breast; and day after day I set out at dawn cheered by the expectation that surely this day must bring the chase to a successful conclusion. As we started at five or six o'clock each morning and kept on the move until 6 p.m., we must have covered altogether well over two hundred miles in the pursuit, as we averaged a mile and a half in the hour. The rogue seemed to know that we were on his track and changed his direction frequently. Strange were the sights I saw and varied the wild jungles we traversed. Sometimes for hours we pushed our way through brakes of tough cane. Sometimes we passed for miles under huge trees in grassy land. Once in the forest Khartoum stopped short so suddenly that I was nearly thrown off her pad. As she backed away the *mahout* pointed to a great snake twelve or thirteen feet long wriggling away from almost under her forelegs. The glimpses I got of it showed it to be the terrible king-cobra.

For the first four days of the chase we had found no droppings left by the fleeing elephant. Then we came on some, small, hard and black with coagulated blood. And only on the sixth day did we discover traces of where he had begun to eat again. And one morning we passed a patch of cultivation in the jungle and a peasant who told us that at daybreak he had found a lame single-tusker elephant feeding on his crops. When the sun rose it moved on again without discovering the man.

At last on the twelfth day since our first encounter I was obliged to give up the chase. We found his trail leading across the wide and rapid river, the Torsa, which pours down its flood from the mountains of Bhutan. My men and animals were worn out by the unceasing pursuit. Although the former suffered less than I did from the want of food, for every village supplied their wants and I had to depend on the kind charity of the planters, yet the irregular meals and the strain told on them. They were not spurred on by the same eagerness to kill the rogue as I. But greatly disappointed as I was at being unable to compass his death, yet I thought that at least we had rid our jungles of his dangerous presence; so, sadly and reluctantly, I yielded to my followers' entreaties and turned our elephants' heads towards home.

We really had deserved better fortune. We had done our best to kill the rogue, and nothing but the most astonishing fortune had saved him. One bullet out of the many half an inch to one side or the other would have given us the victory. And we had shot calmly and steadily. I was sure that not one of our bullets had missed him, which of course was not astonishing, as they had all been fired at the closest range. Yet I have seen a man miss a fourteen-hand *sambhur* at ten yards. But with this elephant I knew that every shot had struck. I have never heard of so long and continuous a pursuit of one animal as ours had been. But the fact remained that with ten solid bullets from my heavy rifle, and seven from the Lee-Enfields, the brute still lived to mock us, and to do worse. For three weeks from the day when we ended the chase on the banks of the Torsa the rogue was back again in our jungles and attacked the tame elephants of an Indian Civil Servant near Buxa Road Station. Needless to say, I was off again after him the moment I heard of this fresh outrage. But all in vain. And a few months afterwards while I was lying dangerously ill in Buxa the brute surprised a Bhuttia and his wife in the jungle three miles from Santrabari and trampled the woman to death; and, for aught I know, still carrying our bullets he yet lives to terrorise the forest. May we meet again! And yet, when I think how narrowly I escaped an agonising death under his terrible feet, I should perhaps be thankful that the chances of our meeting are small; for hundreds of miles of India now divide us.

It is fortunate that in sudden danger one has not time to think; for if, in the nerve-trying moment when a man stands facing the onrush of a charging elephant, a vivid imagination painted to his eyes the awful fate in store for him should the bullet fail to strike home, the rifle would drop from his shaking fingers. But though in anticipation the heart beats quickly and the breath comes fast, yet when the instant of danger comes the nerves turn to steel and the hand never falters. A tiger is not always a formidable foe; and one generally meets him on advantageous terms. But the wild elephant's charge must be met on ground of his own choosing; and the odds are perhaps in his favour. Yet the man who has once stopped him in his headlong rush will long to do battle with his kind again; and the recollections of the peril escaped acts only as a spur.

CHAPTER VIII

IN TIGER LAND

The tiger in India—His reputation—Wounded tigers—Man-eaters—Game killers and cattle thieves—A tiger's residence—Chance meetings—Methods of tiger hunting—Beating with elephants—Sitting up—A sportsman's patience—The charm of a night watch—A cautious beast—A night over a kill—An unexpected visitor—A tantalising tiger—A tiger at Asirgarh—A chance shot—Buffaloes as trackers—Panthers—The wrong prey—A beat for tiger—The Colonel wounds a tiger—A night march—An elusive quarry—A successful beat A watery grave—Skinning a tiger.

WOULD any book on India be complete without a tiger in it? Although he is found in many other Asiatic countries—in China they shoot him in caves, in Corea there is a whole militia raised to deal with him—yet in the popular mind the tiger is particularly associated with Hindustan. No distinguished visitor would consider himself properly entertained if one were not provided for him to shoot. The young subaltern in England pines for the day to come when he will be ordered to India and have his chance to face the striped beast in his native jungle.

The usual conception of the tiger is an animal of infinite cunning, cruelty and ferocity. Cunning he certainly is; but his reputation for ferocity and courage is hardly deserved. He is really rather a harmless and timid creature, of a decidedly shy and retiring disposition, avoiding, rather than courting, notoriety. Sanderson, one of the greatest authorities on sport in India, argues that the tiger is actually a public benefactor, inasmuch as he kills off old and sick cattle which, since the pious Hindu would not put them to death, would otherwise linger on spreading disease among the herds. Natives, near whose village a tiger takes up his residence, betray no fear of him and go about their daily avocations in his vicinity as indifferently as if he did not exist. I have seen women drawing water from a stream not a hundred yards from the spot where half an hour later I drove a tiger from his lair. For, except in rare cases, these animals prefer to give man a wide berth, and, when stumbled upon accidentally, will usually effect a rapid retreat if they can. Of course a wounded tiger followed up is an exceedingly dangerous foe. Furious with pain, exhausted and in agony, he will turn savagely on his pursuers; and then a quick eye and steady rifle are needed to check him in his fierce charge. Even shot through the heart he may retain sufficient vitality to reach and maul his aggressor, then perhaps fall dead on his mangled victim without killing him outright. But few men wounded by a tiger ever recover; for the shock and the blood-poisoning set up by the unclean claws of the carrion feeder are almost invariably fatal.

The man-eater is, fortunately, rare; for, having once learned how easy a prey human beings prove, he is apt to devote himself too exclusively to them; and the total of his victims soon mounts up into the hundreds. The man-eater is made, not born. Sometimes it is an old beast no longer agile enough to surprise the animals of the forest or even bring down a stray cow, but still supple enough to spring upon some unwary wood-cutter or villager. Natives believe that human flesh disagrees with a tiger's digestion, and point in proof to the mangy state of most man-eaters' hides. But the reason of this is that the animal is generally old or sick. Sometimes, however, the tiger who takes to the slaughter of human beings is a young and vigorous beast. He has probably some time or other been disturbed over a kill or foiled in an attempt to carry off cattle by some rashly courageous individual, and in anger or the desperation of hunger has slain the intruder. Finding that after all man is not a formidable enemy and quite palatable, he continues to prey on him and in time almost devastates a whole district. He becomes a public character and attracts more attention than he likes. Government gazettes honour him with a notice proclaiming him. A price is set on his head. White men come from all sides to hunt him down; and the unfortunate animal knows no peace until a lucky bullet lays him low. Scared natives regard him as an evil spirit and set up altars to him. And yet it is extraordinary how indifferent the inhabitants of a district ravaged by a man-eater become to his presence. I have seen a postman jog-trotting along night after night on a road on which two men had been killed and eaten by a tiger the week before. The man's ridiculous little spear and bells would have been no protection against the Striped Death springing on him out of the darkness; but he had his living to make. His orders were to carry the mail-bag along that stretch of road every night; so with true Oriental fatalism he jogged on, seemingly indifferent to the chances of an unlucky meeting.

The man-eater being an exception, tigers may be

classified as game slayers and cattle killers. Those haunting a jungle where *sambhur*, *cheetul*, pig and small antelopes abound take their toll of them. A monkey is quite a delicate morsel, if they can catch an unwary *bunder* on the ground or fetch him from a low bough by an unexpected spring. Those that take up their residence in cultivated country usually prey on the cattle grazing in the scrub jungle near the villages. A tiger generally rules over a stretch of ground about five miles square and keeps strictly within his own domain. Any intruder of his own sex is speedily ejected. But it is a curious fact that when a tiger is shot, another quickly appears and takes up his abode in the defunct animal's dominions. A certain patch of jungle, a particular *nullah*, may be the residence of a tiger which is known to be the only one for miles round. But if he is killed his habitat is almost certain of another striped tenant very soon.

The game slayer is not often seen, living as he does in the heart of the jungle and prowling mostly by night. The cattle lifter levies contributions from the villages in his district in turn, usually killing a cow every two or three days. He takes up his residence for the time being near the carcass in some shady spot close to water. He eats about sixty or eighty pounds of beef at his first meal, goes to drink and lies up during the day to digest his heavy meal, returning at night to feed again. If any villager happens to blunder in on his privacy during his siesta, he gives a low, warning growl which usually suffices to scare the intruder off. The natives pay little heed to him and go about their usual pursuits without heeding his proximity.

On my first introduction to the jungle—it was in the Central Provinces years ago—I had a wholesome respect for tigers. When I learned that one lived in the particular part of the forest where I went shooting, I used to feel anything but comfortable as I wandered about in seach of *sambhur*. I marvelled at the unconcerned way in which even women and children traversed this jungle from village to village. One day I climbed down into a deep, narrow ravine in the hope of finding a stag sheltering in it from the unpleasantly hot sun. Suddenly from a clump of bushes above my head came a deep "Wough! wough!" like the bark of a great dog; and a tiger crashed out of it and bounded up and over the edge of the *nullah*. I swung my rifle round; but he was out of sight before the butt touched my shoulder. My *shikaree* (native hunter) cried "Bagh! Bagh! (A tiger! a tiger!") and rushed up past me after the vanished animal. Rather unwillingly I clambered up too; and I was decidedly relieved when, on emerging from the ravine, I found that the ground was covered with grass six feet high, so that pursuit of the tiger was hopeless. However, on calmly considering the matter afterwards, I came to the conclusion that the beast was even more afraid of me than I of him. So I devoted much time and attention to trying to meet him again. Many a night did I sit up for him over a cow tied up as a bait. Time after time I followed his footprints by day and tried to walk him up near the carcass of some deer he had killed and half-eaten. But never again did I see him.

A few months ago in the Kanera Forests I was wandering about one afternoon, shot-gun in hand, in search of jungle fowl for the pot, about half a mile from the Government *dâk* bungalow—or rest-house—in which I was staying. I was making my way along a narrow path. Just as I reached a spot where it came out on a small clearing in the forest, I heard some heavy animal forcing its way through the undergrowth about forty yards to my left. I stepped out into the open and looked in the direction from whence came the sound, which stopped as soon as I appeared. I stood still for a couple of minutes. Suddenly a tiger, which had evidently been watching me, gave a deep roar and crashed off through the thick jungle. It was useless to try to follow him up even if I had had a rifle instead of a shot-gun. The setting sun warned me that I must hurry home; so I continued on my way. Two hundred yards further on the path led down into a narrow *nullah* with steep banks. Here I found the fresh prints of the tiger's paws in the mud, the water just oozing into them. Had I come along a few minutes earlier we would have met face to face in the narrow way; and the chances were that, in his hurry to escape, he would have charged me and knocked me down. And a blow from a tiger's paw is not a caress to be courted. But the two incidents will show that these animals are generally anxious to avoid men.

Native *shikarees* frequently sit up over water for tigers; but European sportsmen usually adopt one of the three following methods. The first and most effective is to shoot them from elephants; but this does not often fall to the lot of the average man. I was fortunate in having the opportunity in Buxa. The second method is to mark down where the animal is lying up after a kill and have him driven by a line of beaters to the spot where the sportsman is concealed.

In the Central Provinces I went out one day with a friend who had arranged such a beat for a tiger which had killed a cow tied up as a bait for him near a village. After a ten miles' drive we reached this village; and, having had an early start, we breakfasted under a tree on a hillock just above a long *nullah* which seamed the bare, brown fields with a winding line of green. Below us the hundred and sixty coolies collected as beaters squatted and smoked until the Sahibs were ready. Just as we had finished our meal, a cow burst out of the jungle in the *nullah* and dashed in among the groups of men. They caught her and became very excited over her. We could see them crowding round her, talking volubly. Then the cow was led up to us; and we found that she was bleeding from a wound in the throat. All down her flanks and rump ran long scratches as if from the claws of a monster cat. This told us plainly that the tiger we were in quest of was still in the *nullah* and that the cow had stumbled on him unawares. The tiger had evidently tried to seize it but, gorged with his night's meal, missed the fatal neck-breaking spring and, as the cow fled, struck out and clawed it behind.

The coolies cried "Wah! wah! the *shaitan's* (devil's) last day has dawned. See how the cow has come straight to the Sahib's feet to show her wounds and claim justice!" I am afraid the animal's bovine intelligence was not equal to this, but, in terror, she was only making for her village and safety.

We waited under our tree until the day was at its hottest, so that the tiger, when driven, would be all the more reluctant to face the burning sun in the open and would retreat along the *nullah* in the shade; for where the ravine forked off in two branches *machâns*, strong wooden platforms, had been built for us up in the trees, one commanding each branch. We took a short cut across the open in the terrific heat. The pitiless sun beat down on us as we walked over the shadeless fields, and seemed to boil the brains in our skulls. It was a relief to reach the *nullah* and the cool shelter of the trees in it. We climbed up into our respective *machâns*, which were about a mile away from where the beaters were to begin the drive. I could see my friend perched up in his tree across the bank dividing his branch of the *nullah* from mine. This bank was covered with undergrowth from which sprang a line of trees. In these a number of *làngurs*—the big grey apes with black faces surrounded by a fringe of white whisker, which gives them a comic resemblance to aged negroes, a resemblance increased by their white eyebrows—were playing. They came to look at us, leaping from bough to bough, stooping and craning their necks to see us as we sat hidden by the leafy screens around our *machâns*. Then, their curiosity satisfied, they continued their play and swung through the branches away in the direction of the beaters. For a couple of hours I sat drowsing in the intense heat. The silence was profound. Suddenly loud cries, the drumming of tom-toms, and the tapping of sticks against tree-trunks, told me that the drive had begun. I looked to my rifle and sat ready. The noise drew nearer; every nerve in my body was aquiver. Then in the tree-tops pandemonium broke loose. The *langurs* were coming back towards us, leaping from branch to branch, shrieking, chattering with rage at something moving along beneath them. It was evidently the tiger, their foe as well as ours, which was trying to steal away silently before the beaters. The apes seemed to know his design and to be endeavouring to foil him. I really believe that they realised that our presence boded no good to him; for several looked at me as much as to say:

"Here he is. He is trying to escape. We won't let him creep off unnoticed."

I had read of this extraordinary behaviour on the part of monkeys during a beat in Captain Forsyth's interesting book, "The Highlands of Central India"; but I could scarcely credit it. But now I saw these *langurs* following the tiger's progress and shrieking abuse down at him. He seemed to be coming straight for me; and my heart rejoiced. But suddenly from the change of direction of the apes I saw that he had turned, crossed the dividing bank, and was going down the other *nullah*. Then I heard a deep short growl; and at the same moment my friend's rifle went up to his shoulder and he fired. Mad with excitement and furious at being unable to see what was happening, I did a very foolish thing. I slipped down from my tree and dashed through the undergrowth to the brink of the *nullah*. I saw the tiger rush across the narrow ravine and spring up the opposite bank, which was higher than the one on which I stood. Near the top his strength seemed to fail him. He clung on desperately, unable to pull himself up. My friend fired again; and the brute, struck in the foreleg, dropped back into the *nullah*. He rolled over and over in agony, biting at his paws and tearing them with his teeth. I fired at his shoulder. Even then he rolled about for a few minutes; and then his head fell back, his frame stiffened and he lay still.

The shot drew my friend's attention to me; for he had not noticed me on the ground. He shouted angrily:

"Go back, you fool. Get up your tree. There is a second tiger in the beat."

I well deserved his uncomplimentary epithet; for, had the first animal sprung up the low bank on which I stood we would have met face to face. I hurriedly scrambled up again and sat with my rifle ready, until I saw first one man, then another and another, appear in the *nullah*; and finally the whole line of beaters reached us. There had been a tigress in the drive as well; but she had broken out to one side. She passed a tree in which a man had been placed as a "stop"; but, although he flung his *puggri* in her face, she was not to be turned, and escaped out over the fields. I climbed down again and cautiously approached the tiger, keeping my rifle ready lest there might be some life in him still. I have known a sportsman to walk up to an apparently dead tiger and pull its tail, to be laid low the next moment by a blow from the animal's paw. Some of our coolies threw stones at the body; and as these elicited no response I walked up to the beast and found it dead. As the natives try to steal the whiskers, which they believe to have a certain magical power, I mounted guard until a litter had been made from cut branches to convey the tiger to the village for skinning. Arrived there the local flayers were set to work. The dead brute looked the embodiment of strength; and

I marvelled at the masses of muscle the knives disclosed in the thick limbs. The first bullet had struck behind the shoulder; and when the carcass was cut open we found a hole the size of a florin right through the heart. Yet even with this wound the animal had been able to dash across the *nullah* and spring up the bank. It showed that a tiger shot through the heart could reach and kill a man before falling dead itself. The other wounds were in the foreleg and ribs. The natives did not leave a scrap of flesh on the bones. For it and certain parts of the tiger are supposed to endow anyone who eats them with courage and vigour; and crowds of women came to carry off their husbands' share of the meat. The fat —such layers of it, white and firm, on the well-fed cattle thief—is boiled down for oil, which is considered a sovereign remedy for rheumatism. The skin was pegged out, hair downwards, on the ground and scraped clean, then covered with wood ashes. And the last stage of the proceedings consisted in the beaters being assembled and paid their wages—fourpence a man. Had the drive been unsuccessful, they would have only received twopence each. It seems little reward for disturbing a sleeping tiger; but the coolies were quite satisfied.

The cause of the *langurs'* rage was evident when a beater brought us the half-eaten body of one of their number which he had found near the spot where the tiger had been sleeping. My friend told me that he was able to mark the brute's progress through the undergrowth by the movements of the apes above him. The tiger had come out from the cover into the clear bed of the *nullah* with his head turned over his shoulder glaring up at them in anger. And the deep growl I had heard was uttered against these betrayers of his flight.

This is a fair example of the second method of tiger shooting. But neither it nor the first are possible in very dense forest; and then "sitting up" must be tried. This consists of tying up a cow near a *nullah* or patch of jungle in which the tiger is suspected or known to be. If he kills and eats part of it, a *machân* is built in a tree close to the carcass and concealed by a tree of leafy branches. On this the sportsman takes up his position in the afternoon and tries to shoot the tiger when he returns to feed on the kill at dusk or later on moonlight nights. Sometimes he is obliged to wait till dawn. This is the method which least often proves effective. It is particularly tantalising and demands the patience of a Job. From about 4 p.m. to 6 a.m. the hunter must sit still in a cramped position. He scarcely dares to move his limbs, must make no noise, cannot smoke; if he has brought food with him he must consume it quietly. The dead cow, specially in the hot weather, offends his nostrils with a terrible stench. And thus, sickened by the awful odour, tormented by mosquitoes, he must sit through the night, every sense on the alert. He dare not drowse, for he cannot tell at what moment the quarry may appear. And the tiger is a cautious beast. If he does return to the kill, he will generally prowl around for some time before approaching it; and if he scents the waiting man in the tree above or anything arouses his suspicions, he will melt away without a sound into the darkness, leaving the hunter's vigil unrewarded.

Yet sitting up is not without its charm. While daylight lasts it is interesting to watch the carrion feeders hastening to snatch a mouthful of the feast Chance has provided for them, always on the alert lest the rightful owner of the banquet should suddenly appear. High overhead a dim speck is seen against the sky. It grows larger and clearer, sinks down and, wheeling in great circles, reveals itself as a vulture. Another and another follow and, gradually descending, perch on the trees around. An impudent grey-headed crow pushes in before them and alights close to the dead cow. Then hopping on to the carcass it cocks its head impertinently at the less courageous vultures and begins to dig its beak into the putrid flesh. The big birds flop heavily to the ground and with much rustling of wings, shoving, hustling, angry squawks and vicious pecks at each other, begin their meal. But up fly the birds as a couple of jackals make their appearance and slink furtively to the kill. While they feed they look around apprehensively and start at every sound. The vultures flap over towards the dead cow again and demand their share of the good things that Chance has provided. The jackals snarl and snap at them, driving them off with short rushes. But suddenly they bolt themselves, as a dozen fox-like little beasts with reddish skins, sharp ears and handsome brushes trot up to the kill. These are the dreaded wild dogs which decimate the game in the jungle. They hungrily tear at the flesh, quarrelling and snapping at each other, ready to fly if the tiger appears. If the carcass is near water a white-and-black, long-legged bird is certain to be hovering about, crying plaintively and incessantly: "Did he do it? Did he—did he—did he do it?" until the exasperated watcher in the tree longs to shoot him. Then the sun sets, the noises of the day sink into silence; but the jungle wakes.

In the forest below Buxa lived a very large tiger which vexed my soul exceedingly. Generations of commanding officers had pursued him in vain; and the task was handed down as a legacy from each to his successor for years. Fired at once, and possibly wounded, over a live cow tied up as bait, he was never to be tempted to approach another. Inspired to compass his death by the impressions of his huge paws, which I often found in the sand of river-beds, I had three cows tied up for weeks in different *nullahs*. In the daytime a man whom I employed for the purpose took them to graze and water and fastened them up again before dark. At first I used to sit up in a tree over one or other of them night after night without result. Then I resolved to wait until he had killed one. It was equally fruitless. For, although his "pugs" or footprints, were often to be traced coming up the *nullah* and diverging towards the cow tied up in it, they always showed that he had turned abruptly and made off as soon as he discovered the nature of the bait.

At last one day news was brought to me that he had killed a *sambhur* hind in the forest. As it was just at full moon, I gave orders that a *machân* should be built in a tree near the carcass. Leaving the fort early in the afternoon I descended into the jungle and reached the spot about 6 p.m. when there was still some daylight. I found that the *sambhur* had been killed in a *nullah* a hundred yards off while drinking, and had been dragged by the tiger over the top of an almost perpendicular bank, up which I found it necessary to pull myself by my hands, and then over a small and steep hill. As a full-grown hind stands thirteen hands high and weighs five hundred pounds or more, this gives one some idea of a tiger's strength. The jungle here consisted of high trees with little undergrowth. As it was now the hot season when most of the leaves are shed, I noticed with satisfaction that the ground around below my *machân* would be well lighted when the moon rose. My orderly and two sturdy-limbed Bhuttia coolies were up in a tree over the kill, tying an inverted *charpoy*. or native bed (which makes the best and most comfortable *machân*) in a fork, and hanging leafy branches around it to screen it from sight. I climbed up and tried to enter it. It was awkwardly placed and overhung me. I succeeded in getting my chest on the edge, when the rotten framework broke and nearly precipitated me to the earth, thirty feet below. I managed to save myself and sat astride a branch while one of the coolies cut a few bamboos from a clump close by and repaired the damage. Then I got into the *machân*, laid a packet of sandwiches and my Thermos flask beside me, loaded my rifle and, sending my orderly and the Bhuttias away, settled myself for my lonely vigil. I amused myself at first by watching the birds preparing for the night. A troop of monkeys came to drink in the neighbouring *nullah* and passed overhead, leaping through the branches, hurling themselves from tree to tree, chasing each other in play or pausing now and then for a comfortable scratch. Mothers with tiny babies clinging closely to them sprang across the voids and swung themselves by hand or foot. A peacock sailed down majestically from the tree-tops to the water and gave its weird cat-like cry. The heavy flapping of wings and an eerie wail told of a big owl bestirring itself early. The harsh "honk" of a *sambhur* stag rang out; and the sharp bark of a *khakur* sounded at regular intervals. The sun sank lower and the twittering of the birds faded into silence. The drone of the multitudinous insect-life, unceasing in the day, yet only heard plainly at the hour when the louder sounds of larger life are hushed, seemed to rise now with startling distinctness. But even it died; and only the irritating hum of the mosquitoes around my head was left to break the complete silence. The air was still; and the sudden fall of a withered leaf seemed to echo clearly through the hushed forest. There was yet daylight in the sky; but a dusky gloom deepened under the trees. I lay down on the *charpoy*, peering through my leafy screen at the dead hind. My rifle was uncocked beside me, for I judged the hour too early for the tiger's visit; and I stretched myself at full length to rest before it would be necessary to sit upright with every sense alert for my long watch. Suddenly I was roused by the sound of loud footfalls to my rear passing over the dry leaves which crackled like tin to the tread. They came without hesitation towards my tree; and I thought angrily that it could only be one of my coolies returning to me contrary to orders. Without moving my body I turned my head around at the risk of dislocating my neck, intending to bid him in a loud whisper to go away. To my astonishment, instead of a man, I made out in the gloom of the underwood a huge bulk that I first took to be a baby elephant. Thirty yards away from my tree it stopped; and I saw that it was a large Himalayan bear, which looked immense to me after the smaller species of the Central

Provinces. Fearful of scaring it I lay still in my constrained position. It stood motionless and seemed to be staring up at my *machân*. I hurriedly debated the question whether I ought to take a shot at it and give up all hope of the tiger, whom the sound would alarm, or let it go and wait for the greater prize. I decided on the latter course and simply watched it. Suddenly it turned and walked away as noisily as it had come. This surprised me; for I had imagined that wild animals tried to move silently through the forest. But the bear is indifferent to the other jungle dwellers; he does not fear the ferocious beasts nor attack the harmless ones.

As soon as it had gone I glanced at my watch which showed 6-40 p.m. I sat up, cocked my rifle, and held it across my knees. The daylight died away in the swift oncoming of the tropic night; but the full moon shone overhead and cast the tangled pattern of leaves and branches on the ground. For hours I sat, scarcely daring to change my position or move my cramped limbs. Suddenly from the direction of the *nullah* where the deer had been killed came the tramping of some heavy animal over the dry leaves towards me. The tiger at last! One touch of the hand to assure myself that my rifle was cocked and I sat motionless, though the beating of my heart sounded loud in my ears. Few sportsmen, after long hours of waiting, can hear the approach of their quarry without a quickened pulse. The brute walked straight towards the kill. In another second it must emerge into the full glare of the moonlight. Stealthily I raised my rifle to my shoulder. Alas! just as one step more would have brought it out from under the black shadows of the trees, the tiger stopped. For minutes that seemed hours it remained motionless. Then it moved back so silently that only the sharp crackle of a dry twig farther away told me that the animal had gone. What had aroused its suspicions I cannot tell. Perhaps it had scented me up in the tree or detected the recent presence of humans around its kill. Cursing its cunning, I uncocked my rifle and stretched my cramped limbs. It was then half-past eleven. I was strongly tempted to lie down and sleep; but I knew that the tiger *might* return. So I continued my watch. It is in the small hours that the vigil becomes hardest. About half-past three in the morning I was nodding drowsily, when again from the *nullah* I heard the sound of the animal approaching. His tread seemed even more assured than before; and I made certain of getting him. But once more, just within the shadow, he paused. I strained my ears but could detect no sound. Another few minutes of anxious waiting; and then gradually, almost imperceptibly, he withdrew. This was the climax. I showered maledictions on his head. I had to wait until after six o'clock before one of my elephants came to take me on a long day's shoot in the jungle. Before quitting the spot I searched the ground and found the tiger's two trails leading up from the *nullah*.

The sportsman who tries his luck in "sitting up" must be prepared for many disappointments. He may watch night after night and never once see his quarry. He may select an evening when the moon is full, only to find clouds come up and obscure its light; and then, in the unforeseen darkness, he may be tantalised by hearing the tiger come to feed on the kill, may listen for an hour to the tearing of flesh and the crunching of bones and be utterly unable to get a shot. The adjutant of my regiment, Captain Hore, once paid us a visit at Buxa and went shooting in our jungles. On his first day he came across the carcass of a *sambhur* killed the previous day by a tiger. So he had a canvas chair tied up in a tree over it and climbed up to wait in it for the slayer to return. Before daylight faded he saw some wild pigs come and feed on the kill. But just as the moon rose they fled hurriedly; and he heard some large animal moving in the jungle close by. It prowled cautiously around in cover near the carcass for over two hours, but would not show itself. Meantime heavy clouds drew across the sky, blotting out the moon and shrouding the forest in impenetrable darkness. Suddenly Hore heard the prowling tiger leave the cover at last. It sprang out on the carcass as though the *sambhur* were alive and tore and rent it furiously. The sound of bones cracked to an accompaniment of snarls and growls came clearly to the watcher above; but the darkness was opaque. At last, in desperation, he fired in the direction of the noise but missed; and the tiger bolted. And the next moment, as though the shot had been the signal for the storm, a vivid flash of lightning rent the clouds, a terrific peal of thunder sounded overhead, the sky seemed to open and pour down sheets of rain. Hore's position was unenviable. The so-called waterproof he had with him was wet through in a few minutes. He could not put his rifle away from him, yet feared lest it should attract the lightning. It was hopeless to descend and try to find his way through the forest in the darkness. And so through the weary night, exposed to all the fury of a tropical storm, he was obliged to sit shivering in his chair, forty feet above the ground. And to add to his annoyance the tiger, evidently confusing the flash and report of the shot with the lightning and thunder, returned and fed on the kill again, while Hore on his uncomfortable perch listened, powerless. And when at six o'clock in the morning one of my elephants came to fetch him, it was a very sodden, chilled, and miserable individual that climbed from the tree on to its pad. But not disheartened he ordered the *mahout*, instead of returning to Buxa, to take him for a wide sweep through the jungle in the hope of shooting something to console him for the night's disappointment. The storm had ceased. Within a mile he came upon a herd of six bison with a splendid old bull among them. But the rules of the forest department prohibit their being shot in Government jungle; and so the again baffled sportsman was forced to let them go unscathed, while they stared at him and his elephant for several minutes before they moved away.

Once during the rainy season at Asirgarh I was sitting up over the carcass of a white cow in what should have been brilliant moonlight. But heavy clouds gathered; and soon all I could see of the kill was a faint whitish glimmer. Suddenly this was blotted out, and I heard a crunching of bones and tearing of flesh. I could not see my sights, but I fired in the direction of the sounds. A terrific howl followed by fiendish shrieks and groans told me that I had hit a tiger. I heard him rush off thirty or forty yards and throw himself on the ground, where he rolled in agony, tearing up the earth and sending the stones rattling down into a small *nullah* beside which he lay. I hoped that I was listening to his dying moans; but he got up again and the groaning and snarling died away in the distance. There was a village a mile off; so, giving the tiger time to get well away, I climbed down and made for it. It was a nerve-trying walk in the darkness; for I feared every moment to stumble on the wounded beast. However I reached shelter without encountering him. I gave my *shikaree* instructions to bid the cowherds of the village be ready with their buffaloes at day-break to track the tiger. For these great black beasts are frequently used in this work. Their instinct tells them that the tiger is the enemy of their race; and they regard him with savage hatred. In a herd they do not fear him; for the hungriest cattle thief will not dare to attack a number of them which form round the calves and present to him an impenetrable front of lowered heads and sharp horns. On their backs the small children of the village who drive them to and from the grazing ground are safe. When a sportsman employs them to track a wounded tiger, the herds take them to a point where they can scent his trail. As soon as they have smelt it, they paw up the earth and bellow with rage, then dash off in pursuit. If they come on him lying up wounded and sore under a tree, they will charge him if allowed to. And no tiger would dare to face their savage onslaught; for little avails his strength and cunning against the fierce rush of the infuriated beasts. If he is not too badly hurt, he will invariably fly before their attack. If not, then must the sportsman shoot quick and the herds exert all their authority to keep the buffaloes back; for, if left to themselves, they will rush in on the tiger, gore him and stamp him to death under their hoofs. And the skin will be of little use as a trophy when they are allowed to work their will on the battered carcass.

Having given my orders, I slept in the local police station on a *charpoy* lent me by the *havildar*, or sergeant, in charge. At daylight my *shikaree* woke me and I went out to find about twenty buffaloes collected. They were driven out to the kill. The sight of the dead cow enraged them. They bellowed and stamped, then snuffing up the trail set off at a run across the fields like a pack of hounds. They soon tracked the tiger into the jungle. They crashed through the undergrowth, now and then at fault, but questing round until they picked up the trail again. They followed it up for two or three miles and finally lost it in broken and precipitous ground among the low hills. My *shikaree* assured me that it was useless to search further, as the tiger could not have been badly wounded and was certain to have retreated to a great distance. To my regret I let myself be persuaded; for, a few days after, the sight of vultures gathering from all quarters led to the discovery of the tiger's body not half a mile from where we had left off. But the carcass was putrid and half-eaten, so the skin was useless.

But shooting on chance in the dark is not always productive of the desired result. Once when sitting up on a cloudy night for a panther, I discharged my rifle at some animal which I could hear, but could not see, at the kill. A pandemonium of shrieks and yells told me that by good luck my bullet had gone home. I waited for silence, and then, having reloaded, climbed down and cautiously approached. But to my disappointment, instead of the dead panther which I had hoped to find, there lay the corpse of a loathsome hyena. On another occasion when sitting up in the middle of a village for a daring leopard which used to enter it at night and kill the cattle in their pens, I shot a mangy pariah dog in the dark.

A panther is a much bolder animal than a tiger. He generally returns to his kill earlier, often in broad daylight. I have seen one come out, five minutes after my coolies had left, from some bushes in which he had evidently been watching them. Even when shot at and missed or slightly wounded they will return the same night to a kill. And sometimes one has been known to discover the waiting sportsman in the *machân* first and spring up the tree to attack him unprovoked. So that sitting up for these animals is not without its risks.

The method of shooting tiger from elephants undoubtedly gives the best sport. Seventeen miles from Buxa Fort the great forest ends abruptly. From its ragged edge, five miles above the town of Alipur Duar, the cultivated plains stretch away to the south, seamed with *nullahs* which run from inside the jungle through the open fields. They are generally deep and filled with low trees and scrub, and as they contain water form ideal bases of operation for a tiger issuing from the forest to carry on war against herds of cattle in the villages. The striped thief can lie up within a few hundred yards of a farm and kill the cows when they come to drink. If disturbed, he can retreat up the *nullah* to the shelter of the forest. Consequently the stretch of ground just outside the south border of the Terai Jungle is full of tigers.

During a visit from our Colonel to Buxa for his

annual inspection I received an invitation from Mr Ainslie, the Subdivisional Officer of Alipur Duar, to bring my elephants and join him in a beat for a cattle thief which was lying up in a *nullah* three or four miles from the town. At that time I had only Khartoum and Dundora; as Jhansi had run away to the forest after being attacked by a wild elephant and had been missing for months. However, on our arrival, we found Ainslie had collected seven; so that we had nine altogether. This number was not a great one; but we hoped that it would suffice. Mrs Ainslie was to accompany us; for she was a great sportswoman and had shot five tigers herself, as well as various panthers, bears and bison. We started out in the early morning, crossed the railway line, forded a river—which each elephant carefully sounded with its trunk—and reached the *nullah* in which the tiger was reported to be lurking. It was broad and dry, filled with scrub and low trees. Ainslie took the Colonel in his howdah; and Mrs Ainslie shared mine. Taking up our positions on the bank we sent the beater elephants half a mile further on to drive towards us. At a signal from Ainslie the beat began. The elephants formed line across the *nullah* and advanced, forcing their way through the jungle. An occasional squeal from one of them when the *mahout* struck it on the head for shirking a particularly thorny bit of scrub, the cries of the men and the crashing of the huge beasts through the jungle as they trampled down the undergrowth and broke off branches from the trees, made din enough to scare anything. It soon proved too much for the tiger's nerves. My *mahout* had carelessly allowed his elephant to draw back from the edge of the steep bank. I saw a sudden flash of yellow as the tiger darted through the scrub along under the overhanging brink in such a way that he was sheltered from my rifle. But I shouted a warning to the others, who were posted farther down where the bank sloped less steeply. The Colonel fired and wounded the beast, which dashed up the bank and received a bullet from Ainslie before it was lost to sight in the high grass on the level. The beater elephants emerged from the *nullah*, surrounded it, and drove it in again. They endeavoured to send it to us; but the tiger refused to face the guns a second time and broke through their line, my orderly, Draj Khan, hurling a heavy stick at it and hitting it as it flashed past his elephant. We tried for it again lower down, several times, but without success.

While we were thus engaged it seemed strange to see the mail train pass on the railway line not half a mile from us, driver, guard, and passengers leaning out to look at us. Leaving the *nullah* we ranged through the long grass on the level and put up a number of wild pigs, the Colonel shooting a fine old boar with long tusks as sharp as knives.

Having heard that a panther was supposed to be lying up in another *nullah* a couple of miles away, we took our elephants there and tried a beat for it. This time the howdah bearers advanced along the bank in line with the beaters, spaced across the *nullah*, which was fairly open, with patches of scrub here and there in it. We were unsuccessful in finding the panther but were afforded an excellent example of the terror with which elephants regard tiny, harmless animals. Over some bushes in front of me I caught a glimpse of a hare running through them down into the *nullah.* Its course brought it right across the line of beaters. Then these huge beasts, which had just faced a wounded tiger unmoved, went mad at the sight of it. All trumpeted shrilly, some planted their forefeet firmly and refused to advance, others turned and stampeded, despite the heavy blows showered on them with the iron *ankus* by the enraged *mahouts.* I saw Ainslie and the Colonel, unable to discover the cause of the disturbance, stand up in their howdah, clutching their rifles and looking everywhere for the charging panther, which they imagined must have scared the elephants.

One afternoon in Buxa I received a telegram from Ainslie telling me to be with him early next morning as a tiger had killed in his neighbourhood that day. As Alipur Duar was twenty-two miles away it behoved me to start at once and march through the night. So, filling my Thermos flask and putting a loaf of bread and a tin of preserved meat into my haversack, I shouldered my rifle and walked down the three miles of steep road to Santrabari. Here I found the *mahouts* and ordered them to get the two elephants ready, Jhansi still being a deserter. I bade them put the howdah on Dundora's back, as she was the steadier with a charging tiger. We started off at once; but before we reached the railway station at Buxa Road, darkness had fallen. My elephant stepped out briskly with the swaying stride that is particularly trying in a howdah, the occupant of which is shaken about like a pea on a drum. I kept slipping off the hard wooden seat; so I tried standing up, holding on to the front rail. This was almost worse; for if I forgot for a moment to brace myself up with stiffened arms I was thrown against the side. So for twenty-two miles I had to keep changing my position continually and found it tiring work. Through the forest we lumbered on without stopping. The night was dark. Fortunately, the road ran along beside the railway line clear of the trees, which would otherwise have swept the howdah off Dundora's back. Once or twice a wild elephant trumpeted in the jungle, much to the alarm of our tame ones; so I kept my rifle loaded, ready to drive off any we might meet. When I felt hungry I opened the tin of meat and, as we went along, made a frugal dinner, having to use my fingers as knife and fork, washing the food down with water from my flask. The long march was extremely fatiguing; but by daylight we were clear of the forest. Arrived at the *dâk* bungalow at Alipur Duar I found one of the officers of my regiment, Major Burrard, who had come there on leave from headquarters at Dibrugarh in Assam for a shoot. The Ainslies could not accompany us that day, but had kindly lent us their four elephants. The kill was reported to be in a *nullah* about four miles away, close to the edge of the forest. Burrard and I started for it at once. Our way lay over open bare fields. Our elephants, as is their habit, persisted in tailing off in single file, though a hundred could have marched abreast. Each kept exactly in the footprints of the one in front of it. As we went along, I noticed half a mile to our left a *nullah* fringed with trees. In these, or circling overhead, were a number of vultures. I remarked that every now and then one would swoop down to the ground, only to rise again into the air like a rocketting pheasant without alight-ing. They indicated the presence of a dead animal; and I asked the *mahouts* if our kill was there. They answered that it was about a mile further on. I judged that another cow must have been killed in this *nullah*; and from the fact that the vultures did not dare to settle on it, I concluded that a tiger must be in the immediate vicinity. So I directed my elephant towards the spot. As we drew near I looked at the rows of bald-headed vultures, those repulsive-looking scavengers of India, sitting on the branches. Every few minutes one would fly down towards the ground and, without settling, hurriedly shoot up again into the air. Cautiously approaching the edge of the bank we found, as I expected, the carcass of a cow. We skirted the bank but could not see the tiger, which was probably asleep somewhere in the tangled scrub in the bottom of the *nullah*. So, marking the spot for a visit next day, we went on our way. Arrived at the place where the beat was to begin, we found another *nullah* filled with jungle, with bare, open ground stretching away on either side of it. We took up our positions in it on our two howdah elephants and put the beaters in farther down.

They came on the tiger lying asleep under a tree. He sprang up in alarm and, instead of retreating along the *nullah* towards us, rushed up the bank and broke away over the open past a group of natives who had come out from a farm close by to watch the hunt. As he was not fifty yards from them, they were very scared. It must have been a fine sight to see the big cat bounding across the bare plain until he reached and plunged into a parallel *nullah* a few hundred yards away. But we in the bottom of our ravine saw or heard nothing of him until our beaters came up. We searched the other *nullah* for him in vain. He probably had not stopped until he had reached the shelter of the forest.

That night, when dining with the Ainslies, our host told us of some curious happenings in tiger hunts around Alipur Duar. A former commandant was shooting one day on Dundora. Mrs Ainslie was in the howdah with him. A tiger burst out of the jungle before the beat. The officer fired and wounded it; but, hardly checking in its rush, it dashed forward, being missed by another bullet, and sprang on to the elephant's head. For a second it stood with its hind feet on Dundora's skull, its forepaws on the front rail of the howdah. The officer dropped his empty rifle and, seizing a second gun, shoved the muzzle against the tiger's chest and fired. The brute fell back off the elephant, dead. The whole incident had passed like a flash. The tiger had actually stood right over the *mahout* crouching on the neck; but the man, although he found afterwards a long tear in the shoulder of his coat from the animal's claw, was not touched. On another occasion a tiger was shot in mid air as it sprang clean across a *nullah*, crumpled up and fell into the stream at the bottom. When the sportsmen on their elephants reached the edge of the bank, it was nowhere to be seen; and they concluded that it must have escaped down the *nullah*. But a month afterwards a second tiger was similarly shot in the middle of a spring and was seen from a distance to fall into a stream in the *nullah*, try to struggle out of the water and collapse beneath the surface. So the mystery of the first one's disappearance was solved. It must have been lying under water at the bottom of the *nullah*; but no one thought of looking for it there.

Next morning I came out on to the veranda of the *dâk* bungalow and surveyed with pride the six elephants drawn up in line before me. On the neck of each sat the *mahout*, who raised his hand to his forehead in a salaam. Then at the word of command the six trunks were lifted into the air and the elephants trumpeted in salute. As I looked at them I murmured inwardly: "This day a tiger must die!"

We were to look for the animal that had killed the cow I had found the previous morning. So Burrard and I made an early start and proceeded to the spot I had marked. The *nullah* was narrow, S-shaped, with almost perpendicular banks fifteen feet high. A stream of water filled it from bank to bank. On either side of it was thick scrub jungle and elephant grass eight feet high. I stationed Burrard at one end of the S and took up my position at the other about a hundred yards from him. My elephant was back a little from the *nullah*, along the far bank of which the tall, stiff grass stood like a wall. The beaters started a quarter of a mile from us and drove through the scrub on the other side of the *nullah*. A tiger, as a rule, begins to move at the first sound of the beat; so I stood up in my howdah with my rifle cocked. I may mention that shooting from an elephant, even when it is standing, is not easy, for the animal is never still. It continually shifts its weight from foot to foot, flaps its ears, moves its head and beats its sides or chest with its trunk to drive off the flies.

The line of beaters advanced through the scrub

with their usual din. Now and then, under the tangled undergrowth, I caught a glimpse of my orderly or a *mahout.* They drew nearer and nothing broke out of the jungle in front of them. My heart sank when I saw them not a hundred yards from me. But at that moment a number of small birds flew up from the tall grass and I heard the sound of some heavy animal forcing its way through the tough stems. I held my rifle ready to cover the spot. The next instant I saw the head and shoulders of a large tiger push out through the grass on the very brink of the *nullah.* Though the tall stalks on my side almost concealed my elephant, the tiger saw me at once and crouched for a spring. Its savage face was plainly visible, the fierce eyes fastened on me, the snarling lips drawn back over the white fangs, the bristling whiskers, all forming a fiendish mask appalling in its cruel expression. I threw up the rifle to my shoulder, took a quick aim and fired. The tiger started convulsively, sprang erect for an instant, then plunged head foremost into the *nullah* with stiffened forelegs close to the body, as a man diving holds his arms straight by his sides and hurls himself into the water. I was too far back from the bank to see down to the bottom of the *nullah*; but suddenly the tiger sprang convulsively straight into my view and then fell back again. The *mahout*, shrouded by the high grass, had seen nothing of all this. I shouted at him to urge Dundora forward to the edge of the *nullah.* From the brink I peered down into it; but, to my intense disappointment, no prostrate body of a tiger met my eyes. The banks were sheer; and I could look up and down the *nullah* for a hundred yards. I could not believe that the brute had escaped. I was convinced that I had not missed him, that my bullet had struck where I aimed, right between the shoulders, as he crouched for the spring. It should have been a fatal shot; but the tiger had vanished.

Suddenly Ainslie's stories of the previous night recurred to me. I glanced down the stream and saw, twenty yards from where we stood, a discoloured patch in the dark water. I had the elephant brought opposite it. I stared hard until I believed that I could make out the outlines of a tiger below the surface and see the stripes on the body. I pointed it out to the *mahout*. He gazed unbelievingly for a moment, then gave vent to an excited shout. The beaters had meantime reached the opposite bank and were calling across to ask if I had hit the tiger. When we told them where it was they laughed incredulously. I ordered Bechan to dismount from Khartoum's neck and enter the stream. With the air of one who does a ridiculous thing to please a fretful child, he slid down the bank and walked into the water. Suddenly he yelled in terror and sprang for the dry land. He had put his bare foot on the tiger's body. The animal was lying dead in three feet of water. The others urged Bechan to go in again; and with some trepidation he did so. Reaching down he lifted up the tail and held the tip up above the surface. The other *mahouts* and my orderly shouted with joy, for it meant largesse to them, and jumped in after Bechan. They moved the body easily to the edge of the water but could not lift it up the bank. We called some coolies from huts close by; and it took twenty men to raise the carcass up to the level.

THE TIGER'S LYING IN STATE.

THE TIGER'S LAST HOME.

The tiger was a fine young male in splendid condition, and measured nine and a half feet from nose to tip of tail. After photographing it, we brought the elephants in turn up to it as it lay on the ground and encouraged them to smell and strike it. This is done to show them that the animal is not a foe to be dreaded. We all had to help in lifting the limp body on to Khartoum's back; for a well-grown tiger weighs nearly three hundred and fifty pounds. It was fastened on to the pad with ropes; and we started back in triumphal procession to Alipur Duar, where the beast was flayed and the flesh scrambled for by the women of the neighbourhood, who gathered like vultures. The skin was pegged out on the grass to dry, before being sent to a taxidermist to be dressed and mounted to adorn my bungalow.

CHAPTER IX

A FOREST MARCH

Reasons for showing the flag—Soldierless Bengal—Planning the march—Difficulties of transport—The first day's march—Sepoys in the jungle—The water-creeper—The commander loses his men—The bivouac at Rajabhatkawa—Alipur Duar—A small Indian Station—Long-delayed pay—The Subdivisional Officer—A *dâk* bungalow—The sub-judge—Brahmin pharisees—The *nautch*—A dusty march—Santals—A mission settlement—Crossing a river—Rafts—A bivouac in a tea garden—A dinner-party in an 80-lb. tent—Bears at night—A daring tiger—Chasing a tiger on elephants—In the forest again—A fickle river—A strange animal—The Maharajah of Cooch Behar's experiment—A scare and a disappointment—Across the Raidak—A woman killed by a bear—A planters' club—Hospitality in the jungle—The zareba—Impromptu sports—The Alarm Stakes—The raft race—Hathipota—Jainti.

THERE is a tale told of the Indian Army in the good old days when soldiering in peace time was an easy life and very different to what it has now become. The story runs that a general order was published to the effect that "Officers are forbidden to drill the men from the verandas of their bungalows." For it was said that, attired in pyjamas, they lounged comfortably in long chairs and shouted out the words of command to their companies drilling on the parade ground in front of the bungalows. But those delightful days have gone for ever. Despite what democratic orators say, the British Army has become a professional one; and soldiering in it is a strenuous existence. In India only the Rains, when outdoor work is almost impossible, give rest to the hard-worked officer and man. Musketry, field firing, company training, both winter and summer, keep them fully employed until battalion training leads up to the culminating point of the year—the brigade or divisional manœuvres, or both. And then it begins all over again. And this, mark you, in a tropical climate!

Up to the rank of Colonel every officer must pass difficult examinations for promotion to each successive grade. And generals and colonels sit on the benches of class-rooms in the Schools of Musketry, and in their own commands lecture, or listen to other officers lecturing, on military subjects.

In the good old days I could have sat in my bungalow in Buxa Duar and watched my sepoys drilling in the narrow limits of our small parade ground. But nowadays too high a standard of efficiency is required from the troops for this method of commanding to pass muster. So, for the first month after our arrival, we scrambled up and down the steep mountains, scaled precipices and fought our way through thorny jungle practising hill warfare. Then I determined to take the detachment farther afield, where the men could have more varied ground to work over and learn something of jungle life. So I mapped out a ten days' march, under war conditions, through the forest below. We should go out as a self-contained force, like the little columns that are sent against the savage tribes along our North-East Frontier. We should carry our own supplies with us, find our own transport, move by day and bivouac at night exactly as we should do in an enemy's country. As the route selected would emerge into open country for a couple of days, the men would have a change from jungle work.

I was influenced in my decision to march through the surrounding country and "show the flag" by private representations made to me by civil officers of the district. They pointed out the advisability of letting the natives of the neighbourhood see soldiers, probably for the first time in the lives of many of them. Asiatics have short memories; and the inhabitants of the Bengals, who rarely see troops, are inclined to forget that the British Army still exists. At that time sedition was supposed to be spreading among them. For it is a curious fact that it chiefly makes headway among the unwarlike races of India, probably for the very reason that they have never learned in the field the respect that the brave man feels for the still braver antagonist who has conquered him. And British rule is more popular among the races that we have only vanquished after a hard struggle than it is among those whose ancestors never dared to meet us in battle. In all history the Bengali never was, never could be, a fighting-man. He was the easy prey of every invader; and, like the cowardly Corean, only the extreme suppleness of his back saved him from extermination. If the British left India the cities and rich lands of Bengal would be scrambled for by every warrior race in India; and her sons would not venture to lift a hand to defend themselves. But cowards are ingrates. Forgetful of all this the so-called educated Bengali whispers of the day to come when the English tyrants will be driven into the sea. He does not suggest that he and his kind will do it themselves. The young Calcutta student, crammed with undigested, ill-understood European knowledge, will talk treason glibly. Insulting women, hurling bombs, assassinating in secret or, gun in hand, plundering unarmed villagers even more timorous than himself, he is a hero in his own eyes. But even in the wildest frenzy of his ill-balanced brain he never pictures himself facing British troops in battle. The cowardly agitator allots that task to the native soldiers when we shall have succeeded in seducing them from their allegiance. But the sepoys, recruited from races that hold only the warrior in honour, look on him and his race as something more despicable than dogs. My Rajputs—descendants of the gallant fighters who conquered half India, who struggled through bloody centuries against the Mohammedan invaders, whose women killed themselves when their lords had been slain and preferred death to dishonour—my sepoys regarded the effeminate Bengalis as unsexed beings.

The Duars abound in tea states; and each manager rules six or seven hundred coolies by moral force. Several planters hinted to me that it would be a good thing to let these coolies see the gleam of bayonets for once, and realise that the white man has something more than the baton of an occasional native policeman to rely on if need arise.

Thrown on our own resources as we were in Buxa, the question of transporting the supplies and baggage of nearly two hundred men required some thinking out. We had no funds at our disposal to hire coolies; and all we could depend on was our three elephants. Ten days' food supply for so many men weighs a good deal; and we had to carry with us as well their bedding, cooking-pots, blank ammunition, pickaxes and shovels for entrenching. It needed some careful arrangement to enable three elephants to do the work of ten. I was obliged to send them out to form depots of sacks of flour, grain, and other food-stuffs at places along the route, and bring them back again to accompany us carrying the other things we required with us. Each sepoy was limited to two blankets and a change of clothing and boots rolled up in his *dhurri* or strip of carpet. Contrary to the usual custom on peace manœuvres each man carried a packet of ten rounds of ball cartridge in his pocket; for, had any sudden call for our services come before we could communicate with the magazine in our fort, we would have been of little use with only blank ammunition for our rifles. And in the forest at night we might require ball to protect ourselves against wild animals.

At last, our arrangements complete, we left forty men behind at Buxa to guard the Station; and one morning in February saw us, a hundred and sixty strong, marching through the jungle in the direction of Rajabhatkawa. We moved with fixed bayonets and all the proper precautions of a column passing through an enemy's country. Advanced, rear and flank guards protected us on all sides. These detachments, instead of being thrown out a mile or more from the main body, as they would have been in open country, were not a hundred yards from it. And even that was often too much in the dense jungle. Every man carried at his belt a *kukri*, the Gurkha's heavy, curved knife, and used it to hack his way through the tangle of creepers and under-

" MY SEPOYS DRILLING."

BUGLERS AND NON-COMMISSIONED OFFICERS OF MY DETACHMENT.

growth. The progress was necessarily very slow, and we hardly advanced a mile an hour. We marched by compass, no easy task in thick forest.

At the first fire line, as there was an open space, I halted and closed the detachment to give them their first object-lesson in the jungle. To my men, inhabitants of the sandy deserts of Rajputana or the cultivated plains of the North-West Provinces, forest lore was unknown. And as all the warfare the Assam Brigade, to which we belonged, would be called upon to wage would be fought against savages in thick jungle, I lost no chance of teaching our men all conditions of the bush. I now asked them where, when the rivers were dry, would they look for water in the forest. They mostly replied:

"We would dig for it, Sahib."

I told them that Nature had been too generous to call for such exertion and had kindly provided water in the trees. They looked at me in surprise and evidently thought that I meant to be facetious. I pointed to a thick creeper swinging between the trees in front of me and introduced them to the mysterious *pani bel*. A piece was cut off; and the water flowed from it. That astonished them.

"*Wah! wah!* but that is *jadu* (magic)," they said to each other. "Marvellous is the Sahib's knowledge. Like us he is new to the forest. Then how could he know of such a wonderful thing?"

The water creeper grew freely all round. Permission given, they broke ranks and rushed into the jungle, each resolved to handle the marvel for himself. In a few minutes I was surrounded by scores of sepoys leaning on their rifles with heads well thrown back to catch in their mouths the water dropping from the cut pieces of creeper. The *pani bel* was a great success. They filled their haversacks with it, and all that day, at every halt, pulled it out to taste and marvel at the magic plant.

We moved on again in our original formation. Carrying my sporting rifle I walked a few yards behind the advanced line of scouts. So dense was the jungle that, out of all the hundred and sixty men around me, I could only occasionally catch glimpses of three or four. Suddenly from a hundred yards ahead I heard a large animal forcing its way through the undergrowth. Fearing that it might be a wild elephant I pushed on in front of the scouts, as my rifle would be more effective than theirs. The animal retreated before me without my being able to see it; and I followed, glancing over my shoulder now and then to sight the sepoys behind and ensure that I was keeping the proper direction. But neglecting this precaution for five minutes, I completely lost the whole detachment. The beast I was pursuing had gone beyond hearing; so I turned back to rejoin my men. But search as I might I could not find one of them. It seemed absurd to lose in a few minutes a hundred and sixty men spread out in a loose formation. But I had succeeded in doing it.

It was a ridiculous position for the commander who was supposed to be instructing his soldiers in jungle training. But, fortunately, I already knew the forest in the neighbourhood fairly well; and guiding myself by the sun, I succeeded in getting ahead of my warriors and rejoining them at the place on which they were marching by compass without any of them realising that they had lost me. We halted for the night and bivouacked close to Rajabhatkawa Station.

The next day's march brought us out clear of the forest. As we emerged on the cultivated plains to the north of Alipur Duar, it seemed quite strange to be on open ground again and able to swing along at four miles an hour. The sepoy is a faster marcher than his British comrade and will do his five miles in the hour on a road if wanted. In his own home he thinks nothing of covering forty miles a day, shuffling along at the native jog-trot that eats up the ground.

After Buxa Alipur Duar seemed almost a city, though it is not an imposing town. The houses, when not made of mud or bamboo and thatched with straw, are built of brick and roofed with corrugated iron. But it boasts a jail, a hospital, a *dâk* bungalow and a sub-treasury. And the last was the cause of my including it in our itinerary; for the detachment was in the throes of a financial crisis. None of the officers or men had received their pay for December and January; and we had not five rupees between us. But the long-delayed pay-cheque on this sub-treasury had just reached me; and I was anxious to cash it at the earliest opportunity. Unfortunately we arrived at Alipur Duar after office hours and were forced to wait another day for our money, instead of marching on next morning as I had intended.

The town had no amusement to offer us Britishers. The only Europeans who resided in it were the Ainslies; and they were then absent; for throughout the winter the district officials are out in camp, moving from village to village in their districts, and administering the law and carrying on the ground work of the Government of the land.

However, Alipur Duar boasted among its public buildings that useful institution, a *dâk* bungalow. In little Stations and dotted every ten or fifteen miles along the highways of India, the *dâk* bungalow is there to shelter the European traveller whom Fate or his work leads far from cities and railways. It is a humble, one-storied building, erected by Government, and containing one two or three scantily furnished rooms. It is in charge of a native attendant, who sometimes provides food for the hungry traveller, though as a rule the latter has to bring his own with him. Luckily India is the land of tinned food.

The Alipur bungalow boasted a *khansamah*, or butler, who was able to furnish us with meals. We found already installed in it a native sub-judge who had come from the headquarters of the district to try some cases in Ainslie's absence. I got into conversation with him and found him a cheery, pleasant little Bengali, a follower of the new reformed *Brahmo Samaj* faith and consequently free from the caste prejudices of the orthodox Hindu, which do so much to keep him and the Englishman apart. Finding that our new acquaintance had no scruples about eating with Europeans, I invited him to share our dinner. He held very decided opinions on what he termed the hypocrisy of the educated Brahmins who, in public, profess to adhere strictly to the severest caste restrictions in the matter of eating with others, particularly with Europeans.

"Sir, I am not possessed of patience to endure them," he said in his quaint English. "In the town where I have the habit to reside, the Brahmin lawyers and under-official strappers invite to the farewell entertainment of a garden-party our much-to-be-regretted late Deputy-Commissioner, when being about to depart from us. They request me to pose as a host with them. I say to them: 'No; I am not willing. You ask to Mr and Mrs ——, an English gentleman and lady, to come partake of your hospitality. But you put on a table in corner of tent cakes, tea and other cheering refreshments and tell them to eat alone while you turn your faces, lest to see them eat would break your caste. It is all a bosh! I have seen many of you in strange places to eat of forbidden food at the restaurants of railway stations where you sit cheek-by-jowl with unknown Englishmen. And yet you cannot indulge in cake, refreshment, etcetera, with the esteemed departing Deputy-Commissioner. It is all a bosh!'"

He more than repaid our hospitality that night by his amusing remarks and shrewd comments on Indian and European manners. He said that, never having come in contact with military officers before, he had watched us all that day and was astonished to see that we were on friendly terms with our native subordinates, knew the names of all our men, and did not treat them with disdainful hauteur, as alleged by the Bengali journals. And I thought of an untravelled Englishman who had told me in a London drawing-room that we British officers were in the habit of beating our sepoys!

Next day we visited the court-house to watch our little friend dispensing justice from the bench. We were amused to see how quickly he disposed of long-winded native lawyers who, in a case involving a matter of a few shillings, were prepared to deliver a speech in high-flown English lasting five hours. He cut them very short with his favourite phrase: "It is all a bosh!"

The pay having been disbursed that afternoon, our men asked me for leave to engage a troop of dancers and enjoy a *nautch*, that entertainment dear to the heart of the Indian but wearisome beyond measure to the European spectator. It was held at night on the open ground behind the *dâk* bungalow. As is customary in native regiments we were invited to witness it and, much against our will, went to it after dinner. The sepoys squatting in a wide circle round the performers rose to their feet; and the Indian officers welcomed us with the usual formalities. After we had shaken hands with them they hung garlands of flowers round our necks, thrust small bouquets on us and liberally besprinkled us with scent. When we sat down small plates were offered us on which, wrapped up in leaves, were various pungent and aromatic spices to chew. Then we were given cigars, cigarettes, and whiskies-and-sodas—these a concession to European tastes. The performance, interrupted by our arrival, continued. Two fat women with well-oiled hair, jewelled ornaments in their noses, gold bangles on their wrists and ankles, their toes adorned with rings, swayed their fleshy bodies and shuffled a few inches forward and back on their heels, singing the while in high falsetto voices. Wrapped from throat to ankle in voluminous coloured draperies as they were, the propriety of their costume was a reproach to the scantily clad dancers of so-called Indian dances in the English music-halls. The musicians squatted on the grass behind them, two men producing weird and monotonous sounds from strangely shaped instruments, while a third beat with his hands on a tom-tom, the native drum. And this is the famous *nautch* at which the Indian will gaze with rapture all night. The flaring oil-lamps shone on the ring of eager dark faces and eyes glistening with enjoyment, as the sepoys watched intently every movement of the ungainly dancers. Fortunately we were not obliged to remain long and soon took our leave of the native officers. Although we were to march at seven o'clock in the morning I heard the monotonous drumming and the shrill voices throughout the night; for the entertainment did not end before five o'clock. And it was a hollow-eyed detachment that tramped behind us on the dusty road that day. Our route lay at an angle to our former course which had been due south; for now we headed north-east towards the jungle and the hills again.

On the left hand lay the ragged fringe of the forest stretching east and west beyond the limit of vision; and high above it towered the long rampart of the mountains. Far away as we were we could see the white specks of the Picquet Towers at Buxa. And back among the jagged peaks rose up the snow-clad summit of a mountain in Bhutan, its gleaming crest seeming to float like a cloud in air above the darker hills. Over the level plain we spread out in fighting formation, one company forming an advanced guard and driving back the skirmishing line of the other which acted as the rear guard of a retreating enemy. And here and there the peasants working in the fields, knowing nothing of the harmlessness of blank cartridges, fled in terror at the sound of the firing.

We halted for our bivouac near a village in a mission settlement of Santals, a wild tribe recently civilised by hard-working missionaries and taught the dignity of labour and the joys of agriculture. We met the clergyman and his wife who were in charge of the settlement and invited them to dinner with us. They showed us a large iron church in the village, the materials of which had been purchased by money willingly subscribed by the Santals, who had erected the building with their own hands. Our guests told us that their half-tamed flock, when they saw us marching in, had deserted the village and fled into the jungle. They explained to their wondering pastor that we were soldiers, and soldiers were folk whose one object in life was to kill people—and who easier to slay than the poor Santals? It took him hours to induce them to return to their homes. But before night they had lost all fear and flocked inquisitively round our bivouac.

Next day we marched through outlying patches of jungle, the advanced guards of the great forest; and we hailed the trees as old friends. After an attack by one company on the other in position on a low hill, we found our way barred by an unfordable river. Along the banks lay logs and trunks of trees swept down from the forest; so we turned to to make rafts, binding the timber together with the men's putties and *puggris*—for their head-gear is made of strips of cloth nine yards long. On these rafts the few non-swimmers, the rifles, clothing and accoutrements were placed; and the swimmers towed and pushed them across the stream. With the same rude materials we made an excellent flying bridge which, moved by the swift current, floated backwards and forwards across the river on ropes made from the *puggris* and putties. The men revelled in the work. Stripped to their loin-cloths they sported like dolphins in the clear, cold water flowing down from the melting snows of the Himalayas.

Then we marched on again until I halted the column on the outskirts of a tea garden and sent Creagh galloping to ask the manager's permission to encamp on it and draw water for my men from the wells. While awaiting his return, I stretched myself along a squared log of timber and, despite my hard couch, fell asleep, awaking with a start to find Khartoum standing over me staring at me with curiosity out of her little eyes, as she flapped her big ears and brushed away the flies from her sides with a branch. For a second I fancied I was in the forest under the feet of a wild elephant; and I sprang up hastily. Then Creagh returned with a cheery, hospitable Englishman, who invited me to consider the tea garden my own. In a few minutes the fires were going, the *bhistis* fetching water from the wells, and the cooks rolling up the balls of dough, deftly patting them out into thin cakes and spreading them on the convex iron griddle over the flames. Sentries posted and guards mounted, the rest of the men piled arms, took off their accoutrements; and, while some hungrily watched the cooks, others lay down on the ground and slept contentedly until food was ready. The coolies gathered to see the novel sight of soldiers; and the inevitable pariah dogs hung about the cooking places and quarrelled over the scraps thrown to them. At every bivouac some of these four-footed recruits joined us; and when we reached Buxa again I found that at least a dozen nondescript curs had adopted the detachment and marched into the fort with the air of veterans.

That night we invited the planter to dine with us. Our meal was laid in my small 80-lb. tent; and, as this measured seven feet by seven feet with a sloping roof, there was not much room for four of us and the servants. Our guest told us of a daring daylight attack by a tiger that morning. While some villagers were driving their cattle on a road which passed along the edge of the tea garden, the animal had sprung out from the jungle skirting it and tried to carry off a cow. The men, being fairly numerous, rushed shouting at him and scared him away. When I heard this I determined to beat up that tiger's quarters in the morning and told the other officers of the detachment, who were delighted with the idea. While discussing it after dinner we were startled by fiendish growls and howls from the darkness outside; for a minute we were puzzled by the awful noises and then recognised them as the sounds of two bears fighting close by. Creagh, Smith and I seized our rifles; and, followed by servants carrying lanterns as the night was very dark, we sallied forth to find the disturbers of the peace. The noise came from a spot about two hundred yards away. We reached a high bank below which was thick scrub and long tiger grass. We climbed down it and formed line with the servants close up behind us holding the lanterns over our heads to throw the light in front. As we pushed our way with difficulty through the scrub a bear gave a sudden growl five yards to our left. We swung round and made for the spot; but the animal did not await our approach. After searching for half an hour without result we gave up the chase and returned to the camp. Next morning daylight showed us that we had been down in a *nullah*, the ground on either side of it being quite open. Had we known this at the time we could have divided our forces, gone along both banks and probably got the bears as they scrambled up out of the *nullah*.

At daybreak we started out with the elephants to look for the tiger. As we possessed only one howdah, it was strapped on Khartoum's back and we all three crowded into it; for the tall grass rose higher than the head of a man sitting on an elephant's pad. Having thoroughly beaten the wide strip of long grass we pushed on and came out on a very broad, empty river-bed. This was the River Raidak, which formerly brought down an immense volume of water from the hills only a few miles away. But a few years before it had grown tired of its old road and suddenly changed its course, flowing into the bed of a smaller stream parallel to it, which became greatly enlarged and was now itself generally known as the Raidak. This was the river we had crossed on rafts.

As our elephants passed over the wide strip of sand, a curious animal broke out of the jungle a couple of hundred yards from us and bounded away up the *nullah*. It was apparently a hornless deer with black back and white belly and looked like a "black buck"; but as these inhabit open plains and do not shed their horns we were puzzled as to its identity. It halted and looked back at us, and then went off again in a series of high leaps and bounds strangely like a black buck's motion. Some months afterwards the Maharajah of Cooch Behar told me that several years before he had turned loose a number of black buck and does into the forest near the Raidak as an experiment, being curious to know what effect life in dense jungle would have on these dwellers of the open plains. Apparently the animal we had seen was descended from these and for some reason of acclimatisation Nature had deprived their progeny of horns. This should interest naturalists.

Our search for the tiger ended in a scare and a disappointment. First, when passing through another patch of tall grass on our way back to camp, one of the two pad elephants, Dundora, trumpeted shrilly and charged some animal in the cover. Her alarm communicated itself to the others, who squealed and tried to bolt. We thought that it was the tiger and, with rifles at the ready, attempted to stand up in the swaying howdah, which was no easy task as Khartoum was plunging violently. When at last we got her near Dundora, the latter's *mahout*, viciously belabouring her thick skull with the *ankus*, told us that the cause of her fright was only a small pariah dog. We passed on into more open jungle and to our joy saw a herd of wild buffaloes. As we were not in Government forest these were fair game for the hunter; and we urged the *mahout* forward. The animals were grazing and did not see us. Cautiously approaching up wind we got within range and were raising our rifles, when an old cow lifted her head and we saw a bell hung round her neck. We swore loudly. They were tame animals; but, as these are like the wild species and we were deep in the jungle, our error was pardonable. Half a mile further on we came on the huts of their owners.

Our course next day lay north-west; and I intended to recross the new Raidak at a point near the hills at a ferry, close to which was a club-house where the planters of the neighbourhood gathered once a week. This was the day of their meeting; so I resolved to make our bivouac there. The march lay through very dense jungle; but at last our advanced guard came out on the bank of a wide river, a swift-racing torrent of clear water that eddied and swirled over the pebbly bottom. On the opposite side was the ferryman's hut, his boat drawn up near it. Behind, in a clearing, stood a long wooden building which was evidently the club-house. Our shouts brought Charon out of his abode; and he ferried us over in driblets. As elephants are excellent swimmers ours made their own way across.

In the jungle, not far from the club, I marked out the spot for our bivouac around which I ordered a zareba to be constructed. As everything was to be done under war conditions, scouts were thrown out on every side. The rest of the detachment piled arms, drew their *kukris* and proceeded to clear the jungle. The small trees and undergrowth cut down were dragged to form a belt, ten yards deep, of entanglement breast-high around the camp. The stems of the trees and bushes were fastened to pickets by creepers to prevent their being pulled away. Thorny branches and a shrub which causes an intense irritation when t uched were thrown in among them; and the zareba thus constructed formed a formidable obstacle. Then parties were told off to erect shelters of leafy boughs; others made the cooking-places or dug latrines; and the *bhistis* were taken down under escort to the river to fill the goat-skin bags, or *mussacks*, in which they carry water. Then guards and inlying pickets were mounted and the scouts withdrawn. Bathing-parties went down with their rifles, only half of the men in them being allowed into the river at a time, while the others kept guard against sudden attack.

By this time the planters were beginning to assemble at the rough wooden building which they proudly called their club. And certainly I believe it saw more jollity and good-fellowship within its timber walls than one would find in any of the palatial club-houses of Pall Mall. From gardens lost in the forest for miles round they gathered. Some dashed up to the opposite river-bank on their smart little ponies and kept the ferryman busy. The host that day was our friend Tyson of Hathipota, which now lay between us and Buxa Duar. He cordially invited us to eat our share of the sumptuous cold lunch he had provided, and introduced us to the other planters of the district, who welcomed us warmly.

During lunch one of our new friends told me that the ferryman, whom we could see busy at his boat on the beach, had lost his wife under tragic circumstances. The woman had gone across the river to a village a couple of miles away to buy provisions. On her return she hailed him from the opposite bank. As he was shoving his boat into the water he saw to his horror a huge bear emerge from the jungle and steal silently up behind the woman. At her husband's warning cry she turned; but before she could move the animal rose on its hind legs and felled her with a blow from its great paw. When the terrified man reached the bank, the bear had disappeared and the woman lay dead with a fractured skull.

After lunch, the planters, most of whom were keen Volunteers, asked me to let them inspect our fortified camp. They were much impressed by the rapidity with which it had been placed in a state of defence and with the ingenuity of our sepoys, who had already made comfortable little huts. Then the senior among the planters told me that he was commissioned by the others to express the gratitude of them all for marching the detachment through their district. He emphasised the fact that the sight of our armed men sweeping through the countryside would have a good effect, not only on the thousands of unruly coolies on the tea gardens around, but also on the lawless dwellers over the border on the hills above us. He said that he and his friends had subscribed on the spot a sum of six or seven pounds and asked my permission to offer the money as prizes for sports to be held by our men that day. I thanked them all heartily and drew up a programme.

The sepoys were delighted and flocked down to the open beach where the sports took place. Of the two events which interested the planters most, the first was called "The Alarm Race." Teams from each section lay undressed and apparently sleeping on the ground beside their uniforms and accoutrements. On a bugle sounding they sprang up, dressed, put on their belts and bandoliers, rolled and strapped up their bedding, and fell in ready to march off. We inspected them; and the team first ready and properly dressed won the prize. The other event was very popular among the spectators.

Teams of men in full marching order were ferried across the river and landed on the opposite bank. At a signal they started to collect driftwood and build it into rafts, tying the logs together with their *puggris* and putties. Then some with long bamboo poles took their places on each raft, while others of the team undressed, placed their rifles, belts and clothing on the raft and, springing into the water, swam alongside and helped to bring it across to our bank. The current ran swiftly and the excited men made their rafts swing round like teetotums. The first party to reach the spot where I stood on the beach and form up properly dressed were the winners.

After the sports some of us played tennis on the courts made in the clearing. As the sun set, after a parting drink and hearty invitations to visit their estates, our friends bade us good-bye and rode off.

On our next day's march our faces were set homewards. We passed several tea gardens until we reached Hathipota, where the hospitable Tyson welcomed us. and placed the resources of his estate at our men's disposal and entertained the British officers in his bungalow. Parties of our non-commissioned officers and men were taken over the factories and withering sheds, and were as deeply interested as we were in the ponderous machinery and clever contrivances. We left Hathipota next day. Later on, we were to see it again under more tragic auspices, when we were conveying a murderer to his doom.

Thence to the end of the ten days' march we worked through the forest back towards home. We passed almost dryshod over a wide river at Jainti, which during the Rains can only be crossed by a cradle running on an iron cable from bank to bank. At Jainti ends the little railway by which we had arrived. The next station to it was Buxa Road.

From Santrabari we climbed our hills again, sorry to have finished our pleasant and instructive march. The men had learned much of jungle conditions; and I had acquired a knowledge of the district which was to stand me in good stead in days to come.

CHAPTER X

THROUGH FIRE AND WATER

India in the hot weather—A land of torment—The drought—Forest fires—The cholera huts burned—Fighting the flames—Death of a sepoy—The bond between British officers and their men—The sepoy's funeral—A fortnight's vigil—Saving the Station—The hills ablaze—A sublime spectacle—The devastated forest—Fallen leaves on fire—Our elephants' peril—Saving the zareba—A beat for game in the jungle—Trying to catch a wild elephant—A moonlight ramble—We meet a bear—The burst of the Monsoons—A dull existence—Three hundred inches of rain—The monotony of thunderstorms—A changed world—Leeches—Monster hailstones—Surveyors caught in a storm—A break in the Rains—The revived jungle—Useless lightning-conductors—The Monsoon again—The loneliness of Buxa.

THROUGH the long months of the Indian summer the cool Hills look down in pity on the Plains steeped in the brooding heat, where the sun is an offence and a torture, where the hot wind, like a blast of fiery air from an opened furnace door, mocks with the thought of pleasant breezes in a temperate land, where night brings only the breathless hours of darkness when the parched earth gives out the heat it has stored by day, and only dawn affords a momentary relief.

From early March to the end of June India is indeed turned into a place of torment. In the crowded quarters of the cities millions of natives swelter and endure with the dumb resignation of animals. Shut up in darkened houses from morning to evening thousands of Englishwomen and children suffer through the weary months. The fortunate ones fly to the Hills; but Hill Stations are expensive and not for the poorer classes of Europeans. And the white men of all ranks and professions must carry on their work. His drill done, the British soldier lies on his cot under the punkah of the barrack-room, thinks with regret of the cool land he has left and forgets the misery of the unemployed in the rain and frosts of England. And his officer, whose work takes him more frequently out into the sun than the soldier, envies the lucky mortals who can obtain leave and fly to Europe or the Hills. Through the hot night he tosses on his bed placed under a punkah out in his garden and dozes fitfully until the punkah coolie drops asleep and the faint wind of the overhead fan is stilled. Then, bathed in perspiration, devoured by mosquitoes, he wakes; and who can blame him if his language to the neglectful coolie, who can sleep all day while his master works, is as hot as the climate?

From our little post on the face of the Himalayas we gazed to the south over the lowlands, seen dimly through the heat haze, and pitied the suffering millions in the India that stretched away from the foot of our hills to the far-distant sea. Buxa is usually cool. The Monsoons which sweep up from the equator and bring the welcome Rains towards the end of June are here forestalled by other currents that deluge mountain and forest with tropical showers as early as February. But for our sins in our first year they failed us. And the heat crept up from its kingdom in the Plains below and laughed at our boasts of the coolness of our Hill Station. In March the only comfortable man in the detachment was a prisoner whom I had sentenced for desertion to two months' confinement in the one cell of the fort. For while we sweated on the hot parade ground below, he gazed at us through the barred window of his cool, stone-paved apartment beside the guard-room; and since I could find no hard labour for his idle hands, he must have laughed as he watched us, officers and men, toiling bare armed in the hot sun, digging earthworks and erecting stockades on the knolls around. It seemed hard to believe that only a few weeks before cheerful wood fires had burned in the grates of our bungalows and after dinner we had pulled our chairs in front of the comforting blaze and defied the cold with jorums of hot punch.

But soon we had more than enough of other fires. The vast forests stretching through Assam, Bhutan, the Terai and Nepal, were dry as tinder owing to the unusual drought. From our eyrie in the hills we looked down at night on the glow in the sky, east, south and west, that told of jungles blazing around us. By day columns of smoke rose up in the distance and spread until a black pall covered the landscape. The hot wind brought the acrid smell of ashes and burning wood to us; and soon the air was full of smuts. From Assam and Bhutan came the tale of leagues of forest devoured by the flames. The dwellers in the pleasant Hill Station of Darjeeling, seven thousand feet above the sea, complained of the pall of smoke that veiled the mountains around them. Day after day I gazed apprehensively on our happy hunting-grounds in the forest below and feared to see them invaded by the conquering fires. I pictured with dismay the game destroyed by the rushing flames or driven far from us. And at last doubt became cruel certainty. Our forests blazed. The legions of the victorious fire king swept through the jungles we loved and denied them to us.

But at first we did not realise that danger threatened us, that our small Station was itself imperilled. On a wooded spur below the fort stood two long bamboo-walled buildings, intended as a segregation hospital for cases of infectious disease. One afternoon news was brought me that the forest fires had crept up to the base of the hill on which they stood. I ran down to the fort and ordered out the whole detachment. The men in whatever garb they were wearing at the moment turned out; and we raced through the back gate and down a zigzag path cut on the face of the precipice on the south side of the fort. Then we struggled up the steep hill to the threatened buildings. Below us the forest blazed. The flames were sweeping up the slopes towards us. The sight was a fine one; but we had little leisure or inclination to admire it. Breaking branches from the trees we fell upon the advancing enemy and endeavoured to beat it back. The wind was against us. Sparks and burning embers flew past and set alight to the hill-top behind us. It was curious to see how the flames ran up the trees and, leaving the trunks unscathed, seized on the masses of orchids on the boughs. Their leaves and stems blazed fiercely as if filled with oil. Scorched by the heat, grimed with the flying ashes and smuts, officers and men fought shoulder to shoulder against the encroaching flames. In a long line we descended to meet them and beat down the burning undergrowth. Suddenly a sharp gust of wind carried a burst of fire against us. Smothered by the smoke, our clothes alight from the red cinders, we were forced back. The flames lit up a patch of tall grass, dry as tinder, which went up in a sheet of fire. We turned and ran up to the summit. But one unfortunate sepoy stumbled and fell; and the wave of flame swept over him. It passed him by and then died as suddenly as it had risen. He stood up and staggered towards the hill-top. The moment he was seen a dozen men rushed down over the smouldering ground to help him. They carried him up to the crest and, as he was badly burnt, took him to the hospital as soon as a litter could be brought for him.

The flames began to circle round the base of the hill and threatened to cut us off; so I was forced to abandon the position and order a retreat. Hardly had we reached the zigzag path to the fort when the huts went up in pillars of flame.

In the evening I visited my unfortunate sepoy. Though in pain, he was conscious and able to speak to me; and I thought he would recover. But during the night he collapsed suddenly and died. This was the first death we had had in the detachment; and it cast a gloom over us all. The sepoys regretted a comrade; while the loss of one of his men always affects an officer. And in our isolated Station the death of one of our small number was acutely felt.

There exists more sympathy between the British

officers of an Indian regiment and the sepoys than between the latter and the native officers. Where the men imagine, not always without reason, that these last are swayed by considerations of different race or caste, of favouritism towards some and a dislike to others, of village and family feuds in their homes—for the Indian officers are generally promoted from the ranks—they know that the British officer is unaffected by such influences. Consequently, the men have far more confidence in his justice. When a sepoy is to be arraigned before a court martial for an offence, he is allowed to choose whether he will be tried by British or by Indian officers. In all my service I have known only one case in which the man elected for the latter. And when he came before the court and found it composed of native officers, he objected strongly and declared that he wished to be tried by the Sahibs. When it was pointed out to him that he had been given his choice of judges, he protested that he had not understood, and that he had no wish to be tried by men of his own nationality.

There is perhaps even a greater bond of union between the sepoys and the white officers of a native regiment than between the soldiers and the commissioned ranks in a British corps. In the first place the Indian Army is a long-service one; and so officers and men remain longer together. Many of my sepoys have watched me advance from subaltern to captain, from captain to major; and youngsters I knew as recruits are now native officers under me. Then the Indian soldier leans more on his British officer. He comes to him with all his troubles about lawsuits over land and his fields—

for every man is a land-holder—and confidently expects that his Sahib will fight for justice for him. Some continental armies would be horrified to see the sepoy off parade talking with friendly freedom to his British officer or playing hockey with him on terms of perfect equality.

The flag of the fort was half-mast high, as the funeral-party marched out to pay the last honours to their dead comrade. As the deceased sepoy was a Rajput his body was carried down to Santrabari to be there placed on a pile of wood and burned with all the ceremonies of his religion; for, while Mohammedans are buried, Hindus are cremated.

But we had little leisure to brood over the dead man's fate. The position of the fort and of the Station of Buxa was very precarious, now that the fires had reached the hills. The former I safe-guarded by burning the grass on the isolated mound on which it stood. But our bungalows, hemmed in by the jungle which grew to within a few yards of them, were in constant danger. The diary of parades which I was obliged to furnish every week to the brigade office in Shillong for the information of the General bore for a fortnight the words "fighting fires," instead of the usual entries of "company drill," "musketry," "field training," and the like. Day and night whenever the bugles rang out the alarm, we had to turn out to fight the intruding flames. Once we had to battle the whole day to save the forest officer's bungalow from being burned. I well remember how, while we officers and men toiled in the heat and smoke to beat back the fire, the Bengali clerks, whose houses were also in danger, stood at a safe distance, weeping and wringing their hands, but never attempting to help.

At night the burning forests below were a gorgeous though pitiable sight. And when the fires, repelled from Buxa, swept past us upwards, and the semicircle of hills around blazed to the summit of Sinchula one night, the spectacle was sublime. In one spot, high overhead, the trees had been felled and left lying on the ground after a half-hearted attempt at cultivation by the Bhuttias. Here the long sparkling lines of fire from the burning undergrowth were changed to pillars of flame, as the huge, dry tree-trunks blazed fiercely up in the darkness.

But life was not pleasant in Buxa during those days. The atmosphere was filled with smoke which veiled the sun. The heat was intense. So when the danger had passed our Station, I took the detachment down into the burned-out forest for a week's training in camp. The jungle was a sad sight for a sportsman's eyes. The big trees stood scorched, their trunks blackened and the branches charred where the masses of orchids that clothed them had burned. Some of the hollow stems were still on fire inside and sent out smoke among the tree-tops as from a steamer's funnel. Dead trees, long supported by creepers, now lay smouldering on the ground. The undergrowth which sheltered the game was gone. It was strange to be able to see for a hundred yards or more between the tree-trunks, where formerly ten paces was the limit of vision. The earth was covered ankle-deep in ashes, which rose up in suffocating clouds at every breath of hot wind. And above them was strewn a thick layer of dead leaves; for the trees shed them in the hot weather. And these I soon found constituted a fresh danger.

To my surprise I discovered that the little corner in the foot-hills around Forest Lodge had been spared by the fire and my bamboo hut, twenty-two feet up in the air among the branches, was intact. So I halted the men and established the bivouac here. We had marched on ahead of the baggage, which was loaded on the elephants. While these were following us from Santrabari the masses of dry leaves underfoot caught fire from some smouldering log; and a long line of flames swept down on the terrified animals. Fortunately they were near a broad, dry river-bed; and the scared *mahouts* drove them into it for safety. A mile away the crackling of the burning leaves aroused us to our new danger. Breaking off branches, officers and men set to work to sweep the leaves around the bivouac into heaps and leave the ground bare for a couple of hundred yards on every side. By the morrow the fire had died out, all the leaves having been consumed.

As we manœuvred through the forest every day I was astonished to still find traces of animal life in it. The destruction of the undergrowth and creepers having left the jungle more open, I determined to try a beat through it. On our last afternoon I sent all the men of the detachment a mile away across a broad river-bed with orders to drive towards it in a long line through the trees. On the near bank, which rose sheer to a height of thirty-three feet above the sand, the British and native officers, armed with rifles, took up their position.

Lying flat on the ground at the edge of the bank, we listened to the shouts of the men coming nearer and nearer. The branches of the trees across the *nullah* became violently agitated; and a large troop of monkeys swung through them, leaped to the ground, and rushed over the sand on all fours. Then a barking deer broke out about a hundred and fifty yards away, and I fired at it. I was using a ·470 cordite rifle; yet, struck just behind the shoulder by a soft-nosed bullet, the little animal ran a furlong before dropping dead. Nothing else followed it. Soon the men came into view between the trees and halted below us. Draj Khan, who was managing the line of beaters, was berating his comrades vehemently. He told me that they had come across a large tusker elephant; and instead of shepherding it gently towards the guns, a number of foolish young sepoys, armed only with sticks, had rushed boldly at it with wild yells. Luckily it did not attack them, but escaped out to one side of the beat. At the other end of the line the men had come on a small herd of *sambhur*, including two stags, and in their excitement had valiantly charged them in the absurd hope of taking them alive. A *sambhur* stag with his sharp horns and the driving-power of his great weight behind them is no mean foe; and it was just as well that the deer had fled from the men and broke out through a gap in the line.

We tried a beat lower down the river, which resulted in the men putting up a panther. But again some foolishly daring spirits rushed at it to attack it with their sticks; and the animal got away at one end of the beat. Draj Khan caught a young *sambhur* fawn, a week old, and brought it to me in his arms. This and the *khakur* were our whole bag.

I was surprised to find that the burnt forest still sheltered so much life. As the fires do not advance very rapidly the wild beasts can generally keep ahead of them and escape. But I cannot understand how the harmless animals support existence when all their fodder is destroyed.

One night when Creagh and I were sitting in the bivouac after dinner in the dim light of a half moon, the idea occurred to me to take one of our elephants and wander along the bed of a river a few hundred yards away, in which, as there was still some water left, we might come upon wild animals drinking. So we got our rifles, and a pad was strapped on Khartoum's back. On her we passed out of the zareba surrounding the camp, in which most of the men lay asleep on their *dhurries* stretched on the ground; for the native requires no softer bed and can repose contentedly on paving stones. A couple of the Indian officers still sat talking by a fire near the shelter of boughs erected for them by their men. We answered the sentry's challenge and turned Khartoum down a path from the bivouac to the water. It lay faintly white in the misty moonlight which barely lit up the ground under the leafless trees. Not a hundred yards from the camp the *mahout* stopped Khartoum suddenly and pointed to a black object which indistinctly blurred the path.

"A bear, Sahib," he whispered.

It was too dark to see my rifle-sights; but I rapidly tied my handkerchief round the barrel and tried to aim at the shadowy outline of the animal.

Unluckily at that moment it moved off the path and entered a patch of shadow under a tree which still kept its leaves. I fired both barrels in quick succession without result and the bear scuttled away among the trees. We tried to follow it but could not find it again.

When we reached the river-bed, down the middle of which a narrow stream still ran, we wandered up it for a couple of miles in the misty light. It was a curious sensation to be roaming noiselessly—for Khartoum's feet made no sound on the soft sand—in the dead of night through the silent jungle. Far away a *khakur's* harsh bark rang out suddenly once or twice, giving warning of the presence of some beast of prey; but otherwise all was still. We disturbed a few deer drinking; and they dashed away up the *nullah* in alarm. But we saw no wild elephant or tiger, such as I had hoped to come upon; and so we turned and made for camp again.

On our return to Buxa the hills near us were bare and blackened; but farther away the fires still blazed. The heat and the oppression of the smoky atmosphere were still almost unendurable. But one night in the first week of April I was awakened by a terrific peal of thunder right overhead, which shook my bungalow and echoed and re-echoed among the hills. Another followed, as the intense darkness was lit up by a blinding lightning flash. And a dull moaning sound advancing from the plains below and steadily increasing to a roar made me sit up in bed and wonder what was about to happen. It drew near; and then a torrential downpour of tropical rain beat down on the Station. My iron roof rattled as if millions of pebbles were being flung on it. The noise was so great that I lay awake for hours.

The storm raged all night; and when I rose for parade I looked out on a changed world. The rain still descended in sheets. The parade ground was a swamp. Down the *nullah* beside my garden raced a tumbling torrent of brown water flecked with white foam. Our rainy season had set in nearly three months earlier than throughout the greater part of the Peninsula of India. And now began the dullest time of our life in the outpost. In the five months that followed nearly three hundred inches of rain fell in Buxa. Work was at a standstill, save for physical drill in the men's barrack-rooms and lectures to the non-commissioned officers. To walk from my bungalow to the office in the fort every day was almost an adventure. Wearing long rubber boots to the knee and wrapped in a mackintosh I paddled across the swampy parade ground in drenching rain, and even in the short distance was wet through. And at night I struggled up the hill to dinner in the Mess along the steep road which was converted into a mountain torrent a foot deep, fearing at every step to find some snake, washed out of its hole in the ground, clinging affectionately round my legs to stop its downward career. All night long and most of the day storms swept down on us; and thunder growled and grumbled among the hills. Dwellers in temperate lands can form no conception of the awful grandeur of a tropical tempest, the fury of the wind, the vivid lightning that spatters the sky and runs in chains and linked patterns across its darkness, the awful sound of the crashing thunder that seems to shake the world. But, terrifying at first, they became actually wearisome from their frequency. When a thunderstorm has raged about one's house for eighteen hours, circling round the hills and returning again and again, one gets simply bored with it—there is no other expression to describe the feeling.

It was wonderful to see the revivifying effect of the rain on the parched ground. One could almost watch the grass grow. Where a few days before was only bare earth, now the herbage stood feet high. All traces of the devastating fires were washed away. On the hill-sides, fertilised by the ashes, the undergrowth sprang up more luxuriantly than ever. But it brought with it the greatest curse of the rainy season in the jungle. Every twig, every leaf, every blade of grass, harboured leeches, thin threads of black and yellow which waved one end in the air and seemed to scent an approaching prey. Walk over the grass, brush past the bushes, and a dozen of these pests fastened on you. Through the lace-holes of one's boots, between the folds of putties, down one's collar they insinuated themselves unnoticed; and you did not feel them until, bloated with blood and swollen to an enormous size, they were perceptible to the touch under the clothing. After a walk one was obliged, on returning to the bungalow, to undress and was sure to find several leeches fastened to one's body. I saw one sepoy with a leech firmly fixed in his nostril. Another time I noticed a man's shirt sleeve stained with blood from elbow to wrist, and, on examining the arm, discovered that, unknown to the sepoy, two leeches were fastened on it and had punctured veins.

Sometimes hailstorms alternated with the rain. I

had heard stories of the size of the hailstones in the Duars. Planters had assured me that animals were often killed and the corrugated iron roofs of the factories perforated by them. I declined to credit these assertions; although in other parts of India I have seen hailstones an inch in diameter. But one night in Buxa, while we were at dinner, a hail-storm rattled on the roof of the bungalow; and I really believe that if this had not been made of thick sheets of iron it would have been drilled through. My orderly picked up one hailstone outside and brought it in to us. We passed it from hand to hand; and then it occurred to me to measure it. It was a rectangular block of clear ice containing as a core a round, whitish hailstone of the usual size and shape; and, using the tape and compass, we found it was two and a quarter inches long, one and a half broad, and one inch thick. And this after it had lain for a few minutes on the ground and had been handled by several persons. Next day a native survey party, under the command of a European, arrived in Buxa on its way to inspect the boundary marks along the Bhutan frontier, as these are frequently moved back into our territory by the wily Bhutanese. The Englishman in charge told me that he had been caught by the fringe of this storm on the previous evening. He had only a few yards to run for shelter but put up his umbrella as he did so. It was drilled through by the hailstones as if they had been bullets. I heard afterwards of several animals killed in the hills by this storm.

Shut up in our small Station by the relentless rain the days passed wearily during the long wet months. Often in the afternoon the rain ceased for a couple of hours; and we were able to get out for a little exercise. So steep were the slopes, so rocky the soil, that in half an hour after the cessation of the downpour the road and the parade ground were comparatively dry. But we could not wander off them without the risk of being attacked by scores of leeches.

In July came a break of nearly a week. I took advantage of it to descend into the forest. Wonderful was the transformation there! No longer could I complain that there was no shelter for game. The undergrowth was higher and denser than ever. Save for an occasional blackened tree-trunk, half hidden in the greenery, there was no trace of the devastation wrought by the fires. The ashes had only served to fertilise the ground, and the vegetation pushed more vigorously than ever. Orchids again clothed the boughs. And, sporting in the unusual sunshine, myriads of gorgeous tropical butterflies, scarlet and black, peacock-green, pale blue, yellow, all the colours imaginable, rose up in clouds before my elephant. The creepers again swinging from stem to stem writhed and twisted in fantastic confusion. The rivers were in flood and rolled their masses of brown, foam-flecked water to the south.

Despite the awful storms I saw no trace in the forest or the hills of damage wrought by lightning. When we arrived in Buxa I had thought the buildings well protected, as conductors ran down every chimney in bungalow and barrack. But just before the Rains an engineer of the Public Works Department had visited us to inspect them. To my alarm he informed me that none of them were properly insulated, and that so far from being a safeguard, they were a positive danger. Then, having cheered me by saying that possibly in a year or two his Department would put them to rights, he left. So when the thunderstorms broke over us I used to wonder in pained resignation which building would be the first struck. But we weathered them all successfully. Probably the hills around saved us by attracting the electric fluid.

Our brief glimpse of fine weather was soon gone. Then the clouds rolled up from the sea before the breath of the south-west Monsoons, the storms again assailed us, and the floodgates of the sky were opened once more. In England one complains of the dullness of a wet summer. Think of five months' incessant rain in a small Station that never boasted more than three European inhabitants, cut off from the world and thrown entirely on their own resources! Smith had long since left us and we had no doctor. In the middle of the Rains Creagh was ordered off to command the Trade Agent's escort in Gyantse in Tibet; and I was left the only white man in Buxa. Life was not gay. Even the relief of work was denied us; and sport was impossible, for malaria and blackwater fever hold possession of the jungles during the Monsoon. And even when the Rains moderated in September, we were not allowed to shoot until the close season ended in October. The wet season is not really over in India until near the beginning of November; and in Buxa we sometimes had rain in that month and in December.

But still we managed to survive the trial by fire and by water; and the winter found us as ready for work and sport as ever.

CHAPTER XI

IN THE PALACE OF THE MAHARAJAH

The Durbar—Outside the palace—The State elephants—The soldiery—The Durbar Hall—Officials and gentry of the State—The throne—Queen Victoria's banner—The hidden ladies—*Purdah nashin*—Arrival of the *Dewan*—The Maharajah's entry—The Sons' Salute—A chivalrous Indian custom —*Nuzzurs*—The Dewan's task—The Maharani—An Indian reformer—*Bramo Samaj*—Pretty princesses—An informal banquet—The *nautch*—A moonlight ride—The Maharajah—A soldier and a sportsman—Cooch Behar—The palace—A dinner-party—The heir's birthday celebrations—Schoolboys' sports—Indian amateur theatricals—An evening in the palace—A panther-drive—Exciting sport—Death of the panther—Partridge shooting on elephants—A stray rhinoceros —Prince Jit's luck—Friendly intercourse between Indians and Englishmen—An unjust complaint.

THE long arcaded front of the Palace of Cooch Behar gleamed in the glow of torches held by hundreds of white-clad natives. From the broad steps of the entrance to the lofty dome above it was outlined with lamps flickering in the night breeze. Before the great portals were ranged two lines of elephants with the State silver howdahs and trappings of heavily embroidered cloth of gold. Their broad faces streaked with white paint in quaint designs, their tusks tipped with brass, the great beasts looked like legendary monsters in the ruddy torchlight as they stood swinging their trunks, flapping their ears, and shifting restlessly from foot to foot. Up the lane between them came carriages and palankeens bearing the officials and nobles of the State to do homage to their Maharajah, who this night held his annual Durbar. The flight of broad steps in front of the great doorway was crowded with swordsmen and spearmen; while on the ground below were the uniformed State Band under a European conductor, and a Guard of Honour of the red-coated Cooch Behar Infantry with muzzle-loading muskets.

The large circular Durbar Hall running up to the high domed roof and surrounded by a balustraded gallery seemed set for a stage scene. The floor was covered with the seated forms of officials and gentry clothed in white and wearing their jewels. On a dais under a golden canopy stood an empty gilt throne, one arm fashioned into the shape of an elephant, the other a tiger. Beside it was a large banner, the gift of the late Queen Victoria, heavily embroidered in gold with the same animals, which are the armorial bearings of the State. Behind the throne stood a number of swordsmen and halberdiers. One portion of the gallery was shrouded by latticed screens, from behind which came the rustle of draperies and the murmur of female voices; for they hid Her Highness the Maharani, her daughters, and the ladies of Cooch Behar—*purdah nashin*, that is, "hidden behind the veil" and never to reveal their faces to any men but their near kin. In another part of the gallery were a few British officers and civilians gazing with interest on the brilliant spectacle below. Through the great entrance could be seen the crowd outside, the soldiery and the lines of restlessly swaying elephants. Through them up the broad roadway came a palankeen borne on the shoulders of coolies and surrounded by torch-bearers and swordsmen. A cheer went up from the crowd; and all inside the hall rose as the palankeen stopped, and from it emerged a frail old man, clothed in white and adorned with splendid jewels which flashed in the ruddy glow of the torches and the clearer light of the electric lamps. It was the *Dewan*, the Prime Minister of the State. As he entered the Durbar Hall the mass of white-robed officials swayed like a field of ripe grain in the wind, as all present bowed to him. He took his place before the empty throne.

Then the assemblage bent lower and a murmured acclamation went up from all as their Maharajah entered, followed by a procession of Indian aides-de-camp in white uniforms with gold aigulettes, white spiked helmets and trailing swords, similar to the summer dress of British officers in India. His Highness was clothed in a beautiful native garb of pale blue, with a *puggri*, or turban, of the same delicate hue with a diamond-studded aigrette. From the broad gold belt around his waist hung a jewelled scimitar. His breast glittered with orders and war medals, for he had seen active service with the British Army. His jewels flashed in coloured fire in the lamps.

With slow and stately step he passed through the great chamber and seated himself on the golden throne; while silver trumpets pealed a welcome and the State Band played the National Anthem of Cooch Behar. Then came a silence and an expectant pause; and there entered four gallant young figures, the Maharajah's sons. Foremost came the heir, Prince Rajendra Narayen, in the scarlet tunic of the Westminster Dragoons, and his brother, Prince

Jitendra, in the beautiful white, blue and gold uniform of the Imperial Cadet Corps. Then followed Prince Victor, a godson of the late Queen Victoria, in the same magnificent dress, and the youngest son, Prince Hitendra, in a fine Indian costume of cloth of gold. The four young men halted and fronted their royal father. Then the heir apparent walked forward to the steps of the throne and held out his sheathed sword horizontally before him in the splendid Indian salute which means "I place my life and my sword in your hand." His Highness bent forward and touched the hilt, the emblematic sign meaning "I accept the gift and give you back your life." Prince Rajendra let fall the sword to his side, brought his hand to his helmet in military salute and took his place on the dais beside his father. Each of the other sons came forward in turn, did homage likewise; and then the four stood two and two on each side of the throne.

Never have I looked on a more picturesque ceremonial or magnificent spectacle than this scene of the Durbar. It seemed too splendid, too glowing with colour, to be real life. The brilliantly lit chamber, the flashing of jewels and gold, the dense throng of white-clad officials, the glittering weapons of the armed attendants; and then the four richly apparelled princes pledging their fealty to their Sovereign and Sire in the historic Oriental custom that has come down to us through the storied ages of Indian chivalry. I could hardly realise that this gorgeous pageant was not some magnificent stage scene.

The staff officers now came forward and offered their swords. Then the *Dewan*, followed by the swarms of officials and nobles, advanced one by one to the steps of the throne and presented their *muzzurs*, the Indian offering of gold or silver coins, which His Highness "touched and remitted," as the quaint phrase runs. Each, after salaaming profoundly before the throne, retired backwards and brought his gift to an official, who counted the amount of the offering, for next day the donor would be dowered with a present of equal amount, a profitable transaction as his own was returned to him.

An attendant brought forward a splendid embossed gold hookah two feet high and placed it before the throne. The long snake-like gold tube and mouthpiece were handed to the Maharajah, who smoked during the remainder of the proceedings. For now a quaint ceremony began. The accounts of the various parts and departments of the State were brought solemnly to the *Dewan*, who sat on the floor surrounded by piles of account-books, which he examined. When he had concluded his lengthy task the Durbar came to an end. The assemblage rose and bowed low as the Maharajah, attended by his sons and his aides-de-camp, passed in procession out of the hall.

Half an hour later the few military and civilian guests assembled in the beautiful State drawing-room, where we were joined by the Maharani and her two pretty daughters attired in exceedingly artistic native costumes and wearing delicately tinted *saris* draped most becomingly over their heads. Her Highness looked almost as youthful and lovely as on the day when the Maharajah first saw her and lost his heart to her. For, unlike most Indian marriages, theirs was a true love-match. She was a daughter of the famous religious reformer, Mr Sen, the founder of the *Bramo Samaj* faith, which substitutes for the mythology and the seventy thousand deities of the Hindu worship, a purer belief in one God. The Maharani has the fair complexion of high-class Brahmin ladies, and an individuality and a charm of her own that makes her hosts of friends. The pretty young princesses seemed more to be masquerading in an attractive fancy dress than wearing their national costume; for they had been brought up by English governesses and educated in England, had danced through the ball-rooms of London and Calcutta in the smartest Parisian toilettes, and were as much at home in the Park or at a gala night at the Opera as in their own country.

Owing to the Durbar, dinner was served at a late hour in the State dining-room, a spacious apartment in white and gold. At one end hung full-length portraits of our host and hostess in the gorgeous robes they wore at the Diamond Jubilee of Queen Victoria in the celebrations in London. Table and sideboard shone with massive silver cups won at race-meetings and shows by the horses of the Cooch Behar stable. Native servants in scarlet and gold waited on the guests; but with all the luxury of a banquet served on silver there was no formality about the meal. The Maharajah and his sons had changed their magnificent attire for a comfortable native dress; and listening to their conversation in colloquial English on polo, shooting, and London theatrical gossip it was hard to realise that an hour before they had been playing their picturesque parts in such a stately Oriental pageant. All the family generally used English as their speech. The boys had been educated at Eton; and Victor, in addition, had done a course at an American University.

After dinner we adjourned to the Durbar Hall again to witness from the galleries a *nautch*; and real Indian dancing is a spectacle of which the European soon has his fill. And somewhere about three o'clock in the morning, fatigued with the monotonous chant and the lazily moving fat figures of the *nautch* girls, overpowered by the heated atmosphere heavy with scent, I gladly hailed the suggestion of Prince Rajendra to escape from it all and go for a mad rush in his motor-car through the surrounding country in the brilliant moonlight. His brothers followed us in their cars. *Nautches* and motor-cars, the brilliant spectacle of the Durbar and these Eton-bred Indian Princes; what a fantastic medley it all seemed! And the swift sweep through the park in the cool morning air back to an Indian palace and a guest-chamber fitted like the best bedroom in a European *hôtel de luxe*. But when next day I left, in response to an urgent message bidding me come to shoot a tiger near Buxa, even the prospect of the sport scarcely reconciled me to quitting the lavish hospitality of my hosts.

The Maharajah of that day is unfortunately no longer alive. The descendant of a hill race, he had all the fighting spirit of his ancestors who left their mountains to carve out a kingdom for themselves among the unwarlike dwellers of the Bengal plains. He took part in the Tirah Campaign with our troops, and held the rank of colonel in our Indian Cavalry. A sportsman, he was regarded throughout India, that land of sportsmen, as one of the best authorities in the world on big-game shooting. He had not his equal in the art of managing a beat with elephants; and it was a marvellous sight to see him working a long line of them through thick jungle with the skill of a M.F.H. with his hounds in covert. He was a splendid horseman. Excelling in all games, he brought up his sons in the love of sport and athletics and made them fine polo players, first-class cricketers and footballers and crack shots. But, in addition, he was an extremely clever and well-read man and a most interesting talker. He had been everywhere, seen everything, and knew most of the interesting personalities of the day. His hospitality was proverbial. In his residences in Calcutta and Darjeeling, in his Palace of Cooch Behar, he kept open house. His courtesy and charm of manner endeared him to all who knew him.

On my first visit to Cooch Behar in response to an invitation of His Highness, Creagh and I were met at the railway station by Captain Denham White, then temporarily acting civil surgeon of the State. He drove us through the town which, though small, is well planned. The streets are broad, well laid, and shaded with trees. In the centre of it lies a large square tank or pond surrounded by roads bordered by public and official buildings. Here afterwards I often saw the invalid permanent civil surgeon, for whom Captain White was then acting, sitting in a chair on the bank fishing, with a table beside him on which his servant laid his tea. And undisturbed by the endless procession of bullock carts, coolies, and natives of all ages, the old doctor sat and cast his line, hooking some extraordinary large fish at times.

The poorer houses of the town were built on posts

with bamboo walls and thatched roofs, similar to the Filipino dwellings in Manila, cool and airy and far healthier than the awful abodes of the lower classes in an English city. Cooch Behar could boast a fine college, a good civil hospital and quite a comfortable prison. I visited it once and found the thieves, highway robbers, and murderers, anything but miserable despite their chains, making soda water, grinding corn, cultivating vegetables or eating better and more plentiful meals than they had ever got in their own homes.

Beyond the town we drove through the open tree-shaded park to the palace, a long two-storied building with arcaded verandas above and below. It was shaped like a T laid on its side; and at the junction of the two strokes was the portico leading to a large hall, off which opened the great Durbar room surmounted by its lofty white dome. On the left of the entrance, as one approached, were, on both stories, the long series of guest-chambers. On the right along the lower veranda was the State dining-room. Off the entrance hall to the right a broad staircase led to the upper story. Its walls were crowded with trophies of sport which had fallen to the Maharajah's rifle all over the world. Heads of bison, Indian and Cape buffaloes, moose, wapiti, *sambhur*, cheetal and roe deer from Germany—relics of many lands. To the right lay the State drawing-room and the splendidly appointed billiard-room carpeted with the skins of tigers. It occupied the front end of the short stroke of the T, and so from its windows and doors gave a fine view over the park on three sides, which made it a popular apartment for the afternoon tea rendezvous with the ladies of the family and their European guests. Behind, lay the private apartments of His Highness, the Maharani and her daughters, from the flat roofs above which, reached by a small staircase, one could see for many miles over the flat country beyond the English-like park. From here the Maharani could look down unseen, for in deference to the customs of her husband's subjects she and her daughters were *purdah* in the State outside the palace, and watch her sons playing football with the Cooch Behar team in the annual association tournament for a cup given by His Highness. The ground was situated in the park close under the walls of the building.

At the time of this visit the Maharajah was the only member of the family in Cooch Behar. He had issued invitations to a dinner-party in our honour that evening, at which we met his staff and some of the principal gentlemen of his State. He joined us at dinner himself; for, being a follower of the *Bramo Samaj* faith, he had no religious prejudices that prevented him from eating with Europeans. I have hunted, shot, played polo and pigsticked with Hindu Princes who yet could not sit down at the same table with me when I dined at their palaces. At most they entered the room when dinner was over and filled a glass of wine to drink our Sovereign's health. But this meal in Cooch Behar was enlivened for me by the interesting conversation of my host, whom I was meeting for the first time. The State Band played outside the dining-room. After dinner we adjourned to the billiard-room or made up a bridge table. The Maharajah was practically the first Indian Prince to adopt English customs and was a frequent visitor to England, where he and his consort were great favourites of the late Queen Victoria. For her and the then reigning monarch King Edward VII. he entertained the warmest personal regard and admiration; and his loyalty to the British rule was founded on his sincere conviction of the benefits it conferred on India. I remember that during dinner that night he said to me:

"If ever, during my lifetime, the British quitted India, my departure would precede theirs; for this would be no country to live in then. Chaos, bloodshed and confusion would be its lot."

I drew him out on the subject of big-game shooting, of which few men living knew more, and listened with interest to his tales of *shikar*. Then the conversation ranged to art, the theatre, war, and politics; and on each he could speak entertainingly. He was deeply interested in developing the resources of his State and was anxious to introduce scientific methods among his farmers. Among other plans he was anxious to improve the quality of the native tobacco grown largely in the State, and had got for the purpose the best species of American and Turkish plants. His third son Victor, after finishing his course at an American University, was sent to Cuba to inspect the plantations and factories, and study the methods in use there.

On the following day my subaltern and I were obliged to set our faces towards Buxa again; and it seemed like turning our backs on civilisation when we left the luxury of Cooch Behar Palace behind us and wended our way to our solitary little Station in the hills.

On another occasion I was present for the celebrations of the birthday of the eldest son, Prince

Rajendra, best known to his friends as "Raji," who is now the Maharajah.* In the palace park the annual sports of the Cooch Behar Boys' School were held. To a European new to India the sight of the native youngsters competing in sprint, hurdle and long-distance races and doing high and broad jumps like their contemporaries in England would have seemed strange. But wherever the Briton goes he takes his sports and games with him and imbues the race he finds himself among with his own love of them. So Chinese lads play cricket and football; and swarthy-bearded Indian sepoys rush round the obstacle course in their regimental sports or play side by side with their white officers on the hockey ground.

Among the marquees in the enclosure for the spectators who were watching the schoolboys' competitions was one which was shrouded by *chikks*, or bamboo latticed blinds which enabled the occupants to see all that was passing outside and remain invisible themselves. It was intended for the use of the Maharani and her daughters, who, as I have said, were *purdah* in their own State in deference to the prejudices of the Cooch Beharis. This custom among the Hindus sprang up at the time of the Mohammedan invasions, partly from imitation of their conquerors, but probably more to shield their women from the licentious gaze of the victorious Mussulmans, who would have had small scruple in seizing any female whose beauty attracted them.

The Maharani and the young princesses emerged heavily veiled from the palace and entered a motor-car which was shrouded in white linen in such a way

* He died in A.D. 1913, and was succeeded by his brother, Prince Jitendra.

as to hide them from sight. It took them through the park to the sports enclosure, where servants held up white sheets to form a lane through which the ladies could pass unseen, to the seclusion of their marquee.

Among the celebrations in honour of the day—how English customs are seizing in the East!—was an amateur theatrical performance by the Young Men's Club of Cooch Behar. After dinner, Prince Raji motored me into the town to see it. The play was in Bengali, the plot being an episode in the history of the State several hundred years ago and containing much bloodshed and tragedy. It was excellently well staged and the acting was capital. Being ignorant of the language I was dependent on my companion's explanations. Like all Oriental plays it was of inordinate length; and having witnessed six or seven acts I was quite ready to depart without waiting for the end when my friend suggested it.

Once when staying at the palace I was fortunate in having an opportunity of witnessing the Maharajah's skill in handling a line of elephants in a beat. The previous night at dinner he told us that he had received information of a "kill" by a panther near a village five miles away, and that he had given orders for his elephants to be ready on the spot next morning. The male guests present hailed the news with joy. We happened to be a curiously assorted party in race and in costume round the table that night. The Maharajah and his family wore Indian dress, as they usually did in the palace; though elsewhere they invariably wore European attire. Two Sikh nobles, officers of the Maharajah of Patiala's Bodyguard, were in correct evening clothes but wore white *puggris* round their heads, which concealed their long hair, which the Sikh is forbidden by his religion to cut. They were tall, handsome men with the good features of their race. As they spoke no English, we were obliged to converse with them in Urdu. The Maharani was not well acquainted with that language and so was forced to appeal to me to interpret for her several times. The Indian aide-de-camp of His Highness wore white mess dress; while a major in a British regiment and I were in the conventional black and white.

After dinner we joined the ladies in the beautiful yellow and gold State drawing-room. We found one of the pretty young princesses seated at the piano, making a delightful picture in the charming Indian dress, the gold-bordered *sari* draped becomingly over her dark hair, her tiny bare feet pressing the pedals as she played—how incongruous it seemed!—a selection from a musical comedy; and, attracted by the melody of the song then the rage in London, her brothers came in from the billiard-room to join in the chorus.

Next morning my orderly woke me at 4-30 a.m. I hurriedly drank my tea and got into shooting kit; for we were to start at five o'clock. When I came out of my room on to the lower veranda I found some of our party already assembled by the great entrance. The Maharajah was seated in his motor-car with his youngest daughter, Princess Sudhira, beside him. To my surprise she was attired in a very smartly cut coat and skirt and wore a sun helmet; for, as she promptly informed me, she did not consider herself old enough—she was only sixteen—to be bothered by the restrictions of *purdah* when it did not suit her. Her father shook his head and smiled at the pretty rebel against Hindu customs.

Major F—— and I went with them in their car; while the Sikh officers followed in another. We sped rapidly through the park and out along rough country roads, by thatched cottages and grass huts, groves of mango trees and dense thickets of bamboo. By the village wells dark-eyed women, poising their water jars on their heads turned to stare at us as we passed in a cloud of dust. From the hamlets tiny naked children rushed out to gaze at the *shaitan ki gharri*—the "devil's car." We soon reached the spot where the elephants were waiting for us beside the road. On the backs of the splendid tuskers intended for the shooters were howdahs fitted with gun rests and seats. Our elephants knelt down for us to clamber up. The Maharajah, with the true spirit of hospitality, left the sport to his guests and went off to take charge of the line of beaters. Princess Sudhira, armed with a camera, shared his howdah. The shooting elephants moved across the fields to a *nullah* filled with small trees and scrub jungle, in which the panther was reported to be hiding, and took up places in or on either bank of it. The beaters made a long circuit and formed line across the *nullah*. Then at a signal from the Maharajah they advanced towards us. As the ground on either side consisted of open, ploughed fields devoid of cover the panther would be forced to come along the ravine to the guns. The loud cries of the *mahouts*, the trumpeting of the elephants, the crashing of trampled jungle and the rending of boughs torn from the trees made a pandemonium of noise. I was posted high up on a bank and had a good general view of the scene. One of the Sikh nobles suddenly raised his rifle and fired; and I saw the lithe form of the panther for a few seconds as it dashed past his elephant and bounded like a great cat along the *nullah*. I caught an occasional glimpse of it between the patches of jungle but could not succeed in getting a shot. The Sikh's bullet had wounded it; but for the time it had succeeded in making its escape.

The Maharajah came up and rearranged the beat. Our howdah elephants were sent along the banks; and we took up fresh positions farther on. Again the line of beaters bore down on us. The panther clung obstinately to the cover, not moving until the beaters were almost on it. Then it slunk cautiously towards the guns and gave the other Sikh officer a chance to wound it again. It turned and dashed against the line of beaters, recoiling almost from under the elephants' feet. For the first time I got a clear view of it but dared not fire lest I should hit anyone in the line. The elephants trumpeted shrilly; and while some tried to charge it and impale it on their tusks, others stampeded. All was confusion; but the Maharajah's voice rang loud above the uproar and made the excited *mahouts* keep their animals in the alignment. The panther, baffled in his attempt to break through, turned again and charged towards us. I lost sight of it in the scrub; but both Sikhs fired, and I saw it spring up the bank towards Major F—— who stopped it with a bullet. I urged my *mahout* forward and came on it rolling on the ground howling in agony and tearing up the earth with sharp claws. It was surrounded by the elephants of the other sportsmen and of the Maharajah. Princess

Sudhira calmly leant over the front of her howdah and snapshotted it as it sprang up and tried to charge, only to be bowled over by a final shot. With a last spasm the beautiful animal sank on the ground and lay still, its yellow and black skin shining in the brilliant sunlight. Several *mahouts* climbed down and approached the body cautiously, while we covered it with our rifles. But it was dead at last; and they lifted it on to the pad of one of the "beater" elephants.

Then, exchanging our weapons for shot-guns we moved off in a long line over the fields in search of partridges. Birds were plentiful. Covey after covey flashed up from the grass under the elephants' feet. A scattered fire opened along the line and the partridges dropped in crumpled balls of feathers. How different it seemed from walking them up over the stubble in the brisk air of an autumn morning in distant England! The Maharajah was shooting now and we soon secured a good bag. We reached the road, found the motor-cars waiting for us, and were whirled back to the palace. Panther and partridges before breakfast—what an attractive programme that would be for a shooting-party in an English country-house!

Though formerly the haunt of every species of big game, Cooch Behar has been so opened up for cultivation that it no longer affords cover for the larger animals of the chase. But in recent years the Maharajah's second son, Jitendra, had an unexpected bit of good fortune in *shikar*. His father was absent in Assam organising a big shoot, and had taken with him all his elephants except one. "Jit," then little more than a schoolboy, was the only member of the family at the palace and was very disgusted at being considered too young to be taken on the shoot. But the Fates were good to him. One day an excited peasant repaired to the palace with the information that a rhinoceros had appeared in a village not five miles from the town. Jit was incredulous. Such a thing seemed impossible; for a rhino had not been seen in Cooch Behar State for many years. But the man stuck to his story. So the boy sent the solitary elephant out to the spot, mounted his bicycle and rode to the village. Here he found a crowd of peasants surrounding, at a respectful distance, a small clump of bamboos in the middle of a large bare field in which several cows were grazing. It seemed impossible that a rhinoceros, which in India always inhabits dense jungle, could have come into such open country. But the villagers declared the animal was there in the bamboos. Jit, still half incredulous, mounted his elephant. Hardly had he done so when a large rhinoceros burst out from the tiny patch of cover, and, apparently objecting to the presence of the cows, charged furiously at them. Up went their tails and off went the cows. Round and round the field they raced, the young heifers leaping and frisking like black buck, while the rhino lumbered heavily after them. The villagers scattered and fled. The scene was so comical that Jit, standing like a circus-master in the centre of the ring, could hardly stop laughing long enough to lift his rifle and take aim. At last he fired; and the rhinoceros checked, stumbled forward a few paces and collapsed in an inert mass on the ground. Then the boy, fearful lest his father might resent his having appropriated the best bit of sport that the State had afforded for years, got on his bicycle and sped home to write a hurried letter of explanation and apology, which had the effect of the proverbial "soft answer."

The late Maharajah of Cooch Behar,* as I have said, was practically the first Indian Prince to adopt English customs, and, with his family, mixed freely in European society. By doing so he helped greatly the cause of friendly intercourse between the two races and did much to break down the great barrier between Briton and Indian. But, be it remembered, that barrier is not of the white man's raising. Educated Indians when in England, complain bitterly to sympathising audiences that in their own land they are not admitted freely into Anglo-Indian society. And the cry is taken up parrot-like and echoed in the British Isles by people absolutely ignorant of Indian conditions. The educated native, fresh from the boarding-houses of Bayswater, claims that he has a right to be introduced to a white man's house, to his wife and daughters. But he would hardly let a European see the face of *his* wife or permit him to enter anywhere but the fringe of his domicile. He has all the Oriental's contempt for women, and yet demands to be freely admitted to the society of English ladies, for whom in his heart he has no respect. And we who live in the land know it. But until he emancipates his own womenkind he cannot reasonably expect to be allowed a familiar footing in an Englishman's home.

* He died in 1911; and his eldest son and successor, Rajendra, died in 1913. Prince Jitendra is now Maharajah.

CHAPTER XII

A MILITARY TRAGEDY

In the Mess—A gloomy conversation—Murder in the army—A gallant officer—Running amuck on a rifle-range—"Was that a shot?"—The alarm—The native officer's report—The "fall in"—A dying man—A search round the fort—A narrow escape—The flight—Search parties—The inquiry into the crime—A fifty miles' cordon—An unexpected visit—Havildar Ranjit Singh on the trail—A night march through the forest—A fearsome ride—The lost detachment—An early start—The ferry—The prisoner—A well-planned capture—The prisoner's story—The march to Hathipota—Return to the fort—A well-guarded captive—A weary wait—A journey to Calcutta—The escort—Excitement among the passengers on the steamer—American globe-trotters—the court martial—A callous criminal—Appeal to the Viceroy—Sentence of death—The execution.

A JANUARY night in Buxa. The last bugle call, "lights out," had sounded in the fort at a quarter-past ten o'clock, and the silence of the mountains hung over the little Station. In the Mess, Balderston and I drew our chairs closer to the cheery wood fire, for the weather was bitterly cold. The glass doors leading on to the veranda were closed. The servants had retired for the night and we were alone, for our Irish doctor was absent on leave. I cannot remember what gave our conversation so gloomy a turn, but the talk ran on cases of murder in the army.

Where men trained to the use of arms and with

weapons within reach are found, there is always the danger of this crime, due to sudden anger or long-smouldering resentment; and no army in the world is free from it. And when a man has committed one murder, too often he is liable to "see red" and run amuck, killing until he is killed himself. Consequently his apprehension is fraught with much danger. Though I have rarely known a case occur in an Indian regiment in which a British officer has been the first victim, yet many have fallen in leading attempts to seize an assassin. At night the sound of a shot in barracks sends a thrill through all who hear it; for it generally means that some grim tragedy has been accomplished. And it may only usher in a series of crimes and a desperate search for an armed assassin in the darkness where death is lurking; not a soldier's glorious ending on the battlefield, but a pitiful fate at the hand of a comrade.

I had just related to my companion a happening which I had witnessed some years before when, at a large rifle meeting and in the presence of hundreds of men, a sepoy ran amuck and shot down a native officer and a havildar or sergeant. A young British subaltern standing close by rushed at him unarmed. The murderer cried:

"Do not come on, Sahib, I do not want to harm you."

But the officer still advanced. The sepoy, to frighten him, sent a bullet close to him, then, failing to stop him, fired again and shot him through the heart. Then, as we around were closing in on him, the assassin placed the muzzle of his rifle to his head and blew his own brains out, rather than be taken alive.

Scarcely had I recounted this incident when I thought I heard the sound of a shot coming from the direction of the fort. I sprang from my chair and ran out on to the veranda. The night was perfectly still. I listened for a few minutes.

"What is the matter, major?" cried Balderston from the mess-room.

"Did you not hear a shot?" I asked.

"No," he replied.

I looked at my watch. It was a quarter-past eleven o'clock. Just then from the parade ground came the short, harsh bark of a *khakur*. It was like the noise I had heard; for I had noticed that, instead of the sharp, clear ring of a rifle-shot, the sound had been a long-drawn-out one. So, laughing at what seemed my nervous fear, I went in again and closed the door. But before I could sit down a bugle rang out loudly in the fort. It was sounding the "Alarm"; and it was followed by loud shouts.

"Good God, Balderston, there has been a murder," I cried. "That *was* a shot I heard. Get your revolver, turn out your orderly with his rifle, and follow me to the fort."

I sprang down the steps into the garden and raced down the steep road. Across it lay a broad stream of light from the window of my bungalow; and as I ran through it I thought that if anyone was lying in wait for me with murderous intent, here was the place for him. As I neared the parade ground I vaguely made out in the darkness two figures approaching me. I called out in Hindustani:

"Who is there?"

No answer came. I shouted again but got no

reply. This was suspicious; but as I was unarmed the only thing to do was to close with them. I ran up to them and found them to be two sepoys with rifles. To my relief they said:

"We are men of the guard sent by the subhedar-major to you, Sahib. Someone has fired a shot inside the fort."

I ran past them across the parade ground and at the gate was met by my senior native officer who stopped me and said in a low tone:

"Sahib, Colour-Havildar Shaikh Bakur has been shot in his bed. The sentry on the magazine, a young Mussulman named Farid Khan, has disappeared with his rifle."

The news stunned me. Shaikh Bakur was one of my best non-commissioned officers. And the murderer was still at large. The sentry's absence from his post pointed to his being the assassin. In that case he had still nine rounds of ball ammunition, and, if he wished to run amuck, held as many lives in his hand. I eagerly questioned the subhedar-major; but he could tell me no more.

The sepoys were falling in in front of the quarter guard and the company orderlies were calling over the rolls by the light of lanterns to see if any of the men were missing. I ordered them to extinguish the lamps, which only served to give a target to the invisible assassin, and bade the section commanders check their sections by memory. The sound of my voice stilled the confusion; and only the low muttering of the havildars and equally low responses of the sepoys were heard. Suddenly from a barrack-room close by rang out shrieks and wailing groans.

"What is that noise, subhedar-major?" I asked.

"It is Shaikh Bakur, Sahib. He is not dead and is crying out in his pain."

As at that moment Balderston arrived I ordered him to examine the rifles of all in the detachment and see if a shot had been fired from any of them. Then I went to the room from which the cries proceeded. The high-roofed, stone-paved chamber was lighted only by a small lantern that cast weird shadows on the ceiling and showed a group of men standing around a bed at the far end. On it the wounded man was writhing in agony, trying with frenzied strength to hurl himself on to the floor; and it required the united efforts of two men to hold him on the cot. He was a dreadful sight. From a bullet hole in his chest the blood welled out at every motion of the body. His face was wet with sweat, the lips drawn back showing the white teeth clenched in pain. His staring eyes saw nothing; and he was delirious. Again and again his awful shrieks rang out through the lofty room and then subsided into meaningless mutterings. In the group by the bed stood an old native hospital assistant, the very inefficient substitute for our absent doctor. He was weeping copiously and seemed utterly helpless. I questioned him about the wound.

"Sir, he has been shot through the body; and the bullet has come out through the chest," he sobbed.

"Have you—can you do anything for him?" I said.

"Sir, it is hopeless. The man will die," he cried through his tears.

I shook him by the shoulders.

"Collect yourself, *babu-ji*," I said sternly. "Try

to do something. Can you not give him an opiate to relieve the pain?"

He wrung his hands in the abandonment of helpless despair.

"Sir, the case is hopeless. The man will die," he repeated mechanically. I could scarcely hear him through the heart-rending shrieks of the dying man, whose handsome bearded face was distorted, and his strong frame convulsed in agony. I turned again to the weeping Brahmin hospital assistant, useless, like so many of his race, in an emergency.

"Oh, for God's sake, drug him into insensibility and let him die in peace," I cried.

But he only sobbed helplessly. As I turned to leave the death-bed, I trod on an empty cartridge-case. I picked it up. It was the one from which the fatal bullet had been fired. It showed that the murderer had reloaded his rifle on the spot and intended that the killing should not end there. I went out into the darkness again. The sepoys were standing silently in the ranks; and the native officers were gathered in a group around Balderston. As the rifle of every man in the detachment, except the missing sentry, had been examined and found clean, it was evident that Farid Khan was the murderer. He had been reprimanded that day, so I learned, by Shaikh Bakur for having his accoutrements dirty on parade. It was a small cause to take a man's life for. But now the first thing to do was to try and find the assassin. This was no easy task on so dark a night, for there was cover for him everywhere in the fort. No one could tell in what corner he might be lurking, ready to shoot down the search-party. Then the means of egress from the fort were easy. The loopholed walls connecting the various barrack-rooms were low; and a man could scale them at any point. As I hurriedly thought over the best means of beginning the hunt, the piteous shrieks of the dying man rang through the silent night and chilled our blood.

I took a couple of armed men with me and commenced to search the empty buildings of the fort. One of the native officers came running to me and called out:

"Sahib, the outer door of my room, which I left open, is now closed and bolted from the inside. Farid Khan must be within."

I went to the room, which was in the same single-storied building as the barrack-room in which the crime had been committed. I tried the door. It was fastened at the bottom. Bidding the sepoys with me load their rifles, I endeavoured to push the door in, sincerely hoping that if I succeeded I would not be received by a bullet. The door resisted, then gave way so suddenly that I fell inside head foremost. I sprang up hurriedly with the uncomfortable feeling that at any moment I might have the murderer's bayonet in me. I groped round the room in the darkness, then lit a match and found the place empty. The door must have swung to in the wind and the bolt fallen down and been caught in the socket. Annoyed at having the scare for nothing I turned to walk out and found myself confronted by the muzzles of my men's rifles, for they could not see who was emerging from the dark interior. Having no desire to be shot by mistake, I quickly let them know who I was. As I came out into the open air, a voice cried:

"Sahib, Sahib! He has escaped. He has left the fort"; and a native follower rushed up breathlessly to say that he had just been passed by a flying figure which had climbed over the back gate.

Calling to my two sepoys to follow me, I ran to this gate and struggled with the stiff bolts. With difficulty we dragged open the heavy iron leaves which grated noisily on their hinges. Outside lay a strip of grass dotted with trees and a few wooden sheds. It ran the length of the back wall but was only forty yards wide, ending on the edge of the precipice which fell sheer for three hundred feet. Down the steep face a zigzag path was cut leading to the hill on which the segregation hospital, burned in the forest fires, had stood. I searched around and inside the sheds and moved cautiously over the grassy shelf, keeping carefully away from the brink of the cliff. I was not carrying a weapon myself; for the night was so dark that the murderer, if he stood motionless, would see us first and could get in the first shot. If he missed I preferred trying to close with him at once, and not engaging in a duel with rifles with him. Should I succeed in grappling with him, the bayonets of my two men would soon end the struggle.

Where the back wall terminated the side walls joined it at right angles; and here our task became doubly dangerous, for they were built almost on the edge of the precipice; and we had to move along in single file, keeping one hand on the wall, for a false step meant a fall on to the rocks far below. I groped cautiously along in the utter darkness, feeling much more afraid of tumbling over the cliffs than I was of the chance of meeting with the murderer.

But, though I did not know it at the time, we had already passed him; for he was standing motionless behind one of the trees near the back wall, watching us as we went by, ready to fire at us if we saw and tried to catch him.

Then, when we had gone by, he stole silently down the zigzag path and climbed the opposite hill, intending to descend on the other side and gain the mountain road leading down to Santrabari.

But when I had completely circled the outer walls I entered the fort by the front gate and at once sent off a party of men under my old Rajput Subhedar, Sohanpal Singh, to go down to Santrabari and hide in the elephant stables. I gave them orders that, if the fugitive came by, they were to cover him with their rifles, call on him to surrender and shoot him down if he attempted to resist. The murderer, crouching on the hill above, heard them passing on the road below him, and turned off in another direction.

Having sent off another party along the mountain-track to Chunabatti, I fell out the detachment and entered the orderly-room to hold an inquiry into the case. The story of the crime was soon told. In the barrack-room there were thirty-three beds, all occupied except the one exactly opposite Shaikh Bakur's. This belonged to the missing sentry, Farid Khan, who was on guard for the night. The men had been awakened by the deafening report of a rifle fired in the room. Although, when they had gone to sleep, the big wall-lanterns had been extinguished and the room was in darkness, there was now a small lamp burning beside Farid Khan's bed. By its light some of the sepoys saw a figure rush out through the open door and heard the clatter of heavy nailed boots on the stone-paved veranda outside. The colour-havildar had shrieked out: "I am shot! I am shot!"

Suddenly the small lamp was extinguished; and the darkness increased the confusion of the room. The men nearest Shaikh Bakur rushed to his bed-side, others called out to him to ask what was the matter; some cried out for the lamps to be lit; and others, not realising what had happened, shouted inquiries. At last a lantern was lighted and re-vealed the unfortunate man writhing in agony on his bed. Meanwhile the sentry on the quarter guard not fifty yards away, hearing the shot and the consequent uproar, awoke the havildar in charge of the guard. He ordered the bugler to sound the "alarm." The guard having fallen in, the *naik* (or corporal) went to the magazine close by and found that the sentry over it, whom he had visited fifteen minutes before, was missing from his post. On the "alarm" being sounded, the sepoys rushed out of their barrack-rooms with their rifles and accoutre-ments and fell in on parade. Still the magazine sentry did not appear, and his absence aroused suspicion. It was remembered that he was a young Mussulman called Farid Khan whom I had checked on parade that morning for carelessness in drill and who had been previously reprimanded by Shaikh Bakur for not having his accoutrements clean.

I discovered that the small lamp, which had been burning when the shot was fired and the murderer ran out of the room, had been put out by a young sepoy who slept in the next cot to Farid Khan's, apparently to help the assassin to escape in the darkness. This sepoy came from the same district as the missing sentry and was his intimate friend. I made him a prisoner.

There was nothing more to be done now until daylight, except to dispatch telegrams to the police and to regimental and brigade headquarters. I sent everyone off to bed and sat alone in the orderly-room by the light of a solitary lamp, planning out measures to capture the murderer. The cries from the barrack-room had ceased; for the poor havildar was dead, and his body had been removed to the hospital. After the recent confusion and bustle the stillness and silence seemed intense. I was haunted by the vision of the murdered man's face and filled with a bitter resentment against his slayer. The odds were greatly in favour of the assassin's escape. In the wild country around us, the broken, jungle-covered hills, the dense forest, a fugitive could hide himself indefinitely, provided only that he could procure food. If he succeeded in making his way to the main railway line the only chance of capturing him lay in his returning to his own country, hundreds of miles away; and I had telegraphed to the police of his village. The knowledge I had acquired of the country about us in shooting and on the march stood me now in good stead. The little railway from Buxa Road would be too dangerous for him; but he might try to make his way on foot to the junction of the main line at Gitaldaha; or a route through the forest led to villages and tea gardens at Kalchini, whence he might eventually reach another railway. But what I feared most was that he might commit suicide somewhere in the mountains or in the jungle and his body be never found, or cross the border to Bhutan, where he would probably be murdered for his rifle. In either case we would always remain ignorant of his fate. Then it would be believed that he had succeeded in effecting his escape. Four or five years before, another murder had been committed in the regiment and the assassin had never been captured. It would be a fatal thing if this murderer also succeeded in avoiding arrest; as it might encourage a repetition of the crime. The hours were interminable. It seemed as if the daylight to help us in our search would never come. My thoughts wandered to the fugitive. I pictured him lying out in the jungle, trembling at every rustle in the undergrowth that might herald the stealthy approach of a savage beast, realising now that his life was forfeit and that henceforth every man's hand was against him. I wondered if in the hours of silent watching in the darkness he had begun to appreciate his deed and its consequences.

At last the wished-for dawn came. I sent out armed patrols in all directions to follow up every track and to occupy every village and hamlet in which the fugitive might try to obtain food. Other parties went by train to Gitaldaha, one to remain there, the rest to go east and west to the junctions of other railways. When these dispositions were complete we had a net, fifty miles wide, around the district. These patrols had orders to take the fugitive dead or alive. I instructed them to shoot him down if he attempted to resist; for I did not want to lose another of my men by his hand.

The day passed wearily. No news came in; and I chafed at the inaction. At noon a sepoy rushed up to my bungalow to tell me that the men of the quarter guard had heard two shots on a wooded hill about half a mile from the fort. I doubled out with an armed party at once and searched the jungle around, without result. To this day I have never found an explanation of these shots, which had been distinctly heard by all the sepoys left in the fort. Night fell without any intelligence reaching me from any of the parties out. The native officers urged us to have a guard placed over the Mess and my bungalow, lest the murderer should be tempted to come back in the dark and shoot me; but I refused, as I wished the men to get all the rest they could in view of the exertions they might be called on to make. I slept little that night; for the memory of the tragedy weighed heavily on me.

Next morning some of the patrols straggled in, exhausted and weary, having found no trace of the fugitive. But in the afternoon Tyson of Hathipota and an officer of the Royal Engineers named Marriott, who had been staying with him in his bungalow, rode into Buxa; and from them I got the first news of the murderer. For on their way from Hathipota they had met one of our search-parties under a havildar, called Ranjit Singh, who told them of the crime and said that he had been informed by villagers at Jainti that a man carrying a rifle had been seen coming out of the jungle early that morning and going east. Shortly afterwards one of Ranjit Singh's patrol arrived and confirmed this. The havildar had sent him back to report to me and tell me that the rest of the party were continuing in pursuit. The news was electrifying. Although the fugitive was going in the opposite direction to where his home lay, yet he was heading towards a river down which he could get by boat to a main railway line. It was imperative to bar his way. I gave orders for a party to start by the first train to Gitaldaha, change to this main line, and proceed to the point where it crossed the river. There they were to detrain and search every boat coming down from the north. A native officer was dispatched on Balderston's pony at once to overtake Ranjit Singh and urge him on the trail. Then I ordered sixty Rajputs, who being Hindus would not be in sympathy with the Mohammedan fugitive, to prepare to start in half an hour and march through the forest to Hathipota, where they were to halt for the night. I determined to take command of this party myself. It was to be spread out into a cordon miles long between the hills and the main railway line. As I had to send telegrams warning the police in the direction in which the murderer was moving and make other arrangements, I sent the party on ahead under a native officer.

Our guests and Balderston volunteered for the pursuit. The latter borrowed a small pony about twelve hands high from a *bunniah*, as he had lent his own to the native officer. Mounting our horses we set off down the steep mountain-road to Santrabari. When we reached the more level ground we galloped the three miles to Buxa Road Station. I expected to overtake my party before we reached this point, but to my surprise found no signs of them. It turned out that they had taken a short cut through the forest.

From the station a narrow track led through the jungle to Jainti. We rode down it in single file.

Night had now fallen, and under the trees the darkness was intense. Marriott was leading and I was immediately behind him; but I could not see even his horse. Our animals stumbled over the fallen trees. Overhanging boughs, invisible to us, nearly swept us from our saddles. A crash and an exclamation from the leader told us that his horse had come to grief. Bruised by the fall, Marriott picked himself up and remounted. And on we blundered in the utter darkness. But there was a greater danger. We were passing through a part of the forest much frequented at night by wild elephants. None of us were armed; and the prospect of meeting with a rogue was not pleasant. Even if it did not attack us it would certainly stampede our horses. And to be bolted with in the thick forest in the dark would be a dangerous experience. Imagination peopled the black jungle with lurking tigers ready to spring out on us; and every sound seemed to herald the approach of a wild elephant. A deer crashing through the undergrowth would have been sufficient to scare our horses. To make matters worse Balderston's tiny pony could not keep up with us. Every time it lagged behind and its rider failed to answer our shouts, we were obliged to halt and wait for them. I shall not readily forget the terrors of that night ride. We were confronted by the constant risk of a fall over a prostrate tree-trunk or of being knocked out of the saddle by a low branch, and by the likely chance of encountering some dangerous wild beast. To keep up our spirits and in the hope of scaring off the elephants, tigers and bears by the far from melodious sounds, we sang choruses loudly in rather shaky voices. The miles through the forest seemed interminable; and I felt that I would sooner face a dozen armed murderers than ride them again.

At last we emerged on the bank of the river at Jainti, on the other side of which was the road to Hathipota along which we had come on our return from the ten days' march with the detachment. Our relief at being clear of the forest was great. We splashed through the shallows and set off at a gallop along the road. Suddenly my horse stumbled and fell in a hole, throwing me over its head. I was badly shaken, but I climbed into the saddle as the others, hearing the sound of the fall, pulled up and came back to me. The hole had evidently been dug in the roadway by a wild boar that night; as it had not been there when Tyson and Marriott came by in the morning. We rode on again. When I expressed to Tyson, cantering alongside, my relief at being out of the forest and safe from the chance of a meeting with wild elephants, I was appalled at hearing that the stretch of road we were then on was a regular thoroughfare for these animals on their way from the hills to the jungle.

We reached Tyson's bungalow about ten o'clock and found that my men had not arrived; and they did not march in until midnight. The native officer in command had tried a short cut through the forest, following a woodcutter's path which led the party into deep *nullahs*, up precipitous banks, and through the densest jungle. The sepoys were utterly exhausted by their toilsome march. The three elephants had started out with them, carrying the men's blankets and rations, but had fallen far behind. But when Tyson showed the party quarters for the night in one of his sheds, no one waited for food or bedding but flung himself on the floor and fell asleep at once.

Ranjit Singh's patrol had reached the village of Hathipota near the tea garden on the previous night. The havildar had learned at Jainti that a man in white dress and carrying a rifle had been seen coming from the forest and crossing the river early on the morning after the murder. Farid Khan, having been on guard, was clad in khaki uniform when he left the fort. But the villagers told Ranjit Singh that this man had a bundle rolled up in a military greatcoat. The havildar guessed that the murderer had been wearing white undress under his uniform and had taken off the latter during the night. So he crossed the river and found in the dust of the road to Hathipota the footprints of a man wearing ammunition boots. He followed them for some miles until they turned off into the jungle, where he lost the trail. Thinking that Hathipota Village was the nearest place where the fugitive could procure food, he pushed on with his two men and hid close to it all night. As by morning their quarry had not appeared, the patrol went on to the ferry over the Raidak River near the planters' club, where the detachment had bivouacked and held sports on the march. Ranjit Singh had brought with him an armed policeman whom he had met at Jainti and who had been sent out to search for the murderer. But this worthy had no desire to meet him and declined to accompany our havildar any farther, alleging that he was fatigued by the previous day's exertions and must stay to rest and refresh himself in Hathipota. But scarcely had our patrol left the village when the policeman, standing with a group of peasants, was horrified by the sudden apparition of a man dressed in white and carrying a rifle. It was Farid Khan. The guardian of the law, though he had a rifle himself, was far too frightened to use it. Farid Khan walked boldly up to him and asked him if any sepoys had visited the village. The terrified policeman, anxious to get rid of him at all costs, told him that a havildar with a party who were looking for him, had just left. He even told him truthfully the direction they had taken. Farid Khan at once disappeared into the jungle.

Meanwhile Ranjit Singh, having reached the river and learned from the ferryman that the fugitive had not arrived there, warned the former not to help the murderer across the stream if he came. Then the patrol turned back to Hathipota. There they were informed of Farid Khan's appearance in the village. They at once retraced their steps to the ferry and found that the fugitive had come to it soon after they had left. He had reached it by a jungle path. When the ferryman refused to take him over the river Farid Khan raised his rifle and threatened to shoot him; and the man was forced to take him across. Ranjit Singh and his men at once followed.

No news of this had reached us. Next morning, as soon as there was light enough to show the way, I marched my party off in a south-easterly direction to reach a point from which we could spread out and form the cordon. Marriott accompanied us, and Balderston was now mounted on a good pony lent him by Tyson, who was obliged to remain behind. As the little column swung along in the light of the rising sun, the excitement of the chase was visible in the sepoys. Struck by their silence, unusual when "marching at ease," I turned in the saddle to look at them. Every man's face was set in a grim, stern look; and as they strode on their eyes swept the country around with quick, keen glances as if they expected to see the fugitive every moment. Absorbing as is the chase of wild animals it is nothing to the excitement of a man-hunt. I forgot that we were tracking a human being to his doom, and remembered only that I had the blood of one of my best soldiers to avenge and that I was pursuing a cowardly murderer. I had given orders to all that Farid Khan, if overtaken and seen to be armed, was to be fired at on the spot; for I was determined to give him as little chance as possible to kill anyone else. Had I come upon him myself I would have shot him down without compunction, and regretted only that my bullet saved him from the gallows.

Some miles ahead of us lay a village which contained a police station. I sent Balderston and Marriott galloping on ahead to give warning to the havildar and constables in it, as they might not yet have heard of the crime. The column tramped on in gloomy silence through fairly open country, until we reached the new Raidak River and found our way barred by the swift-flowing stream. However, at this point there was a ferry consisting of a small dug-out canoe. I halted the detachment and was superintending the embarkation of the first batch of men, when higher up on the opposite bank two horsemen appeared. They were Marriott and Balderston. They called out across the water something that I did not hear. But the sepoys farther along on our side of the river did; and a wild burst of cheering from them startled me. They seemed to have gone mad. They threw their *puggris* in the air and waved their rifles above their heads yelling excitedly. Then a wild rush was made towards me.

"They've caught him, Sahib. Ranjit Singh has caught him," they cried, as they crowded round me. Never in my service had I seen the usually stolid sepoys so moved. Only then did I realise fully their bitter feeling of personal hatred of the treacherous assassin who had slain a comrade, and how keenly they had desired his capture.

Fording the stream the two officers approached me. Balderston waved his helmet, his face aglow with excitement.

"They've got him, major! They've got the brute, thank God!" he cried.

A load seemed lifted off my heart; but a sudden fear gripped me.

"Are the others safe?" I asked. "Anyone shot?"

"No, no. They sprang on him before he could use his rifle," he replied, as his pony scrambled up the bank. Swinging himself out of the saddle he continued: "We met Ranjit Singh on the road bringing him along. They are not far off. They tracked him to a village and overpowered him before he could resist. He had his loaded rifle beside him."

That was the first happy moment I had experienced since the fatal night. The murderer was in our hands; and my poor havildar's death would be avenged.

We stood in silence beside the river, watching the opposite bank intently. At last on it appeared a little group of figures, three in khaki, a fourth in white. Again the cheering burst out from the sepoys and continued as the canoe was sent across the stream to bring over the prisoner and his captors. Farid Khan was in front, his hands bound behind his back by a rope, the end of which was held by Havildar Ranjit Singh, who carried a rifle. As they came down the sloping path to the water's edge, it occurred to me that the prisoner, when in the cranky boat, might endeavour to capsize it and drown himself. So I ordered two or three of my best swimmers to strip and be ready to plunge into the river. But Farid Khan stepped carefully into the canoe and seated himself in the bottom of it and never moved until it reached our side. He laughed amusedly when one of his escort, trying to spring ashore, fell into the shallow water. As the canoe grounded the sepoys crowded round it with menacing looks; and we officers had to drive them back. Had we not been there they would have lynched him. Some cursed and reviled him, while others applauded his captors. But coolly and unconcernedly he stepped ashore with a cynical smile on his face. When the havildar had marched him up in front of me he stood quietly at attention. He was a young man twenty-one years old, with good features and a slight, well-knit frame. He returned my gaze steadily and seemed as little perturbed as though the offence he would have to answer for were of the slightest nature. The havildar handed me a rifle.

"This was in the prisoner's possession when I arrested him," he said.

I examined the weapon. The barrel was fouled; and in the magazine were eight cartridges.

I warned Farid Khan that anything he said might be used in evidence against him, and then asked:

"Why did you run away from the fort?"

"Because, when I had shot the colour-havildar, it was the only thing to do," he replied unconcernedly.

"You confess that you did shoot Shaikh Bakur?" I said.

"Yes, I did shoot him."

"Why?"

"Because he punished me and abused me that day. I knew that I would be on guard that evening and would have cartridges for my rifle. So I resolved to shoot him. At first I did not intend to do it in the night; as it would cause a lot of trouble to the other sepoys of the detachment, since they would be obliged to turn out and try to capture me. But while I was on sentry I thought the matter over and reflected that I might not have as good a chance to kill him in the morning as when he was sleeping. So I determined to make sure of him and do it at once."

He spoke calmly and without the least sign of remorse or apprehension.

"How did you do it?" I asked.

"As soon as the *naik* (corporal) of the guard had visited my post at eleven o'clock that night, I walked across to the barrack-room. I groped my way to my cot, beside which was a small lamp. This I lighted. Then I got my pipe, sat down on my bed and had a smoke. When I had finished it I stood up and took my rifle, which I loaded. Shaikh Bakur was lying asleep opposite me. I shot him and ran out of the room."

I tried to picture the scene with the callous youngster calmly smoking as he watched his unconscious victim. I wondered if the sight of his enemy's face had aroused his anger as he looked at it.

"How was Shaikh Bakur lying?" I questioned. "Was his face turned towards you?"

"I don't know," he replied indifferently. "His head was covered up in the bedclothes; and I could not see it."

The cold-blooded manner of the crime horrified me. The murderer had coolly fired at a huddled mass of blankets. The listening sepoys around us were awed into silence as he calmly related the details of his foul deed.

"What did you do then?" I asked.

"I reloaded my rifle to shoot anyone who tried to stop me, thus putting one cartridge in the chamber and leaving eight in the magazine. I ran out of the room and stood outside near the building until the sepoys began to come out. Then I went to the back gate. While I was climbing it the bolt of the rifle dropped back and let the cartridge in the breach fall out. So you will only find eight in the magazine. Soon I heard the gate open and saw you come out with two men. I got behind a tree and watched you pass within five yards of me."

"Why did not you shoot me?" I said.

"Oh, I had no desire to kill you, Sahib, as long as you did not discover and try to capture me. If you had I would have shot you."

He spoke as coolly about killing me as if it were a most ordinary matter. I was less indifferent, and felt thankful that I had not blundered on him in the dark. I realised fully what a narrow escape I had had.

"Why did you take your rifle with you when you went off?" I asked.

For the first time his indifferent manner vanished. A malevolent gleam shone in his eyes.

"Because my greatest enemy still lived," he said. "The man I most wanted to kill was the subhedar-major. I had gone to his room first that night and tried to enter it. But, luckily for him, the door was bolted. So, as I was determined to shoot someone, I went to the barrack-room and killed Shaikh Bakur. But I took my rifle; for I resolved to escape, hide in the jungle until the pursuit was over, then return at night and kill the subhedar-major."

He announced his murderous intention with the utmost calmness. I thanked God that we had been able to capture him; for if he had returned and shot his native officer, he would then have run amuck and killed until slain himself.

"How did you get away?" I said.

"After you had passed me, Sahib, I went down the zigzag path. I meant to get on to the road to Santrabari, but heard the patrol passing down it below me and knew that you had cut my retreat off that way. So I sat on the hill until daylight and then made my way through the forest to Jainti."

I asked him if he had any accomplices. He denied that he had; and, when I refused to believe him, he said:

"Why should I tell a lie now? I know that my life is forfeit."

"Yes," I replied. "You'll hang for this."

"I don't care. My father has five other sons and can spare me. But my one regret," he said, and again a baleful light shone in his eyes, "is that my worst enemy still lives."

I turned away from him and interrogated Ranjit Singh about the capture.

When the havildar learned that the man he was pursuing had crossed the river after he had been seen in Hathipota, he followed with the two men of the patrol. On the other side they picked up his trail, which led to another village. Near it they met some peasants and learned from them that Farid Khan was in this village. Approaching cautiously they dodged from hut to hut until they saw him sitting on the ground before a *bunniah's* shop, eating food which he had just bought. His rifle lay beside him. They crept up behind him, for they were resolved to take him alive, rushed on him suddenly and tumbled him over before he could seize his weapon. As they held him down and bound him, he said:

"It was lucky for you, havildar, that I did not see you first. I had my magazine full and would have shot you all."

After his capture he seemed resigned to his fate and scarcely spoke again until he was brought before me. I praised Ranjit Singh and his patrol warmly and then fell in my men. We marched back to Hathipota, where we halted for the night. Next day we reached Buxa.

I was determined that our prisoner should not cheat the gallows by escape or suicide. So night and day for the two months that elapsed before he was brought to trial a guard was mounted over him in his cell.

All through those weary weeks of waiting his indifferent demeanour never changed. I visited him every day. To my inquiries as to whether he had any request to make, he always replied respectfully. But he never acknowledged that he had had any accomplices in his crime; and was never able to bring his comrade Gulab Khan to trial.

At last the orders came to conduct Farid Khan to Calcutta to appear before a general court martial. We marched out of the fort and down to Buxa Road Railway Station with the prisoner in the centre of a guard of six men with fixed bayonets. By one of his wrists he was handcuffed to a burly Rajput over six feet high. These precautions were necessary, as the journey would take a day and a night and necessitated many changes; and I was determined to give Farid Khan no chance to escape. At Gitaldaha we had to wait for some time for another train which brought us in the early morning to the banks of the River Ganges. Across this we were taken in a steamer, the passage occupying over an hour. Our appearance excited much interest among the passengers on board, some of whom were American tourists returning from a flying visit to Darjeeling. My party, including the witnesses and the escort, was quite a large one; and I heard one fair daughter of Uncle Sam remark:

"Wa'al, it takes a lot of soldiers to guard that one poor man."

One of her male companions, who addressed me as "Officer!" questioned me as to the prisoner's crime, and seemed quite disappointed at learning that it was only murder.

On the other side of the Ganges we entrained again.

and reached Calcutta by noon. I handed over my prisoner to the care of a regiment quartered in Fort William; and he was safely consigned to their guard-room cell.

On the bank of the broad River Hugli, which flows through the city of Calcutta and up which the ships come from the sea, stands this large fort, which dates back far into the days of the Honourable East India Company. One face fronts the stream, the others look on the *maidan*, a broad open space, tree-studded and seamed with roads, which lies between the frowning, embrasured walls and the nearest houses. Within the wide precincts of the fort, a city in a city, are found barracks, the arsenal, houses for military and civil officers, a church, and the official residence of the Commander-in-Chief, all separated by broad squares and green lawns.

Here next day in the garrison library, a large recreation-room for soldiers, Sepoy Farid Khan faced the court martial which was to try him for his life. When I had given him his choice in Buxa of having either British or Indian officers as his judges, he answered unhesitatingly:

"I want to be tried by Sahibs, of course."

And so, in accordance with his wish, nine British officers in white full-dress summer uniform, swords at their sides and medals on their breasts, sat in judgment on him at a long table. Behind them was a stage on which military amateur actors strut their hour in the garrison theatricals. The drop curtain was up, showing a pretty English country scene. It seemed an incongruous setting for the grim drama of real life which was now to be enacted.

Near the members of the court sat another officer,

the deputy judge advocate general, who was present to see that the trial was conducted in accordance with the rules of military law, and to advise the court on legal points. At a small table to one side Captain Balderston took his place as prosecutor. Then the prisoner, his handcuffs removed, was marched into the room by the guard of the regiment in whose cells he was confined. He walked in with an erect and soldierly bearing and stood to attention as the president of the court read out the charge to him and called on him to plead. And to this charge of "Murder" he answered composedly "I am guilty." But, since with this plea no evidence in his defence or in extenuation of his crime could be given, the court, with the extreme fairness of a military tribunal, advised him to withdraw it and plead "Not Guilty." Then the native witnesses who testified to his desertion of his post, his flight and capture, gave their evidence in Hindustani. After them I repeated his confession of the crime to me. I spoke in English, my evidence being translated to the prisoner by a British officer who acted as interpreter. But I noticed that Farid Khan did not seem to understand this officer, who spoke a purer and correcter Urdu than did the prisoner himself.

I stated my belief to the court. The president, who spoke the vernacular, asked Farid Khan if this were so.

"Yes, it is true. I cannot understand what that Sahib says," he replied; "but I can understand my own major Sahib," pointing to me.

Then, with the court's permission, I repeated to him the evidence I had given.

"Yes, that is all quite true," he said.

Then the president bade me ask the prisoner if he wished to question me on my evidence. I did so.

"No," Sahib," he replied. "What you have said is correct. I only wish to say that on that night I intended to kill the subhedar-major first. I tried his door first but——"

I told him to be silent, as he was only committing himself deeper. Then the court asked me what the prisoner had said and I answered that it was something to his disadvantage; the president told me that in that case I need not interpret his words.

The trial lasted two days and ended in a verdict of guilty. But in accordance with military law it was not announced at the time, as the whole of the proceedings of the court had to be first carefully scrutinised at army headquarters; so that if any illegality had been committed, or the verdict was not justified by the evidence, the case could be quashed and a fresh trial ordered. But in due course the decision of the court martial and the sentence of "Death by hanging" were published. But long before this I had left Calcutta with my party and returned to Buxa, Farid Khan remaining a prisoner in Fort William. His father and a brother came across India from Rajputana to visit him; and, probably acting on their advice, he appealed for mercy to the Viceroy.

But his appeal was rejected. One night at eleven o'clock the adjutant of the regiment which had him in charge was handed a telegram to that effect and informing him that the prisoner was to be hanged next morning at eight o'clock. The officer went at once to the condemned man's cell. Farid Khan was asleep. The adjutant woke him up and said:

"You are to die to-morrow morning."

"Very well, Sahib," was the unconcerned reply; and the prisoner lay down again and was asleep before the adjutant had quitted the cell.

I had feared that Farid Khan would be sent back to Buxa Duar, so that the execution could be carried out in presence of his comrades. But the last act of the tragedy took place in the courtyard of the civil jail in Calcutta. Detachments of all the regiments, British and Indian, in that city were formed up in front of the gallows.

When the condemned man was marched into the courtyard, the adjutant asked if he had any last request to make.

"Yes, Sahib," he replied. "I want to know how many men you have told off to bury me."

"Two," said the officer.

"That is not enough, Sahib; I should like eight."

"Very well, you will have them."

"Thank you, Sahib," replied the condemned man cheerfully. Then with a firm step he mounted the scaffold. As the rope was adjusted round his neck, he looked down at the adjutant and called out to him with a smile:

"Salaam, Sahib. Good-bye."

They were his last words.

CHAPTER XIII

IN AN INDIAN HILL STATION

To Darjeeling—Railway journeys in India—Protection for solitary ladies—Reappearing rivers—Siliguri—At the foot of the Himalayas—A mountain railway—Through the jungle—Looping the loop—View of the Plains—Darjeeling—Civilisation seven thousand feet high—Varied types—View from the Chaurasta—White workers in India—Life in Hill Stations—Lieutenant-Governors—A "dull time" in Darjeeling—The bazaar—Types of hill races—Turquoises—Tiger-skins for tourists—The Amusement Club—The Everlasting Snows—Kinchinjunga—The bachelors' ball—A Government House ball—The marriage-market value of Indian civilians—Less demand for military men—Theatricals—Lebong Races—Picturesque race-goers—Ladies in India—Husband hunters—The empty life of an Englishwoman—The dangers of Hill Stations—A wife four months in the year—The hills *taboo* for the subaltern—Back to Buxa.

SIXTY or eighty miles west of Buxa Duar and seven thousand feet above the sea is the pleasant Himalayan Hill Station of Darjeeling. Less than a day's journey by rail from Calcutta, it attracts to it the fortunate mortals who, in the summer months, can escape from the heat of that crowded city and the Bengal plains and plunge into a whirl of gaieties on the cool heights of the Pleasure Colony. To it I had my first change from Buxa. About a year after my arrival I got fourteen days' leave to Darjeeling in order to meet the officer of my regiment commanding our detachment at Gantok in Sikkim, who was coming there to appear at one of the many examinations that plague the soldier's soul. The month was October, perhaps the unpleasantest time of the year in India, when the Rains are almost ended and the heat is intensified by the dampness of earth and atmosphere.

To reach my destination required a very roundabout journey by rail. First from Buxa Road to the junction at Gitaldaha, where I could get on to the main line which took me to Siliguri at the foot of the mountains again; thence up the toy Himalayan Railway which crawled in spirals and zigzags up the face of the giant hills. The Indian first-class railway carriage is very unlike an English one. It is divided into two compartments, each entered by a door at the end and containing along each side a broad, leather-covered couch, used as a seat by day, a bed by night. Above each is a hanging bed, hooked up until it is required for use. There is thus sleeping accommodation for four in the compartment, off which is a lavatory, which on some lines contains a bath, a luxury much needed on a long journey in India. In the hot weather the carriages are fitted with electric fans, which only serve to stir the heated air, and hardly cool the perspiring occupants. Every traveller carries his roll of bedding, which his servant spreads down at night and in the morning ties up and stows out of the way. Until comparatively recently restaurant cars were unknown; and the trains halted three times a day for half an hour to allow their passengers to descend at stations where meals could be obtained. For long journeys, and in India three or four days in a train is not unusual, the type of carriage I have described is more comfortable than the corridor carriages which are now being introduced. This change is greatly due to the number of running-train thefts and the murder of a Eurasian girl; for of course in the corridor system travellers are less isolated. Recent occurrences have somewhat scared ladies travelling alone. To reassure them the railway companies allow them to have their *ayahs* or native female servants to share the carriage, the window-shutters have been provided with bolts, and the guards have instructions to lock the doors of their compartments.

As my train rolled along through the level country I was surprised to note the number of rivers we crossed. These were the streams which vanish at the foot of the hills and reappear above ground farther south. The country we passed through was typical of Bengal—level plains well cultivated and dotted with clumps of bamboos, numerous villages and prosperous-looking farms.

In the early morning we reached Siliguri where we had to change to the Himalayan Railway. A crowd of sleepy passengers descended and entered the refreshment-room in search of breakfast, while their servants gathered their luggage together. Then we took our seats in the tiny open carriages of the small train which climbs the steep slopes of the mighty mountains. At first it plunged into forest between huge trees clothed with orchids, walled in by dense undergrowth; for we were in the Terai again. Then it wound among the jungle-clad foot-hills and climbed ever higher, while the forest grew thinner and sparser. Anon it emerged on the sides of the open bare mountains; and we looked down on the dark belt of trees and the plains spread like a map below us. We could trace for miles the winding course of the

Tista, the wide river that flows down through the hills from Sikkim. Here and there we passed by long stretches of tea gardens. In one place the railway forms a complete circle, looping the loop; so that, with a long train, the engine would be crossing over a bridge while the last carriage was still under it. Beside the line ran the mountain road, by which heavily laden coolies toiled between the villages of rough wooden huts. At last the greatest elevation was reached at the small station of Goom; and the train ran down for a thousand feet and ended its journey in Darjeeling.

Mark Twain was enraptured by the beauties and marvels of engineering of this Himalayan Railway. But to me it seemed far less wonderful and lovely than the lines over the Rocky Mountains of his own country. I have crossed them by the Denver and Rio Grande route, where in broad Pullmans and big-windowed observation-cars we sat in comfort, and at an elevation of ten thousand feet gazed at the snow-clad peaks towering above us or, lower down in the deep gorges, strove to see the tops of the sheer, two-thousand feet high walls of the Grand Canyon, painted in brilliant colours by the lavish hand of Nature.

But Darjeeling was unique in my experience; for I had visited no other Himalayan Hill Station. A town on the mountain-tops, a town of pretty villas, large hotels, clubs and churches, of big English shops with plate-glass windows, of jumbled native bazaars thronged with thousands of men and women of a dozen different hill races. Broad, well-kept roads run along the ridges and up and down the steep hill-sides, lined with lovely gardens, in which stand fascinating European houses like the villas of Trouville and Deauville under the shade of giant orchid-clad trees. English ladies in smart frocks go by in rickshaws or reclining in chairs carried on the shoulders of strong coolies. Officers and civilians on well-groomed ponies trot past groups of sturdy-limbed Bhuttias or rosy-cheeked Lepcha women hung with turquoise and silver ornaments. British soldiers in khaki stop to chat with small, cheery Gurkha policemen by the roadside. Pig-tailed Sikkimese and Tibetan lamas fingering their rosaries stare into the plate-glass windows of shops that would not be out of place in Oxford Street and which display to the bewildered heathen Paris fashions or the latest pattern of coloured shirts and smart waistcoats.

The central point of Darjeeling is the cross roads at the Chaurasta. Here on one side the ground rises a thousand feet or more to the summit of Jala-pahar, crowded with barracks and European bungalows. To the other the hill-sides slope steeply away covered with tea gardens. Along the ridge the road runs by a trim English Church in pretty grounds, the straggling building of the Amusement Club with tennis courts terraced one above the other, and on to the Lieutenant-Governor of Bengal's summer residence set in a lovely park. To the north the ground falls sharply another thousand feet; and one looks down on the roofs of the bungalows and British Infantry Barracks of Lebong, with its race-course around the polo ground and the rifle-range, seeming like a toy station set out far beneath. Below, the deep valley; and beyond it rises a jumble of mountains on mountains in bewildering profusion. And at dawn and evening above the clouds hangs high in air the long line of the Everlasting Snows. Over it towers Kinchinjunga, twenty-eight thousand feet high, with its jagged white peaks gleaming in the morning or pink-flushed in the rosy light of sunset; forty miles away, yet so clear and distinct that the beholder imagines he would be able to see a man on it, if some climber could scale its untrodden heights.

The abrupt change from the sweltering heat of the Bengal plains, seven thousand feet below, to the cool climate and refreshing breezes of Darjeeling is marvellous. In less than twenty-four hours the English dwellers in the hot and crowded city of Calcutta are borne to this gay Hill Station, which must seem another world to them. In the brisk mountain air the jaded visitors from the Plains revive and are filled with renewed energy; and one and all plunge feverishly into social gaieties. In India only in such places as this does one find the Englishman unoccupied by work; for in the East there is no leisured class of Europeans. Even the Viceroys and Governors are busy mortals, and perhaps the hardest-worked individuals in the dominions they rule. Every white man in India has his employment; for he is a soldier, a civil servant, a judge, a lawyer, a railwayman or a merchant. Each has his work and his place in the scheme of things. But in the Hills, save for those at the military or civil headquarters, he is on leave, and has come to enjoy a well-earned rest.

The life in an Indian Hill Station is unlike anything that we have in England. Gaiety reigns supreme. Games, races, dances, theatricals, and all such entertainments abound. To take Darjeeling as an example. In the mornings and forenoons the roads are thronged with riders or with ladies in chairs or rickshaws, going to pay calls or on their way to luncheon-parties. In the afternoons on the polo ground of Lebong the players on their agile little ponies jostle each other, or race after the ball. The tennis courts in the grounds of the Amusement Club are full. The skating rink inside the Club is thronged in the mornings, and when dusk falls, the lamps are lighted and the tea-tables are set out beside the polished floor. The nights are never dull; dinner-parties in the bungalows, restaurants and hotels, dances and theatricals at the Club, fill them.

In these Hill Stations the summer residents in the bungalows, the visitors at the hotels or boarding-houses, though they come from places in the Plains far apart, are of the same class in life and know each other or of each other. For, except for the lawyers and merchants, the names of all are set forth in either of the two great books of India, the Civil Service or the Army List. And they are linked by the bond of a similar profession. All are members of the Club and see each other there every day. To all are sent invitations to each big festivity. The Lieutenant-Governor of the province has his summer residence in its Hill Station and gives a series of official entertainments to which are asked all those who have written their names in the book which, guarded by red-coat servitors, lies on a table in the veranda of Government House. He is constrained by his position to give dances, dinners, and garden-parties, regardless of his private inclinations. For he is a very important personage, and lives in almost regal state. He has his military aides-de-camp, his military or police guard; the Union Jack flies from a flagstaff on his lawn as a sign of his dignity. He rules over a province as big as England and is supreme in his dominions unless the Viceroy chances to visit them. Think what a change it must be for such a proconsul when he has to retire and takes up his abode in a London suburb or a small country town, where he is unknown to fame, and unhonoured!

Life is indeed gay in these Hill Stations. To them flock the ladies to escape the burning heat of the Plains, leaving their poor husbands to grill and earn their pay while their wives are enjoying themselves up in the cool mountains. And the fair ones must be amused. So the bachelors, who can more easily afford to take leave than the married men, are at their service to ride, play tennis, dance and flirt with them.

The fortnight of my stay in Darjeeling was supposed to be quite a dull time in the Station; for it preceded the holidays of the Poojahs, a Hindu feast, when all the Government and mercantile offices in Bengal are closed and the Englishmen thus set free flock up to the Hills. These holidays lasted two weeks; and an elaborate programme of festivities was prepared for them. Yet during the period of my stay I found that there were to be three balls, four afternoon dances, two days' races and two separate amateur theatricals. So it seemed to me a whirl of gaiety after the hermit-like seclusion of Buxa Duar.

On the first afternoon I rickshawed down into the bazaar or native quarter thronged with representatives of many hill races. Sturdy little Gurkhas, pig-tailed Sikkimese, broad-shouldered Bhuttias, dusky Hindu women and fair-complexioned, red-cheeked Lepcha girls jostled each other in the narrow, hilly streets.

In the open market-place were stalls of vendors of cheap commodities; and harsh-featured old women sat behind trays of rough-cut turquoises or smoothly polished imitations of the blue stone dear to the hearts of the female hill dwellers. In the bazaar many of the dingy native shops were filled with curios to attract the white resident or globe-trotter. Tibetan prayer-wheels, lama devil-dancers' masks, Chinese embroideries and roughly hammered brass gods were heaped in confusion. Trays of cut turquoises and lumps of matrix stood on the counters. The window of one shop was filled with skins of tigers, bears, and panthers; a sight to move the sportsman to wrath, for to him such things are trophies to be won in fair chase, not articles to be exposed for sale to the American tourist. I noticed that tiger-skins were ticketed at £20, the pelts of other animals at lower prices. Beyond the market-place, on a knoll, stood the European sanatorium, in which I was to find myself a patient months afterwards.

As I entered the Amusement Club at sunset, after my visit to the bazaar, I was quite bewildered by the sight of so many white folk. Outside, the tennis courts were emptying as the dusk fell. Inside the building the rink was crowded with skaters. Along one side of it were set out scores of tea-tables, around which sat ladies attired in the latest fashions. The card-room was full. People were changing books in the Club library or looking at the English illustrated papers and magazines in the reading-room. And in the bar was gathered together a festive crowd of men of many professions and callings, though the military predominated, chatting and disposing of the "short drinks" beloved of the Anglo-Indian. Here I met two subalterns of my regiment, one on leave, the other on his way back to headquarters from Gyantse in the heart of Tibet, where he had been commanding the escort to the British Trade Agent. In that isolated spot, thirteen thousand feet above the sea, he had lived for eighteen months, solacing his solitude by stalking the wily ibex. Here, too, I came across the major of the Punjabi regiment whom I had relieved nearly a year before at Buxa Duar. After a cheery greeting he asked me pityingly how I managed to endure the loneliness of my little outpost. When he heard that I liked the existence there immensely he seemed to regard me as a half-demented individual. While I was chatting with him there descended upon me emissaries of a frantic amateur stage-manager who, having heard that I had had much experience in theatricals, besought me to take the place of one of his actors who had suddenly fallen ill, as the performance was to come off in two days' time. The dress rehearsal of the piece, a well-known London comedy, was just about to commence in the Club theatre. Having consented I was borne off to it, a typed book placed in my hand and I dragged into the dressing-room to be "made up." I was already caught in the grip of the amusement machine.

Next morning I was up before the sun to see the gorgeous panorama of the Everlasting Snows. As the day dawned the lower hills were shrouded in clouds; but high above them rose the long line of snow-clad summits, seeming to float in air, unreal, unsubstantial in their beauty; and Kinchinjunga's white and jagged crest towered over them all and was the first to flush with rose colour in the rays of the morning sun. Then a veil was slowly drawn over the glorious picture, as the clouds soared slowly up from the lower levels and hid the gorgeous vision from sight.

I spent the day paying calls, rehearsing my part in the theatricals, and becoming acquainted with Darjeeling. I visited the beautiful Botanical Gardens, picturesquely situated on a steep slope and giving a wide view over the deep valleys below.

I found that the transition from the two thousand feet height of Buxa to the seven thousand of Darjeeling was rather trying at first; as the least exertion of walking and climbing soon left me breathless. In a few days I was quite accustomed to the superior altitude.

That night the bachelors of the Station gave a large ball in the Amusement Club. Their coat-of-arms—a bottle, slippers, and a pipe crossed with a latch-key—was blazoned on the walls. Gay was the revelry, which lasted well into the small hours; and I was glad that I was on leave and no early parade could claim me in the morning.

On the following night came another ball given by the Lieutenant-Governor in his official residence. Government House was filled with the wearers of pretty frocks and varied uniforms; and in the glamour of scarlet and blue mess-jackets the black-coated civilian was for once at a discount. But, alas! for the mercenary nature of the fair sex; if he belong to the Indian Civil Service he is preferred to the soldier as a husband. For he is worth "£400 a year dead or alive"; for his widow will get that amount as a pension. Whereas an ungrateful country dowers a lieutenant's relict with £40 a year, a captain's with £70, a major's £100 and a colonel's £120. So how can the red-coat compete with him in the matrimonial stakes?

The illuminated grounds of Government House and the cunningly-devised "kala juggas," as sitting-out places are termed in India, lured many of the dancers from the ball-room. At supper that night I sat at a small table with a merry little party consisting of the subaltern of my regiment on leave, Prince Rajendra of Cooch Behar and his partner, a pretty Armenian girl. And of the four of us two are now dead. The subaltern died a few months after attaining to his captaincy. Prince Rajendra soon succeeded his father as Maharajah, but only lived to enjoy his dignities two short years.

Next night the Club theatre was filled with a kindly disposed and enthusiastic audience to witness our performance of the comedy. As India is rarely visited by professional companies, which only appear in the large cities, it is mainly dependent on the efforts of its amateur actors. But these often, through natural talent and much practice, attain a degree of excellence that would not disgrace the London stage. And few would gainsay this who saw the performances of "The Country Girl" given by another troop of amateurs before the end of my stay. They were under the direction of His Highness the Maharajah of Cooch Behar, who had lavished money on the production. The scenery and dresses had come from London; and the piece was magnificently staged. The singing, acting, and even the dancing could not be surpassed by at least any first-class touring company in England.

The Maharajah had a house in Darjeeling where his entertainments were princely and his hospitality profuse. The ladies of his family were absent in Simla; but his sons were with him. Prince Rajendra, as befitted the heir apparent, had a separate house and an establishment of his own. Here one night I was present at a merry supper-party, after renewing my acquaintance and dining informally with the Maharajah.

Every day of my short stay seemed to have its particular gaiety. The races at Lebong were a sporting and a fashionable event. Down the steep hill roads from Darjeeling, a thousand feet above, poured the stream of Europeans in rickshaws or on ponies and of natives afoot early in the afternoon to the miniature race-course which is built on the cut-away hill-top. There is scant room for any horse to bolt out of it; for a few yards will bring it to the edge of the precipitous slopes around. In fact, the "straight" for the run home is gained by finishing up the Darjeeling road. Most of the events were for hill ponies, sturdy and plucky little animals; and the jockeys were mainly natives. But the excitement of the crowds of race-goers of many shades of colour, the keenness of the plungers on the totalisator or with the few bookmakers, and the gaiety of the pleasure-seekers, could not be exceeded at Ascot or Epsom. The scene was an animated one. The enclosure was gay with the colours of the English ladies' frocks, the bright hues of Parsee women's *saris*, the white refreshment tents, and the uniforms of the military bandsmen; while outside was the varied crowd of British Infantry soldiers in red, gunners in blue, and natives of a score of different races, each in their distinctive garb. And over it all towered the heights of Darjeeling and Jalapahar; while on three sides lay the deep valleys, beyond which stood the mountains that barred the way to Sikkim and Tibet.

Such is life in a Hill Station. To a man not devoted to social frivolities existence in them soon palls. He tires of the sameness of tennis in the afternoons, the vapid conversation of the tea-tables, and nights spent in the heated atmosphere of ball-rooms. But to the fair sex it appeals strongly; and they gladly hail the approach of the hot weather, which will free them from the monotony of small Stations in the plains and send them flocking to Simla, Darjeeling, Missourie or Naini Tal.

Who would not be an English woman in India?

As Gilbert says:

> "They are treasured as precious stones
> And for the self-same reason—for their scarcity."

But they are not inclined to recognise this, and are apt to attribute the attentions paid them by the men to their own charms and not to the paucity of their sex in the land. Consequently they are too liable to become conceited and over-bearing and forgetful of the fact that courtesy *is* a ladylike quality. It is perhaps not to be wondered at that their heads get turned. The plainest girl, who in England would spend most of her time at a ball sitting with her chaperon, in India can fill her programme thrice over. She, who in her country village sees no men of her own class except the parson and the doctor, out here finds herself among crowds of military officers and better-paid civilians who, prudence whispers, are more eligible *partis*. But the day has passed when any failure in the English marriage-market can be shipped off to India, sure of securing a husband there. Frequent leave and fast steamers have altered all that. When men can find themselves back in England in a fortnight they are not so prone to wed plain-featured and dowerless maidens, sent out in search of a spouse, as were their predecessors in the old days when it took six months in a sailing ship to reach London from Calcutta or Bombay. The attractive but penniless girl in India has still a better chance of marrying than she would in England; for she is thrown in daily companionship with a large number of bachelors. But many a damsel who, dispatched by her parents with a single ticket to distant relatives or mere acquaintances in the East, thinks on first arrival that she has only to pick and choose among the surplus men and give herself airs accordingly, is forced to write home for her return fare and go back reluctantly to the unwelcome existence of an old maid. To my mind there is something almost immoral in the custom which prevails of girls going out to India as paying-guests in the known, if unavowed, hope of securing a husband. But the practice grows every year.

Yet the existence of a white woman in India is not all unalloyed pleasure. Her lot may be cast in some small out-of-the-way Station, where there is little society and less amusement. And even in larger places her life is empty enough. In the morning, perhaps, she goes for a ride and then has to shut herself up in her bungalow on account of the heat, until in the cool of the afternoon she can drive out to play tennis or golf and then go to the club, where she sits on the lawn and talks scandal with her female friends or, possibly, flirts with her male ones. She is not occupied with the cares of the household as is her less fortunate sister in England. Her cook goes to the bazaar early in the morning and then later appears before her to show her his account book and take her orders for the day. And she has little else to do to fill in the long, weary hours in the house from breakfast until tea-time. An occasional caller may come to pay his or her visit; but otherwise the time hangs heavy on her hands. Any accomplishments she may possess are apt to be neglected. Her reading is generally confined to novels from the Club library; and she seldom tries to improve her mind by more strenuous studies. In a land where all the white men are workers, she is idle. And so the English woman in the East is generally uninteresting. The gossip and scandal of the Station are her chief topics. The wonders of the country she lives in, the strange life of the peoples outside her door, the greater questions of Empire, are a sealed book to her; and she is generally as commonplace as her untravelled sisters in English country towns. The clever Mrs Hauksbees that Kipling depicts are rare —more's the pity, for Anglo-Indian society would be brighter if there were more of her type.

The petty squabbles among the ladies of a small Station are pitiful.

The Anglo-Indian wife too often takes little interest in her husband's work, and so cannot prove very companionable to him. And this probably accounts for the extraordinary latitude he allows her in seeking the society of some particular bachelor with whom she rides, drives and sits in the Club every day, who becomes a standing feature in her life. The *mènage à trois* flourishes in India.

Hill stations have much to answer for in the frequency of domestic trouble in Anglo-Indian society.

In the old days before they existed, and passages to England were long and costly, the wives stayed by their husbands' side for weal or woe. What the latter could endure their spouses were not afraid of. Now, at the first signs of the approach of the hot weather, the married ladies, as well as the maidens, fly to the Hills. In Darjeeling I met many who said they had not seen their husbands for eight months—and yet I found them in October booking their rooms in the hotels for the following March. Naturally this separation does not tend to the continuance of conjugal love. And there is a still greater danger. A married woman arriving from the Plains to take up her residence in a hotel probably finds no other woman in it whom she has known before. Among the guests there is sure to be a preponderance of her own sex; and though many ladies may call on her, they will probably be too much engrossed in their own concerns to give her much of their society. She sits by herself at table at meals and spends most of her time alone in her own room. Then some bachelor on leave, and staying perhaps at the same hotel, makes her acquaintance. He finds her pleasant and attractive, offers to join her in her solitary rides and walks, comes in often to chat with her in her private sitting-room, takes her to the many dances, and, as men are scarcer at them than in the ball-rooms of the Plains, engages half her programme and escorts her back to their hotel afterwards. Even from sheer loneliness she accepts his attentions and allows him to drop into the acknowledged position of her *cavaliere servente*. Two or three months of this daily, hourly companionship and—well, another Hill scandal is caused.

The man who brings a pretty wife to India is brave; the one who sends her away from him for six or eight months in the year is, to say the least of it, unwise. It is not fair to her to expose her thus to temptation. Far be it from me to assert that every Hill grass-widow forgets her absent husband. But many do; and all the blame should not rest on them.

The careful commanding officer of a regiment discourages his young subalterns from taking leave to Hill Stations. He knows that in such places mischief is too often found for idle hands. He urges them rather to go shooting in the jungles or in Kashmir. And certainly this latter is a better way for the youngster to spend his holiday than loafing about a Hill Station.

Despite the novelty of the life in Darjeeling and its social gaieties I did not repine when my time came to quit it; and my heart rejoiced as I got out of the train at Buxa Road, mounted the elephant awaiting me, and rode through the silent forest towards my lonely hills.

CHAPTER XIV

A JUNGLE FORT

I decide on Fort Bower—Felling trees—A big python—Clearing the jungle—Laying out the post—Stockades and *Sungars*—The bastions—*Panjis* and *abattis*—The huts—Jungle materials—Ingenious craftsmen—The furniture—Sentry-posts—Alarm-signals—The *machicoulis* gallery—Booby-traps—The water-lifter—The hospital—Chloroforming a monkey—Jungle dogs—An extraordinary shot—An unlucky deer—A meeting with a panther—The alarm—Sohanpal Singh and the tiger—Turning out to the rescue—The General's arrival—Closed gates—The inspection—The "Bower" and the "'Ump"—Flares and bombs—The General's praise—Night firing—A Christmas camp.

THE month of November in Buxa brought the end of the Rains and the beginning of the cold weather. Once more we could descend into the jungles below, for work or sport, without risking the deadly Terai fever. Our open-air military training, which had to be laid aside during the long, weary months of the Monsoon, was resumed.

The warfare which the Assam Brigade would be called upon to wage would generally be against the savage jungle dwellers along the north-east borders. Consequently the training of the troops composing it demanded much practice in forest country; for, in the jungle, wide extensions and thin lines suitable to troops attacking in the open would be replaced by close formations, and the bayonet more often used than the bullet. Timber barriers would be substituted for earthworks, and the axe for the spade. In a jungle campaign, as the fighting column moved forward, stockaded posts would be established on the line of communication, in which convoys of supplies going to the front or of wounded or prisoners sent back to the rear could halt for the night under the protection of the permanent garrisons.

When General Bower announced his intention of coming to hold his annual inspection of our detachment at the end of November, I determined to build such a stockaded post in the forest below Buxa Duar for him to see, and as useful instruction for my men. Consequently, three weeks before his arrival, I moved the double company down into the jungle. While Captain Balderston and I took up our abode in Forest Lodge, the sepoys bivouacked a few hundred yards away on a high bluff over a broad river-bed now almost dry. Here I proposed building our forest fort.

Our first task consisted in clearing away the undergrowth, now denser than ever after the fires and Rains. With curved *kukris* and straight *dahs* the sepoys fell to work on the thick scrub and tangle of thorny bushes. Then came the harder labour of felling the trees for the stockades—and the tools that contractors supply the Government with are not of the best quality. The forest rang to the stroke of axes and the shouts of the sepoys who, delighted at the change from their ordinary routine, vied with each other in bringing the trees crashing to the ground. As I watched them one day I saw a sudden commotion among a group. The men scattered, then closed in again; and vicious blows at the ground, mingled with cries of "*samp!*", told me that they had disturbed a snake. Then on poles bending under its weight they brought me the body of a beautifully marked python nearly ten and a half feet long. Though not poisonous, such a beast would be a formidable antagonist. With the driving-power of its weight and muscle, its head could strike with the force of a battering ram; and a man's body, crushed in its folds, would soon be a shapeless pulp. I kept its skin as a companion to the king-cobra we had killed in Buxa.

The plan I had decided on for the fort was a square, each side fifty yards long. For instructional purposes I varied the design of the faces. That on the river-bank was to be a *sungar*—a loopholed wall, seven feet high and three feet thick, of large boulders from the *nullah* below. The east side opposite it was to be a loopholed stockade of single timbers two feet thick and fourteen feet above the ground. Each of the other two faces was to be a "double stockade" of shorter trees, that is, each two timber walls four feet apart, the space between them being filled with earth. At opposite corners were bastions, or towers, eighteen feet high, projecting out, and thus each giving a flanking fire along two faces of the fort. They were arranged for three tiers of fire, one row of loopholes three feet from the ground for men kneeling, one four and a half feet for others standing, the third above a gallery running round inside the top. Below the galleries the bastions were roofed in and formed barrack-rooms for the guards.

In front of the three stockaded sides of the fort

THE WALLED FACE OF FORT BOWER OVER THE RIVER.

THE STOCKADE AND DITCH AT FORT BOWER.

a broad, V-shaped ditch was dug, five feet deep. On the fourth face the bank fell sheer thirty or forty feet to the river; and built out over the *nullah* on tree-trunks laid horizontally, their butts buried in the ground, was a gallery projecting from the stone wall. It was loopholed for men to fire, not only on three sides, but also directly beneath them down into the river-bed. Entrance to it was gained from a small door in the wall. Close to it, and similarly projecting over the *nullah*, was a device copied from the savage tribes of the frontier. This was a booby-trap, a bamboo platform hinged and held up by thick, hawser-like creepers fastened inside the wall. On it were piled rocks. A couple of blows with an axe would cut through the supporting creepers; and the platform, falling, would shower down an avalanche of huge stones on the heads of enemies gathered close under the sheer bank, and safe from the rifles of the defenders above. These traps are largely used by the Nagas, Mishmis, and other wild races along the borders of Assam and Burma. They are placed over steep and narrow mountain paths and discharged with disastrous effect on foes toiling up to the assault. During the Abor War they were frequently tried on General Bower who was too wary to be caught by them. He always took the precaution of sending parties of Gurkhas to scale the heights to search for and cut the booby-traps away before his column passed under them.

As the shallow stream ran close to the bank we erected, behind the wall, a dipping-pole and bucket to bring up water without danger from hostile fire to the men fetching it.

Our stockades would have proved very unpleasant

obstacles to surmount. They had a forward rake to increase by the overhang the difficulty of escalading them. And along their tops was fastened a tangle of cut and sharp-pointed branches projecting well outwards, so that it was almost impossible to climb over.

In attacking a stockade the assailants try to get close up to it, fire in through the loopholes and hack it down with axes. To prevent this, six-foot *panjis*—sharpened bamboo stakes, their pointed ends hardened by fire—stuck thickly out from the face of our stockades. On the near slope of the ditches lines of *panjis* projected with their points at a downward angle; while on the far side fences of sharpened bamboos were planted. At the bottom of the ditches *chevaux de frise* of long *panjis* were fixed.

These *panjis* inflict ghastly injuries, and are more dangerous than bayonets. An officer of my acquaintance, when leading an assault on a stockade held by dacoits in Burma, ran against a *panji* which transfixed his thigh. He was eleven months in hospital before the wound healed; and for many years afterwards he was lame.

For twenty yards beyond the ditches the ground was covered with a five-feet-high entanglement of felled trees. Their butts were lashed to stout pegs driven deep into the earth. Their thinner branches were lopped off, the thicker ones cut and trimmed with sharp points towards the front. In military parlance this is called an *abattis*.

Anyone endeavouring to rush the defences of our fort would have found it a difficult feat, even if no bullets were showered on him from the loopholes. He would first have to force his way through twenty yards of entanglement, then climb a sharp-pointed fence, pass the *chevaux de frise* in the ditch, get by the downward-pointing *panjis*, evade the six-foot stakes projecting from the face of the stockade, and climb over the stockade itself through the overhead tangle of branches. And to do it under a hot fire would be almost impossible. To attack such a post successfully guns would be necessary—and a well-built double stockade would withstand light artillery.

For our own use winding paths led through the *abattis* to drawbridges before the two gates. These latter were of bamboo, hinged at the top and opening outwards and upwards, supported when open by high, forked poles. In each was a small wicket constructed on the same principle and only wide enough to admit one man at a time. Wickets and gates were stuck thick with projecting *panjis*.

Trees in the interior of the post were left standing to give shade, as were others growing in the line of the defences. And in the latter, forty feet from the ground, were platforms reached by ladders and hidden by the leafy branches. On them the sentries were stationed; and from them, during a night attack, men could fire and hurl bombs down on the assailants who would find it difficult to locate their position. From these sentry posts stout cords of twisted *udal* fibre led to kerosene oil tins hung up in the quarters occupied by officers and section commanders. In the tins stones were put, so that a pull on the cords would rattle the tins throughout the post and arouse the defenders without an approaching enemy being aware that the alarm had been given.

So much for the defences. As such a post would

be constructed with a view to long occupation the question of housing the garrison comfortably remained. In the interior along each face two huts, each to hold a section of twenty or twenty-five men, with huts for the native officers, were built. The roofs were thickly thatched. The back and side walls were made of two rows of bamboo a foot apart, with rammed earth between them. The front walls were lightly made of bamboo and hinged at the top to open outwards and upwards in an emergency, so that the whole section could come out in line. For ordinary use a small door sufficed. Along the back wall ran a sloping guard-bed, with a broad shelf underneath, on which the sepoys' clothing could be laid. Overhead were pegs for their rifles and accoutrements.

Along the cross-roads through the fort were built the storerooms, hospital, and native followers' quarters. And on them were also the Mess and huts for the British officers. These were quite comfortable little cottages, the walls of split bamboo with the latticed windows and the doors screened by blinds of cane strips. The floors and walls were covered with two-inch mats of jungle grass.

The sepoys proved themselves wonderfully ingenious craftsmen and made excellent furniture for our quarters. Out of the ever-useful bamboo they constructed beds, chairs, tables, and writing-desks with drawers and pigeon-holes. And like the fort and everything else in it, the jungle provided the materials for all this furniture, in which not a nail was used; for it was held together by lashings of bamboo bark or *udal* fibre.

All this was not quickly done. The building of

THE GATE CLOSED, WITH WICKET OPEN AND DRAWBRIDGE LOWERED.

CAPTAIN BALDERSTON INSIDE THE STOCKADE.

the defences and the huts and the construction of a military bridge across the river took every day of the three weeks before the General's arrival. Our working hours were from 5 a.m. to 5 p.m. with an hour's interval at noon for food. But the sepoys revelled in their novel labours and looked on them as a welcome change from the monotony of drill. So interested were they that I often found them at work long after the bugle had sounded the "dismiss" in the evening; and when I told them to knock off, they would reply: "Oh, Sahib, we would like to finish this to-day."

Our comfortable and airy little hospital was rarely tenanted. Almost the only patient our medical officer had was a pet monkey which required a surgical operation. The native sub-assistant 'surgeon, who took the proceedings very seriously, was called on to administer the anæsthetic. Chloroform was poured on a wad of wool in a paper cone which, much to the patient's annoyance, was pressed firmly against its muzzle. It scratched and bit for quite a long time before sinking into unconsciousness. And when, after the surgeon's knife had been swiftly and dexterously plied, it came back to life again it looked a very sick monkey indeed. Wrapped up in a towel with only its tiny puckered face showing, it presented such a woebegone and comical appearance that the onlookers were moved to unseemly mirth. But the little beast was too ill to care, though usually it fiercely resented being laughed at.

We were too busy during these weeks to do any shooting. But a curious bit of *shikar* fell to my lot one day. While I was superintending the building of the fort a sepoy who had been gathering stones for the wall ran up to tell me that he had seen some curious little animals in the *nullah*. Borrowing an ancient Martini rifle from a native officer, I ran down to the river-bed and found several wild dogs playing on the sand a few hundred yards away in front of a small island covered with thick undergrowth. On seeing me they bolted. I took a hurried shot at one and missed it, the bullet glancing off a rock behind which the dog had disappeared. To my horror a low wailing cry issued from the bushes on the island behind. Alarmed at the thought that I might have wounded one of my sepoys, I ran to the spot. There to my astonishment I found a barking deer standing up with half its face blown away. The unlucky beast had been struck by my chance bullet. Its shrieks were piteous and almost human, until we put it out of its pain.

Another day a sepoy cutting bamboos was disturbed by a herd of wild elephants. He had the sense to remain motionless; and the animals passed without seeing him.

One evening another man met a more dangerous beast. He had gone down at dusk to bathe in the river just below the fort and came face to face with a panther drinking. The man was unarmed; but fortunately for him the brute only growled and trotted away.

One Sunday afternoon we had a serious alarm. No work being done on that day two of the native officers, taking a few sepoys with them, had gone out with shot-guns to look for jungle fowl. Splitting up into two parties they separated and beat through the undergrowth a few hundred yards away from the fort.

Suddenly one of them came upon a tiger which snarled viciously at them and retreated in a direction which would bring him upon the other party. With this was Subhedar Sohanpal Singh, the sturdy old Rajput who had been my companion in the long chase after the rogue elephant.

A sepoy came running back to the fort with the news. Seizing a rifle, I turned out a number of men with their arms and ammunition and hurried off to the rescue. Reaching the spot where the tiger had been seen, we searched the jungle for it and for Sohanpal Singh's party until dusk, without result. We shouted the *subhedar's* name loudly but got no answer. When night fell we returned to the fort. I was in hopes that the missing party had passed us in the jungle and got in safely. When I found that it had not come back I began to be seriously alarmed. But I reflected that it contained four men and that the tiger could hardly have killed them all and not left one to bring back the news. The missing men returned at ten o'clock. They had not actually seen the tiger but had heard it growling close to them in the thick undergrowth. As one of the sepoys had his rifle with him, Sohanpal Singh took it and tried to get a shot at the animal. The beast retreated slowly before him, growling all the time, but keeping in dense jungle where he could not see it. In vain the *subhedar* tried to get ahead and cut it off. He and his party followed the tiger until night put an end to the tantalising pursuit. Then, when they tried to retrace their steps, they lost their way in the darkness and wandered blindly through the jungle for hours until they struck the river.

On the day of General Bower's arrival I sent two

elephants to bring him and his staff officer with their baggage from Buxa Road Station. Balderston and I awaited him in the fire line about four hundred yards from our fort. When our visitors reached us they dismounted and shook hands with us. After our greetings were over I said to the General:

"You told me last year, sir, to teach my men the art of making themselves and their officers comfortable in the jungle. You have got to test the result of my instruction practically now. You must live in a jungle hut, sleep on a jungle bed, sit at jungle-made tables on jungle-made chairs."

General Bower laughed. "Is the jungle supplying my food too?" he asked.

"Yes, sir; jungle fowl and venison. Captain Balderston wanted to give you wild vegetables from the jungle as well. But I tried them myself once; and as I don't want a bad report of my detachment, I dare not offer them to you."

I led the way along a road which we had cut through the forest. Where it emerged on the clearing around our post I stopped and said:

"There is the fort."

Our visitors looked about them in astonishment. For, at a distance of two hundred yards, the stockades with the living trees in them behind the tangle of *abattis* could not be distinguished from the surrounding jungle. In warfare this would be a great advantage, because it would come as a surprise on an advancing enemy.

When we reached the *abattis*, we passed down the winding path through it and stopped at the edge of the ditch. For, in order to give the General a good idea of the strength of our defences, I had ordered

BRINGING HOME THE GENERAL'S DINNER.

that the gates should be closed and the drawbridges raised. On a board above the gateway were painted the words "Fort Bower," the name given by the sepoys to the post in honour of our inspecting officer. Having allowed our visitors time to be suitably impressed by the formidable stockade and the grim-looking *panjis* in the ditch, I called to the sentry hidden forty feet above us in a tree:

"Open the gate!"

The invisible doorkeeper pulled a string to inform the guard in the bastion. Then the heavy drawbridge fell across the ditch, the gate was raised and held up in position by the supporting forked poles.

"That is very ingenious," said the General as he entered the fort.

The men's huts were first inspected; and then we proceeded to the officer's quarters on the main street. We showed the General the cosy little two-roomed cottage he was to occupy, and pointed out the name painted on it, "The Bower."

"Captain Humphreys' quarters are next door," we told him. "They gave us more trouble to find a title for. When we thought that the brigade major, Major Hutchinson, was to accompany you, the name suggested itself—we'd have called it 'The Hutch.' But when we heard that Humphreys was coming instead we were puzzled—until the idea occurred to us to name it 'The 'Ump.'"

The General seemed to appreciate the mild joke more than his staff officer did. I pulled up the cane blind on the door of "The Bower" and invited the General to enter and see his jungle abode.

"Here, sir, is your hat-rack," I said, showing a bamboo pole stuck in the flooring, its top split open into several points held apart by a cone of wood, thus providing a number of pegs. I drew his attention to an ingeniously-made writing-table with pigeon-holes and drawers. Then we passed into the inner room. Here a comfortable bed had been formed by driving the ends of six forked sticks, arranged in a parallelogram, into the earth. In the forks four light poles had been laid and fastened, making the head, foot and sides of the bedstead. Then across from side to side were tied split bamboos, which formed a bottom as elastic as steel springs. On it was laid a grass mat, three inches thick, as a mattress. The best bed ever turned out by Maple's could not have been more comfortable. Against the walls stood a bamboo dressing-table and a washstand. On the latter was an enamelled iron basin, the only article I could not replace from the jungle. But above it hung a length of hollow bamboo filled with water and pierced near the bottom by a hole now plugged. I withdrew the plug; and the water poured down into the basin.

The General gazed around admiringly.

"These contrivances are very clever," he said; "and there is no doubt that now your sepoys know how to make themselves and their officers very comfortable with the help only of jungle materials. All this is very ingenious and practical."

After lunch the General inspected the defences and asked to see the sepoys man them. I led him up the ladder into the *machân* or platform occupied by the sentry in a tree over the river-bank. The men were all shut up in their huts.

"Give the alarm," I said to the sentry.

He gathered in his hand the strings leading from

the *machân* to the officers' and section-leaders' quarters and pulled them. Throughout the fort we could faintly hear the stones rattling in the suspended tins. Instantly the fronts of the huts were raised; and the men of each section came silently out in line and went straight to the loopholes they had been posted to.

"That is the best device I have seen yet," said General Bower. "The whole camp can be simultaneously aroused at once without any noise being heard by an approaching enemy, who would remain in ignorance of the fact that the defenders were on the alert. Consequently they would come on confidently in fancied security until they exposed themselves to a sudden fire at close range."

Climbing down from the *machân* he inspected the booby trap. At a signal, men inside the wall cut the creepers supporting the outer end of the bamboo platform which fell on its hinges and sent an avalanche of rocks into the *nullah* below.

As soon as it was dark we went out on to the gallery projecting over the river-bed. From it cords led to bombs buried in the sand and piled around with stones. They were made of bamboos filled with powder and fitted with a rifle cartridge so arranged that, on pulling the cord, a rock fell on a nail which struck the cartridge-cap and exploded the bomb.

We fired these off one after another. The explosions hurled the stones in all directions with terrific force. Captain Balderston had devised an arrangement similar to the old Roman catapults for throwing hand-grenades over a hundred yards. He gave us an exhibition of this. On the sand of the river-bed bonfires had been piled to be set on fire by flares ignited by men tripping against cords laid along the ground. These were now worked; and the flames rose high and lit up the *nullah* clearly, so that anyone in it was plainly visible from the fort.

Our dinner that night in the thatched bamboo hut dignified by the title of "Officers' Mess" was quite a festive affair. Our forest fare was much appreciated by our visitors; for it comprised *sambhur* soup, roast jungle fowls and the delicate venison of a barking deer. But the river was not called upon to supply the liquor for our feast. General Bower was as full of good stories as ever; and long after the sepoys had turned in for the night their slumbers must have been disturbed by the hearty laughter of their Sahibs in the Mess.

The next two days were occupied in doing manœuvres through the jungle.

At the conclusion of the inspection General Bower ordered me to form up the detachment and made a little speech to the men. He praised all ranks for their keenness and efficiency and complimented them on the ingenuity displayed in the construction of the fort.

"You have made its defences so strong," he said, "that without artillery it would be almost impossible for an assault on it to be successful. I am very pleased with what you have done and at hearing from your Major Sahib how well and how willingly you have worked. I shall give this detachment a very good report."

The Indians, like other races, love their meed of praise; and at the General's words the sepoys' faces beamed. Contrary to strict ideas of discipline

Subhedar Sohanpal Singh, standing in front of his company, turned to his men and cried:

Three cheers for the General Sahib!"

And as General Bower, having said good-bye to us and mounted his elephant, disappeared in the jungle on his way to the railway station, the hearty cheers of the sepoys followed him.

For the remainder of our stay in Buxa Duar Fort Bower served to accommodate officers and men whenever we went down into the forest for military training. On one occasion we had some useful practice in night-firing from it. In the cleared space around it and in the river-bed targets were placed to represent an attacking army. A hundred yards from the defences bonfires, to be lit by flares ignited by cords leading into the fort, were arranged. When darkness fell these were set alight. The leaping flames showed up the targets, at which the sepoys fired through the loopholes of stockade and wall with very good results. At the time I had an American Cavalry officer on a visit to me. This was his first experience of the Indian Army at work; and he was very much impressed by it.

At Christmas, Balderston and I invited friends to come to us for a shooting camp. Fort Bower served us as a residence; and from it we sallied out every morning into the forest on our elephants. On Christmas Day we added to our usual fare of jungle fowl and venison a plum pudding and mince-pies sent out from England, brewed punch, and in the heart of the jungle, thousands of miles from home, kept the feast in the good old fashion.

CHAPTER XV

FAREWELL TO THE HILLS

The Proclamation Parade—An unsteady charger—"Three cheers for the King-Emperor!"—The Indian Army's loyalty—King George and the sepoys—A land held by the sword—An American Cavalry officer's visit—Hospitality of American officers—Killing by kindness—The brotherhood of soldiers—The bond between American and British troops sealed by blood—U.S. officers' opinion of us—A roaring tiger—Prince Jitendra Narayen—His visit to Buxa—An intoxicated monkey—Projected visits—A road report—A sketch fourteen feet long—The start—Jalpaiguri—A planters' dinner-party—Crossing the Tista River—A quicksand—A narrow escape—Map-making in the army—In the China War of 1860—Officers' sketches used for the Canton Railway survey—The country south of the hills—A sepoy's explanation of Kinchinjunga—A native officer's theory of the cause of earthquakes—Types on the road—After the day's work—A man-eater—A brave postman—Human beings killed by wild animals and snakes in India—Crocodiles—Shooting a monster—Crocodiles on land—Crossing the Torsa—Value of small detachments—The maligned military officer—A life of examinations—The man-killing elephant again—Death of a Bhuttia woman—Ordered home—A last good-bye to a comrade—Captain Balderston's death—A last view of the hills.

WHEN our Christmas shoot ended I returned to Buxa with our guests in time to hold the Proclamation Parade; for on 1st January, 1877, Queen Victoria was proclaimed Empress of India, and on this date every year the event is celebrated in military Stations throughout our Eastern Empire by a parade of

"I WAS MOUNTED ON A COUNTRYBRED PONY."

"AN ELEPHANT LOADED WITH MY STORES AND BAGGAGE."

troops in garrison. Even in our little outpost we did not forget to honour the day.

On the drill ground a flagstaff had been erected, from which flew the Union Jack. The two companies of the detachment, officers and men in their full-dress uniform of scarlet and blue, were drawn up in line facing it. Captain Balderston rode a pony recently purchased from a planter, which strongly objected to soldiers and refused to go near the troops. No persuasions of its rider could induce it to approach the line; and when Balderston called the men to attention on my arrival and the rifles were brought smartly to the "slope," his disobedient charger swung round and bolted with him off the parade ground, jumping a ditch and nearly ending both their careers in a deep *nullah*. I was mounted on a country-bred pony which I had brought from Darjeeling and trained to troops. Deprived of the assistance of my second in command I started the parade. After the royal salute had been given, the men fired the *feu de joie*, when the rifles are discharged one by one along the front rank from right to left and back again in the opposite direction down the rear rank. Then taking off my helmet I gave the command "Three cheers for the King Emperor!"; and the hills re-echoed the shouts of the sepoys. A useless ceremony this, to the Little Englander; yet one fraught with deep meaning and stirring the heart to the core; for at that moment throughout the Indian Empire from the Himalayas to Colombo, from Aden to Mandalay, the cheers of His Majesty's soldiers, white and black, were ringing in loyal chorus.

Fifty years ago, in the dark days of the Mutiny, the revolted sepoy regiments faced their erstwhile comrades in battle; but the guilt of that black crime has long ago been purged in blood and obliterated by faithful service; and to-day the Kaiser-i-Hind has no more loyal soldiers than the men of his Indian Army. Until a few years ago the Sovereign was only a name to the warrior races that fill its ranks. But King George by his visits to India has made them realise his existence. He has given his Indian subjects what Orientals always desire, the knowledge that they have a living monarch. And by so doing he has changed the vague loyalty of the sepoys into a real and affectionate attachment to the person of their ruler. The native troops whom he reviewed, who lined the streets or formed his Guards of Honour in Bombay, Delhi and Calcutta, rejoice to have actually seen their "*Badshah*" (Emperor) and proudly boast of it to others who have not been so fortunate. Only we officers of the Indian Army can fully realise how much this means, how wise were the councils that dictated his visits to India.

For, despite the politician and the civil servant, we hold the land, as we won it, by the sword. No concessions to the clamour of the *babus* of Bengal will retain the loyalty of this country. It rests on the weapons and in the hearts of the gallant warrior races that aided us to conquer India and help us to retain it. Would that the Englishman in England could realise the fact!

Shortly after the departure of our guests who had come for the Christmas shoot, I received a long-expected visit from an American officer, Captain Brees, 1st United States Cavalry. Years before, in China, Japan, and California I had foregathered with a cheery Irish subaltern of his regiment,

Lieutenant Coghlan, who had won his commission in the fierce fighting in Luzon. And when Captain Brees, their corps being then in the Philippine Islands, arranged to visit India on his way home on leave to his native country, Lieutenant Coghlan guaranteed him a warm welcome from me. For I felt that I owed a debt of gratitude to every officer of the American Army for the kindly hospitality I had received from them in the United States—from the Pacific to the Atlantic. Before I landed in San Francisco, Coghlan, then stationed in Los Angeles and unable to come to meet me, had written to friends of his in regiments quartered in the Army Post in the Presidio, the Golden City's splendid park, and asked them to welcome me in his stead. As soon as I arrived not only they, but a score of other officers of the garrison, had made their way through the ruins of the city not long before devastated by earthquake and fire to give me that welcome to their country. They offered me all the hospitality of their camp and clubs. A Cavalry regiment on the point of departing for their summer training in the famous Yosemite Valley extended a cordial invitation to accompany them and promised me a horse, a tent, and rations. The Field Battery offered to mount me whenever I liked to march out with them. I was asked to every military entertainment; and at every regimental dance my hosts saw that I had my programme full.

One night at a magnificent entertainment at the Fairmont Hotel in celebration of the first anniversary of the earthquake and San Francisco's phœnix-like rising again from the flames, a civilian asked me if I belonged to the Indian Army. On my replying in the affirmative he begged to be allowed to introduce me to two friends of his present that night, American officers on leave from another Station, as they were anxious to meet an officer of my Service. As shook hands with them, one said:

"We've been looking for a fellow in the Indian Army."

"Which one?" I asked.

"Anyone. It doesn't matter who. We want to kill him," was the alarming reply.

"Good Heaven! why?" I queried apprehensively, backing away from him.

"Say, don't be afraid," he answered, laughingly. "We only mean to kill him with kindness. The fact is that we have just been on leave through India and Burma; and your fellows were so good to us everywhere we went that we have been looking for any stray officer of your army to give us an opportunity of returning their hospitality."

"That's so," said his companion. "Now, what can we do for you? Dine you, wine you, or lend you money?"

And when I told them that the unbounded kindness of their comrades in San Francisco had left me nothing to desire, they were very disappointed.

Between the soldiers of every nationality there is a bond of brotherhood; and never have I found it so strong as between American officers and ours in the too few occasions on which they have met.

"Blood is thicker than water"; and in the China War of 1900 Uncle Sam's troops and the British seemed to form one army. Side by side they fought in the grim combats around Tientsin. On the day when the city was stormed, when the pouches of the gallant 9th United States Infantry were empty, their brave colonel, Liscum, and a score of men killed, and four officers and seventy-two men wounded out of total of two hundred Americans engaged, a British officer, Ollivant, was killed in trying to replenish their ammunition, another, Major Pereira, was wounded in trying to bring in their injured, and Lieutenant Phillimore and his blue-jackets of H.M.S. *Barfleur* helped them to hold their ground, and brought back their wounded.

In less strenuous days in North China after the fighting, our American friends there told us that they found us very different to their preconceived ideas of the English officer, whom they had pictured as a languidly haughty individual, inseparable from his eyeglass, and prefacing every remark by "I say, by Jove!" They frankly admitted that they had come prepared to dislike us, but had found us on acquaintance not such bad fellows after all.

Similarly Captain Brees confessed to me that he had been obliged to reconstruct all his preconceived ideas of British military men as soon as he had met them. Before his departure from Manila I had sent him letters of introduction to many of our officers in Hong Kong, Singapore, Colombo and Calcutta. He told me that on arriving in Hong Kong he had hesitated to avail himself of them but, hardening his heart, had at last dispatched them to the addresses.

"I can tell you, major," he said, "that, with the ideas I had of what your fellows would be like, I was considerably surprised when several of them swooped down upon me in my hotel and insisted on my transferring myself and my baggage at once to their quarters, where they entertained me royally for the rest of my stay in Hong Kong. The same in Singapore. And when my ship reached Calcutta, two British officers came on board as soon as the anchor dropped, took me ashore, and gave me a bully time there. I tell you that after this you can just inform any of your army friends that, if they visit America, their address is '1st United States Cavalry.' And don't you forget it!"

"Jimmy" Brees was one of the most charming men I have ever known; and everywhere he went in India he made a most favourable impression on all our officers who met him. In Buxa we could not offer him any social gaieties; but we made him free of the jungle, taught him to ride on and shoot from elephants, and did the little we could to entertain him.

Once, after a long day in the forest on Khartoum's back, we climbed up into Forest Lodge to dine and sleep. Exhausted by his tiring experience, Brees had just fallen asleep and I was preparing to follow his example, when I heard a tiger roaring in the jungle close to my lofty tree-dwelling, and apparently approaching us. I was delighted to give my guest the opportunity of at least hearing a tiger and possibly shooting it in the moonlight if it came close enough. So I sprang out of bed, seized my rifle and, posting myself at the window, called out over my shoulder:

"Wake up, Jimmy, wake up! There is a tiger close by."

"Eh? What?" came the sleepy reply.

"Get up, man, get up!" I whispered excitedly. "I tell you there's a tiger near us. It may come close enough to give us a shot at it."

But the fatigues of the day had been too much for him. A loud snore was his only answer; and although the tiger roamed around the house for half an hour, uttering its peculiar snorting roar, it never woke him. However, he lost nothing but the noise; for, though I sat eagerly expectant by the window for a long time, the brute never came within range.

My next visitor was Prince Jitendra Narayen, now through the death of his eldest brother Maharajah of Cooch Behar. Before Darjeeling came into existence as a Hill Station the rulers of his State possessed a house in Buxa Duar, to which they used to come in the summer to avoid the heat of the Plains. But this was before the day of the present generation of the family, none of whom, except the then Maharajah, had ever visited Buxa. So Prince "Jit" was glad of an opportunity of seeing our small Station, and spent several days with me. As he belonged to the Imperial Service Cadet Corps he was keenly interested in military matters, and passed much time in watching our detachment at work. Like his father, he was an ardent sportsman and good shot; and, used to the more open country south of the forest, he enjoyed wandering on one of our elephants through our dense jungle in search of *sambhur*. His cheery manner made him popular with everyone in Buxa—except our pet monkey. For that little beast, having a severe cold, was given whisky-and-milk one day, and, imbibing too freely, became absolutely drunk. Its antics as it reeled about the mess-room were extremely comical and made us all roar with laughter. It seemed to pardon its owners' want of good manners but resented Prince Jitendra's mirth as an impertinence in a stranger. Swaying drunkenly as it tried to stand on its hind legs, it chattered and shrieked with rage at him and endeavoured to stagger across the room to bite him, falling down and rolling helplessly on the floor on its way. And next morning it was plain to see that it suffered from a bad headache. But when Jit entered the Mess at breakfast-time and condoled with it on its evident pain, it flew at him and attacked him savagely.

When my guest returned to Cooch Behar I accompanied him. At the Palace his account of the beauties of Buxa Duar made the ladies of the family eager to see the place; and it was arranged that Her Highness the Maharani and her two daughters, the Princess Pretiva and Sudhira, should pay us a visit in our outpost. The Maharajah's four sons were also to come at another time, bringing all the elephants belonging to the State, to join me in making a systematic search for a rogue which was committing havoc in the forest near Buxa. But the Maharajah's illness, which necessitated his going to Europe for medical treatment and which resulted in his lamented death the following year, deprived me of the pleasure of these visits.

Shortly after Prince Jitendra's departure an order from the brigadier to report on and sketch eighty-four miles of road and country across Eastern Bengal afforded me an opportunity of seeing something of this province south of the Terai Jungle. The task was no light one. The military sketch was to be executed on a scale of two inches to a mile; so that I had to make a map fourteen feet long! It was to begin more than twenty miles west of Jalpaiguri, a town on the railway to Siliguri and

Darjeeling, the route running parallel to the mountains and thirty or forty miles south of them, and ended at Alipur Duar.

As the ground to be traversed contained no towns where I could purchase supplies, I had to make my own arrangements for food as well as transport. I might find an empty *dâk* bungalow here and there; but it behoved me to carry a tent with me. So, dispatching my pony and an elephant loaded with my baggage and stores to march across country and meet me at Jalpaiguri, I went by train to this station, reaching it of course several days before my animals could arrive. There I borrowed an elephant from the police officer, bought some tinned provisions and flour, and set out west along the twenty-four miles of road to the spot where I was to begin my sketch. I was fortunate in finding *dâk* bungalows on it every ten or twelve miles in which to shelter at night. At the first of these I was informed by the native in charge of it that on a tank—as ponds and lakes are called in India—about six miles away I would find hundreds of duck. So I shouldered my gun and set out across the fields. I discovered the tank and from a distance saw that the water was dotted with birds. Cautiously stalking them, with glowing anticipations of wild duck for dinner, I reached the bank to find that they were coots and "divers." Not even a snipe rewarded me for my long walk; and I returned to the *dâk* bungalow to give my misinformant my candid and unflattering opinion of him.

Next day I reached the spot where my sketch was to begin. My starting-point was near another *dâk* bungalow, perched on a little hill overlooking a broad river flowing through thin jungle and well-cultivated fields. Here I turned my face towards Jalpaiguri and commenced my task. Cavalry sketching-case in hand I walked along the road through open and uninteresting country, counting my paces as measurement and filling in the meagre details of the country on either hand on my map. I completed the mapping of the twenty-four miles in two days.

Arrived at Jalpaiguri I had to wait there a day for my elephant and pony, which were accompanied by my butler and a sepoy orderly, as well as the *mahout* and a *syce*; so that with Draj Khan, who was already with me, I had quite a following. Jalpaiguri is built on the west bank of the broad Tista River, which flows from Sikkim through the Himalayas to the plains of Bengal. The civil Station contains the usual Anglo-Indian community of such a town, the deputy commissioner, a judge, a settlement officer, a Public Works Department engineer, a police officer and a few more Europeans. There are no troops there. The engineer who had visited me at Buxa, which was in his charge, kindly offered me the shelter of his bungalow; and I was hospitably entertained by everyone in the Station. I came in for a very merry dinner-party given at the club by a number of planters of the neighbourhood to two members of their community who were leaving India for England. Near midnight we escorted the guests to the railway station and considerably delayed the mail train by our lengthy good-byes and parting libations. In vain the stationmaster, the guard, and the engine-driver in turn stormed, argued, and pleaded with the two departing planters to take their seats and let the train start. Sleepy and irate English passengers put their heads out of the carriage windows and cursed the causes of the delay. One of our party had to be stopped by main force from pouring a whisky-and-soda into the interior mechanism of what he declared to be "a poor thirsty engine that nobody thought of offering a drink to." The native stationmaster, torn between his dread of official reprimand for delaying the mail and his fear of displeasing the Sahibs of his town, almost wept as he implored the party to end their farewells and let the train depart.

My transport having arrived that night I continued on my way next morning. I had to cross the Tista, which here, though the banks were more than a mile or a mile and a half apart, was at that season shrunk to a stream half a mile in breadth flowing between wide stretches of sand, over which I rode on my pony to reach the ferryboat. This was a broad, flat-bottomed craft, loaded with natives, cattle, bullocks and a cart which carried the baggage and camp equipment of a civil official going out to tour his district. The cart was festooned with wicker crates containing hens and ducks destined to supply "master's dinner in jungle," as the servant in charge informed me. With sail, oar and pole the ferry-boat made its way across the stream, until it reached a wide stretch of sand lying between the water and the bank. My pony, after much urging, jumped out; and I mounted. I had ridden four or five hundred yards when the animal stopped suddenly and its legs began to sink. To my horror I found that we were in a quicksand. The pony plunged and struggled wildly. I slipped from the saddle to ease it of my weight and sank at once up to my knees. Visions of a horrible death engulfed in the yielding mass of sand flashed across me as I struggled against the invisible monster that seemed to clutch me and drag me down. Luckily the pony got its forefeet on to firmer ground and fought its way out of the quicksand, pulling me out with it by the reins to which I clung. It stood terrified and quivering while I tried to soothe it. Fifty yards away was a group of natives who had been watching the incident phlegmatically and had made no move to come to our help. When I was safe they called out to me.

"That is a very dangerous place, Sahib. A cow was swallowed up there the other day."

Having told them forcibly what I thought of them for not warning me in time, I cautiously led my pony forward to the firm earth bank, which I was delighted to reach after the treacherous sand. Here the road to Alipur Duar began again. I swung myself into the saddle and continued my sketch on horseback, thus covering the ground much more quickly than on the first days. I was able to get my measurements by having previously counted the number of paces my pony took to cover a distance of a hundred yards at a trot.

In the old days knowledge of map-making was, in the army, confined to the Royal Engineers. A late inspector-general of fortifications, General Sir Richard Harrison, R.E., told me that in the China War of 1860 only two officers, he and Captain, afterwards Lord, Wolseley, in the Anglo-Indian Army there could make a military sketch, and very few others were able to understand it when made. Nowadays every officer can map any country and during the drill season is called upon to furnish at least one sketch. The civil engineers brought out in 1905-6 to Hong Kong to survey the route of the railway to Canton told me that in the British Hinterland they made no maps, and contented themselves with such annual military sketches of the country done by officers of the garrison. And these they found accurate enough for railway laying. The task that I was now engaged on, which was for the purpose of revising the military route-book of Eastern Bengal, was set me as part of my ordinary work; I being the nearest available officer.

The country through which my road lay for the next sixty miles was open, level, and well-cultivated, dotted with groves of feathery bamboos and the typical, compact, thatched villages and farm-buildings of Bengal. As usual, in India, the fields were not divided by hedges or any obstacles. Even at that season of the year the country-side looked green, in striking contrast to other parts of the land then when the hot weather was drawing near. And always along and parallel to my route lay the wall of the mountains thirty or forty miles away, rising abruptly from the plains in a confused jumble of rugged hills overtopping each other until they culminated in the long white crest of Kinchinjunga, which now and then at sunset or dawn towered over them all above the clouds and seemed to float detached in the sky.

At the first *dâk* bungalow which sheltered me after leaving Jalpaiguri we had a splendid view of this magnificent mountain; and I overheard my orderly, Draj Khan, who had been with me in Darjeeling and had seen it from there, explaining to the Rajput sepoy with us that it was composed entirely of ice. The latter, a man from the sandy deserts of Bikanir, never having seen snow or more ice than a small lump in some native liquor-dealer's shop in the bazaar, refused to believe Draj's statement and appealed to me. I found it no easy task to explain the mystery of the Everlasting Snows to the intellect of this more or less untutored savage; and I fear that he understood me even less than he did Draj Khan's explanation. Natural physical phenomena that we accept as articles of belief we find not so easy to make clear to the minds of uneducated people. The Pathan subhedar-major of my regiment rejected my account of the causes of earthquakes in favour of his own theory that they arise from the movements of a dragon slumbering in the centre of the earth and occasionally shaking itself or turning round in its sleep.

I found my journey day by day along the road interesting from the many types of natives whom I passed. Brown-skinned peasants, many clad simply in a cotton cloth wound round the waist and between the legs, and *puggris* tied loosely about their heads, saluted me respectfully as I rode by. Native women, nose-ringed and glass-braceletted, modestly drew their *saris* over their dark faces to hide their problematical beauty from my profane gaze. Naked little brown urchins with them stopped to gaze, finger in mouth, at the Sahib and scampered off in simulated fear when I waved my hand to them, but halted at a safe distance to wave back laughingly. Bearded Mohammedans uttered a "Salaam Aleikoum"* and grinned with pleasure at the correct reply "Aleikoum salaam." † Groups of lean-shanked jungle-dwellers shuffled by, the men unencumbered, the ragged women laden with cooking-pots, babies, and other possessions. Once or twice I passed a tall, stately

* "Peace be with you!"
† "With you be peace!"

Pathan, long-haired and hook-nosed, clad in baggy trousers, gold-laced velvet waistcoat and voluminous turban. These gave me a cheery salutation, with no trace of servility; for the Pathan is of a haughty race and thinks himself any man's equal. These individuals had wandered far from their homes among the mountains beyond the North-West Frontier to make small fortunes as usurers among the simple peasants of Bengal. Small boys herding cattle drove their black buffaloes to one side of the road to let me pass, fearlessly beating with shrill cries the savage-looking animals which seemed inclined to charge my pony. Heavy carts, their wheels solid discs of wood, drawn by stolid white bullocks, lumbered noisily along, the drivers twisting the *byles'* tails to accelerate their speed. Although I was in so-called disaffected Eastern Bengal I met with no rudeness or black looks; for the sedition carefully fostered among the feather-headed young Bengali students has not affected the simple cultivators of the soil, who still respect the white man and look confidently to the Sahibs for justice. Even well-fed *babus* on the road stopped and closed their umbrellas, a native sign of respect, and were always ready to answer my questions or enter into a chat.

Every day after completing ten or twelve miles of my sketch I halted at a *dâk* bungalow or pitched my tent. My servants and elephant had usually arrived before me; and I found my breakfast of biscuit, tinned meat and tea, occasionally supplemented by eggs from the nearest village, awaiting me. My orderly, scouting on ahead on my bicycle, had sought for information of sport; and, if the prospects of it were good, I took my gun or rifle and went out in search of something to shoot. But in such well-cultivated country there was very little game.

At one village near which I halted for the night I heard that a man-eating tiger was lurking in the neighbourhood. It had killed two natives on the road within the week. Of course I went out to look for it, but with scant hope of finding it, as I could only stay a day in the place. Mounting my elephant I started after breakfast and beat through all the small patches of jungle for miles round and along the banks of a small stream flowing by the village. But, though I hunted until after dusk, I found no traces of it, and returned disappointed to the *dâk* bungalow.

As I sat smoking after dinner out in the compound under the stars I heard the tinkle of bells coming along the road and drawing nearer and nearer. Then past the gate of the enclosure around the bungalow a native postman shuffled by at a dog-trot, his spear and bells over his shoulder. I stopped him and asked him if he had heard of the tiger.

The little old man, bent almost double under the weight of his mail-bag, wiped his brow, as he answered:

"Yes, Protector of the Poor, the *shaitan* (devil) killed two men of this village on this very road by which I come each night."

"Are you not afraid of meeting him?" I asked.

"That is in the hands of God, Sahib. I must earn my pay by carrying the *dâk* (mail) along that road every day."

"But why come by night?"

"The *dâk* only reaches my post office after nightfall, and must be sent on at once. *Hukm hai.* It is the order." And with a farewell salaam he trotted off into the darkness and danger of the night; and the tinkle of the bells died away down the fatal road.

Next morning I moved on, deeply regretting that I could not afford the time to remain and make a systematic search for the man-eater. It was tantalising to be in its hunting-ground and yet be unable to stay longer and devote myself to its destruction. To shoot an ordinary tiger is not much of an achievement; but to circumvent and kill a murderous beast, grown daring and wily in the slaughter of human beings, is something to be proud of, and a good and useful deed. The hunter must pit his brains against its cunning and risk his life freely; for the man-eater is acute beyond all others and has lost the wild animals' usual dread of man. It is fortunate that such are rare; for last year tigers killed eight hundred and eighty-five persons in India, one being credited with forty-one deaths. Other wild beasts were far behind in the grim count. Wolves killed two hundred and fifty-five; while panthers slew two hundred and sixty-one human beings. But these figures fall far short of the havoc caused by venomous reptiles. In 1911 over twenty-five thousand persons died from snake-bite; in 1912, twenty-one thousand four hundred and sixty-one deaths were recorded from the same cause. But it must be remembered that in villages far from police investigations and coroners' inquests, snake-bite is a very convenient explanation of a sudden and violent death.

As I rode along day by day busy with my sketch I had not time to feel lonely; though, with the exception of my brief stay in Jalpaiguri, I had not exchanged a word with one of my own colour for over a week. But in India one grows accustomed to that. Soldiers, planters, forest and civil officers are used to being cut off from their kind; and on detachment I have passed months without seeing another European. The evenings, when the day's work is done, are the hardest to bear; and now in this long and solitary ride, when I sat in my tent or a *dâk* bungalow after dinner by the flickering light of a hurricane lantern I did occasionally wish for a white man to talk to.

My road, running parallel to the hills, crossed many rivers flowing from them. Most of these were, at that season of the year, easily fordable; though in some the water was up to my pony's girths. Warned by my experience at the Tista, I kept a sharp look-out for quicksands. At one broad stream villagers bade me beware of crocodiles; and fording a river in which these brutes lurk is not a pleasant task.

The crocodiles of India are divided into two species. The *ghavial*, or fish eater, attains a length of eighteen feet and is reputed not to attack human beings. Yet with their long, narrow snouts studded with a serrated row of sharp teeth they look much more formidable than the man-eating, blunt-nosed *muggers*. The latter are similar to the alligators of the New World and the crocodiles of Africa, though they do not reach the length of the latter. The largest I have known was an old veteran twelve and a half feet long, which I shot in the Jumna near its confluence with the Ganges at Allahabad. The latter river is full of *muggers*; but the former is reputed locally to contain only *ghavials*. My crocodile may have been a stray. From a boat in which I was drifting down stream I saw it, looking like an immense log, lying on the bank; for these brutes are in the habit of coming ashore to sun themselves during the heat of the day. They are not easy to shoot, as at the least sign of danger they are prone to dive into the river. Even if wounded they are hard to secure; for they nearly always lie at the water's edge, so that the least movement takes them into the stream and, if they die below the surface, their bodies do not float for some time.

Having spotted the crocodile in question from a distance I landed on the opposite bank and, cautiously stalking it, managed to get within two hundred yards without its being alarmed. I was armed with a ·303 carbine and, aiming at its neck, luckily paralysed it by my first shot with a bullet in the spine. To make sure of it I fired several more rounds at it, then, hailing my boat, crossed over to where it lay. It feebly snapped its huge jaws at me as I approached, but was unable to move otherwise; and a final bullet laid it out. It was an old and immensely powerful brute, broad out of all proportion to its length. Its thick hide studded with bosses was like armour-plate, and over its back impenetrable to bullets. Its teeth were large and blunted and its nails long and thick.

At the sound of my shots a number of natives had run out from a village close by. When they saw the *mugger* lying dead, they streamed down to the bank and to my surprise swarmed round me, hung garlands about my neck and lauded me to the skies. I learned from them that the dead monster had closed a ford from their village to one on the other side of the river for two years, had carried off several women bathing or drawing water (this was a minor offence to the native, women being cheap in India); but, worse still, had killed several of their sacred and valuable cows. Hence my ovation. The brute was so large and heavy that it took fourteen villagers to drag and push it up an inclined plane of planks into my big native sailing-boat. We brought it down the river to the Lines of my regiment, which were built close to the bank. There we landed it and cut it open. In its stomach were seven metal anklets or armlets of different sizes, ornaments such as are worn by native women and girls, and—a horrible sight!—the entire body of a child about a year old. It was in the process of being digested; and, when exposed to the air, the flesh fell away from the bones. The stench was unforgettable.

The rivers of Bengal are full of these unpleasant saurians. And crocodiles do not always confine themselves to the water; for they are reputed to have an undesirable habit of wandering across country by night from stream to stream and, if these are far apart, hiding by day in any convenient tank. I have seen a large one in quite a small pond which was rapidly drying up and would contain no water in a week. A friend of mine in the Civil Service told me that once, riding into a village in his district in Eastern Bengal, he found it in a state of commotion and the whole population gathered in front of the local post office but keeping a respectful distance from the building; for on the steps of it was a crocodile about six feet long, snapping fiercely at anyone who approached it. It must have been overtaken by daylight when passing through the village on its way from water to water. My friend shot it, to the intense relief of the besieged postal officials inside the building.

A crocodile would certainly be an unpleasant animal to meet on the land in the dark. However, I forded all the streams I came to without mishap. When I reached the Torsa, a broad and rapid river, across which, some thirty miles to the north, I had driven the man-killing rogue elephant months before, I found it unfordable. A large ferry-boat was plying across it; and in company with two carts and their bullocks and drivers, a wandering Pathan, several peasants and a gipsy family, I embarked on it. We had an adventurous voyage. Heavy squalls sweeping down from the mountains churned up the dark surface of the river and drove our shallow, top-heavy craft back. The few boatmen, striving with paddles and poles, to propel it against the wind, were helpless. I seized a long bamboo and tried to aid them. The Pathan followed my example, while the other natives on board sat watching our efforts apathetically. This infuriated him; and he fell upon them with kicks and cuffs until they rose, took up other bamboos and helped to pole the boat across. But such was the strength of the gale that it took us two hours to force a passage against it; and once or twice we were nearly capsized.

Another couple of days or so brought me to the end of my task. When I saw the tin-roofed buildings of Alipur Duar rise before me on the road, I struck spurs to my pony and finished my sketch at a gallop. And the next day saw me back in Buxa Duar, glad to be among the friendly hills again, for the charm of the mountains was upon me. And on them I hoped to spend another year; but the gods willed otherwise.

Such outposts as ours may not be as good for the training of the rank and file as service in large garrisons. But for the individual officer there is no better way of developing his power of initiative and teaching him to rely on himself than the command of these small detachments. And in these jungle outposts the sport to be found is an additional advantage. Save only active service what better education can he have than the pursuit of big game, when every sense is trained to be on the alert, and quick decision becomes a second nature? An eye for country, readiness of resource, generalship and courage is needed in this "image of war." The time he spends in the jungles is not wasted.

The British military officer is a much-maligned individual. It seems an article of faith among civilians in England to believe that he leads a life of luxury, is ignorant of the science of his profession, and leaves the training and instruction of his men to be done by the sergeants. As to luxury—see him in his plainly furnished one room in barracks in the British Isles or his rat-infested Indian bungalow for which he pays an exorbitant rent! Examinations all through his service up to the rank of colonel; examinations for promotion to each grade, signalling, transport and musketry classes, each with its final examination, examinations in Indian and other foreign languages keep his brain from rusting for want of exercise. I have had to pass nine professional, and three obligatory language examinations myself during my service; and there are many who have passed more. That there is no army in the world that has as many officers qualified as interpreters in foreign tongues as ours was well exemplified in North China during the Boxer War of 1900. And as for leaving his work to be done by the non-commissioned ranks, only a person absolutely ignorant of our army to-day would venture to make that assertion. Who created the auxiliary armies throughout the Empire, who made the Indian, the Egyptian, the West and the East African Armies? Not the drill-instructor, not Sergeant What's-his-name, but the British officer!

Little did I think as I rode into Buxa, after making my sketch, that my time among my beloved mountains was drawing to a close. One day, not long afterwards, when out tiger-shooting I was taken suddenly ill and was barely able to remain in the howdah long enough to fire my rifle and bag the tiger. Hardly capable of sitting in the saddle I made my way on my pony back to my Station, there to lie on a sick-bed for over a month. And I raged at my helplessness when news was brought me during that time that the man-killing elephant I had fought with was back in our forests again. Within a few miles of us he surprised a Bhuttia woodcutter and his wife encamped in the jungle. He came upon them at dawn. They fled before him; but he overtook the woman, struck her down, and crushed her into a shapeless mass under his feet. When I heard of it I longed to be well enough to go out to meet him again. But the Fates forbade it.

Thanks to the devoted care of our Indian doctor, Captain Sarkar. I.M.S., I recovered sufficiently to be sent to England on sick leave, much against my will, for I had no desire to quit Buxa. But four sturdy *kahars* (bearers) carried me in a litter down the steep road from our little outpost through the forest to the train. Beside me walked Captain Balderston wishing me farewell and a speedy return to health. I little knew that I was never to see him again, as he shook my hand for the last time. Four months afterwards his sorrowing sepoys laid my cheery little comrade to rest in his grave in the deserted cemetery of Buxa. He died there all alone.

As the train bore me out of the forest and through the green plains of Eastern Bengal, I raised myself from my couch in the railway carriage and with sadness in my heart looked back to where the white Picquet Towers shone out on the purple background of the fast-receding hills.